D1021046

LAURA
WERLIN'S

CHEESE
ESSENTIALS

LAURA WERLIN'S

CHEESE ESSENTIALS

AN INSIDER'S GUIDE TO BUYING AND SERVING CHEESE

{ *With 50 Recipes* }

LAURA WERLIN

photographs by
MAREN CARUSO

STEWART, TABORI & CHANG
NEW YORK

TO THE CHEESEMAKERS

Published in 2007 by Stewart, Tabori & Chang
An imprint of Harry N. Abrams, Inc.

Text copyright © 2007 Laura Werlin
Photographs copyright © 2007 Maren Caruso

Library of Congress Cataloging-in-Publication Data:
Werlin, Laura.
Laura Werlin's cheese essentials : an insider's
guide to buying and serving cheese : with 50 recipes.
p. cm.
Includes index.
ISBN 978-1-58479-627-5
1. Cookery (Cheese) I. Title.

TX759.5.C48W49 2007
641.6'73--dc22
2007015459

Editor: Julie Stillman
Designer: The Engine Room
Production Manager: Jacquie Poirier

The text of this book was composed in Warnock Pro and Geometric

Printed and bound in China
10 9 8 7 6 5 4 3 2 1

HNA
harry n. abrams, inc.
a subsidiary of La Martinière Groupe

115 West 18th Street
New York, NY 10011
www.hnabooks.com

Acknowledgments

Not only does the process of writing acknowledgments help bring the concept of gratitude into focus, it also puts those who have been helpful along the way front and center. This time, as I reflected on those people, I was struck by the number of individuals in the publishing arena who have been with me since I wrote my first book. In this business, such continuity is a rarity. For that and so many reasons, I am humbled and grateful.

Among those individuals is my agent, Carole Bidnick, whose unwavering support, infectious optimism ("it *will* happen"), and generosity of spirit have opened doors to professional opportunities and a personal bond that no contract ever could have included; Stewart, Tabori & Chang vice president and publisher Leslie Stoker, a rarity both within and apart from publishing because of her vision, fine character, and unwavering support; and my editor, Julie Stillman. This is the one time when my typical wordiness eludes me, for I can't possibly adequately express my gratitude for her skill and patience.

Photographer Maren Caruso and food stylist Kim Konecny are masters at turning food into art and still make it look like food. Their considerable talent and restraint makes this so. My deepest thanks to them as well as to Maren's fantastic photography assistant, Scott Mansfield, and to aspiring photographer Ron Armstrong.

I loved watching The Engine Room's principal, Dave Braden, "engineer" his creativity by taking my words and Maren's images and transforming them into a beautiful design that made sense.

The beautiful cheese photographs would not have been possible without the cheeses themselves. For this I have Ray Bair, owner of the magnificent San Francisco shop Cheese Plus, and Sara Vivenzio, the founder of the popular San Francisco Cheese School, to thank. Ray and Sara spent an inordinate amount of time ensuring that I got the cheeses I wanted and that they were in perfect shape. Ray also allowed us to bring our photo equipment into his busy store to bring you the cheese shop photos you see in this book. I can't thank him enough.

There are many others in the cheese world who have been immensely helpful along the way. From the world of academia, my deep appreciation goes to Dean Sommers from the Center for Dairy Research in Wisconsin and Marc Druart, cheesemaker at the Vermont Institute of Artisan Cheese, for answering my technical questions with nontechnical verbiage I could actually understand. My thanks to Dave Leonhardi of the Wisconsin Milk Marketing Board, who shuttled me across the Wisconsin plains, introducing me to cheesemakers along the way; and to Bob Kenney of Context Marketing in Sausalito, California, and Nancy Fletcher of the California Milk Advisory Board for their ongoing support of all things cheese. My deepest gratitude to Cindy and Liam Callahan, cheesemakers and owners of Bellwether Farms in California, who once again endured my relentless questions and Maren's shutter-clicking in the midst of making crucial cheesemaking decisions. Thanks also to cheesemakers Jennifer Bice, Allison Hooper, Judy Schad, and Joe Widmer. You and all American cheesemakers are my heroes.

I shudder to think what the recipes in this book would have been without phenomenal cook and de facto Southern humorist Sheri Castle, who enthusiastically tested each recipe and weighed in with experience, grace, the aforementioned humor, and essential tips. Thank you, Sheri.

Once again, my dearest friend Cheryl Gould took the lead on the hobbyist recipe-testing front, marshaling testers into their kitchens to make my nascent recipes. My deepest thanks to Cheryl and the "troops," Lori Ayre, Barbara Ayre, Renee Vollen, Sara Farandini, Lisa Krieshok, Pam Asselmeier, Julie Reich-King, Chuck King, Rose Zamudio, Sharon McAuley, and Dana Whitaker. Thanks also to chef Matt Colgan from À Côté restaurant in Oakland, California, and Top Chef Harold Dieterle for their recipe contributions.

An integral part of this book lies within the Appendix. A huge thank-you to fellow cheese fanatic Kate Brady for her painstaking work to compile a list of cheese shops we can really use.

Sometimes people are just there and don't have any awareness that they're helping, but they are. To these people, I say thank you: Kim Müller, Greg O'Byrne, Tim Gaiser, Gail Simmons, Christina Grdovic, Steve Dveris, Barbara Smith, Kevin Karl, Lynne Devereux, Jeff Roberts, John Folse, Michaela York, Kurt Dammeier, David Gremmels, Carole Palmer, Noah Marshall-Rashid, Peter O'Grady, Michelle Kiley, Dave Halverson, and my friends Faye Keogh, Beth Roemer, and Kevin Donahue, who ate recipes in the rough and made me feel as if it was the best food they ever tasted.

Finally, where would I be without my family? To my mom and dad, my sister, Andi, and to Valerie, all of whom once again contributed to the recipes, the stories, the very fiber of this book, and to me. You are my foundation, encouraging and inspiring me today.

CONTENTS

INTRODUCTION

If only our voracious appetite for cheese and our knowledge of it could find a peaceful intersection! At least that is the message I have been hearing as I travel the country educating the cheese-hungry about one of the world's oldest foods. This thirst for knowledge about cheese is encouraging because learning comes on the heels of desire. But I am also noticing that as the number of cheeses grows so does the intimidation factor. This troubles me because cheese is a humble food, the representation of the magical transformation of milk, as rustic in its appearance as it is in its appeal.

In itself, cheese is a paradox. It is unpresumptuous yet capable of inspiring extreme exhilaration in its taster. I suppose it's this tension that makes cheese and its study so compelling. We love a food that we cannot master, one that continually reveals itself but never really allows itself to be known. Each experience, each taste of cheese is different, making it intrinsically indefinable. In short, a cheese's elusive quality is responsible for its relentless grasp on the palate and on our souls.

In many ways we know "cheese" in the generic sense as well or better than any other food because of its ubiquity. It is on pizzas, in sandwiches, and on hamburgers; it is half of the macaroni duo, the precursor to "and crackers," an essential ingredient in a soufflé. Now, however, instead of generic cheeses, we are adorning our hamburgers with Emmentaler, our pizzas with Gruyère, and our macaroni with Vermont cheddar. Yet sometimes having too many choices can be confusing, particularly as our lives become more complicated. In the face of confusion, we look to the familiar and away from what is not. Although we appreciate having choices, the sight of, say, 300 cheeses to choose from is downright daunting and sometimes even maddening.

That's why I set out to help bridge the gap between the growing passion for cheese and our knowledge of it by writing a comprehensive easy-to-follow guide to buying, understanding, cooking, and entertaining with cheese. My goal is to make you "cheese wise." It is one thing to know the cheeses you like; it is quite another to venture into unknown cheese territory and feel confident on the journey. You just need some basic knowledge, and the rest is easy.

ABOUT THIS BOOK

Let's start at the beginning. In Chapter 1 you'll learn how to navigate a cheese counter, whether at the cheese shop, the supermarket, or the club store. You'll also learn some cheese basics: the characteristics of the different types of milk used for cheese—cow, goat, sheep, and water buffalo; information about rinds and mold; tips on cooking with cheese; and a word about the progress—indeed explosion—of American cheese, a movement I have long championed and am wildly passionate about.

The heart of the book consists of individual chapters on the eight styles of cheese—fresh, semi-soft, soft-ripened, surface-ripened, semi-hard, hard, blue, and washed-rind. It is my firm belief that if you understand these eight basic styles you will have a very good idea of how *all* cheeses taste. These chapters give you all the essential information you need to be an informed cheese buyer and consumer. Here's how the cheese style chapters are set up.

USES Because it is helpful to know how to use each style of cheese, I begin each chapter by telling you what those particular cheeses are best suited for. Are they good with vegetables? In salads? With meat? On a cheese board?

WHAT ARE THEY? is a list of the cheeses in that style that you're most likely to find when you go cheese shopping. In most chapters this is followed by a second list that I call Off the Beaten Path. These are cheeses that are not widely available or perhaps are seasonal, but worth knowing about should you see them. These lists specify the country the cheeses come from, and cheeses that are made of goat's milk or sheep's milk; the rest are cow's milk cheeses.

You will see the phrase *"See also"* in some of the listings. This is because not all cheeses fit neatly into just one style. A cheese like the Spanish Mahón might start out as a semi-soft cheese, but some cheesemakers choose to age it; depending on how long it's aged, it will become a semi-hard or even a hard cheese. For this reason, you will find Mahón listed in the semi-soft, semi-hard, and hard style chapters.

YOU KNOW IT'S A ___ CHEESE WHEN. . . This section gives you a list of visual characteristics that distinguish that style of cheese. As you will learn, being able to identify a cheese by how it looks will give you a very good idea of what that cheese will taste like without ever taking a bite.

THE EXPLANATION The explanation section describes how each style of cheese is made, the type of milk used, and other information specific to that style. Having a little insight into the "why's" of a style is key to remembering that style and once again, its distinctive flavor components.

Next, you'll learn **WHAT TO LOOK FOR WHEN BUYING** each style. To help you, I have provided **VISUAL, TEXTURAL, AROMA, AND FLAVOR CUES** and explain how to tell whether the cheese is in good or not-so-good shape.

There's also information on the **MOUTHFEEL** and **FINISH** for that style. The term "mouthfeel" is fairly literal, indicating how the cheese feels in your mouth. Is it creamy? Gritty? Chewy? The finish is the length of time and quality of the flavors and texture of the cheese that last long after you have swallowed it. A long finish generally indicates a more complex cheese.

A FEW NOTEWORTHY CHEESES Although there are hundreds of cheeses that are noteworthy for one reason or another, I wanted to bring special attention to a few cheeses within each style that I think are standouts.

IF YOU CAN'T FIND ___ USE ___ Is there overlap between styles of cheese? You bet. Although certain cheeses do not fall neatly into one style or another, they usually have enough of the characteristics of one particular style to clue you in to what style the cheese is likely to be. Just in case, I have provided substitutes for a number of cheeses within each style. For example, if you can't find a harder-to-get triple-crème cheese such as Brillat-Savarin, you can look at the list and feel confident that the more easily sourced St. André is a fine substitute.

STORING CHEESE Knowing how to care for cheese is just as important as knowing how to buy it. That's why every chapter includes instructions for how to care for cheese once you get it home.

CHEESE AND WINE PAIRING For many people, including me, cheese and wine are the ultimate pair. That's why I have included cheese and wine pairing tips in each chapter. I have also ranked each style of cheese based on its overall wine compatibility — reflected in the number of stars I have assigned it. The rankings range from one to five stars, with five being the best.

TAKE-HOME TEST Experimenting with cheese is truly the only way you can develop a visceral memory of it. The good news is that there are ways to develop that memory. One way is by doing a little homework. I have provided "take-home tests" at the end of each style chapter to give you practical tasting experience. Don't worry, these assignments are fun, not taxing. You can do them with friends and family or just on your own. They are designed for four people but you can customize them to suit your needs. You can even turn your homework assignment into a cheese-tasting party. The idea is that by doing a specific tasting assignment, you are much more likely to remember those cheeses and whether or not you like them. But it isn't just about individual cheeses. Each lesson is intended to teach you about an entire style of cheese, so when you shop for cheese, you will be able to identify each style just by looking at the cheeses. You will also have a broader understanding of the flavors you can expect within each style. If only school had been this much fun.

RECIPES I have created fifty recipes to showcase how to use the different styles of cheese. These are found at the end of each chapter.

APPENDIX At the back of the book you'll find an alphabetical list of cheeses, a basic cheese glossary, and resources for buying and learning about cheese.

Now that I've told you generally what to expect in these pages, I want to tell you what *not* to expect. This is not an encyclopedia, nor a guide to every cheese made in the world. Instead, this book is a comprehensive guide to *understanding* the styles of cheese you will find in places that offer average to very good cheese sections as well as stand-alone cheese shops. Your understanding of these styles will ensure you are happy with your cheese choices.

As the interest in cheese grows, you can get in on the excitement simply by getting started. Take out your cheese knives (see pages 238–239), dig out your cheese board (see page 236), and get ready to understand cheese in a way that will serve you whenever and wherever you buy it, even if it's in a cheese shop in France. You may not know the spoken language, but you will know the language of cheese and how to choose it. Best of all, you'll almost certainly love your choice because it is an informed one. You are now in command of the *Cheese Essentials*.

Chapter 1

Getting

to Know

Cheese

Your first point of entry into the cheese world is the cheese shop or cheese aisle of the grocery store. After you've arrived there, it can be a huge leap to actually decide on a particular cheese to buy. This chapter is designed to help you make that decision with confidence and ease by introducing you to different means of navigating the cheese counter as well as provide you with basic but essential cheese information.

Navigating the Cheese Counter

Does this sound familiar? You casually walk up to the cheese counter at your local market or cheese shop where at least 50 and upward of 300 cheeses are beckoning. You came just for cheddar, but then the other 299 cheeses catch your eye. You haven't heard of most of them, let alone tasted them, and the cheese that you came in for now seems elusive. You'd rather run—or go to the block cheddar section—than make an uninformed choice. Still, you're intrigued. What *are* all these cheeses anyway?

Buying cheese these days is more challenging—and more fun—than ever before simply because of the sheer number of choices in cheese shops as well as the increasing number of grocery stores that carry a wider variety of cheeses. For people whose sun rises and sets on cheese, the ever-growing selection of cheese is nirvana. For those who are new to the cheese world, it is a mixed bag. You want to know more but it is almost overwhelming.

If you find buying cheese intimidating or downright scary, you are not alone. In fact, you are like most cheese buyers. Think about it: just how much can anyone know about a food category that boasts well over a thousand varieties? This begs the question, where do you start?

The Cheese Shop

In almost all cases, designated cheese shops or counters are the most shopper-friendly places to buy cheese. Not only is the selection more varied and extensive, this setting also gives you the opportunity to have a conversation with a knowledgeable person who can lead you to good choices. As part of that, you have the essential opportunity to taste the cheese. Cheese shops and staffed cheese counters are also the places where you will find the majority of cheeses in excellent condition, because the shop goes through them quickly and the staff knows how to take care of them.

In addition, a cheese shop is where you are most likely to get the answers you're seeking about cheese. Because most cheese shop owners have a passion for their product, they like to travel the world sourcing cheese and quite often have relationships with cheesemakers and *affineurs* (cheese agers) in other countries. Those relationships yield hard-to-get and even unique cheeses, making your trip to the cheese shop all the more worthwhile — you never know exactly what you'll find. Part and parcel of this is also that the owner has effectively endorsed each cheese on the shelf.

One of the downsides to shopping for cheese in a cheese shop is that you may feel as if you have *too* many choices. Variety may be the spice of life, but really, do you need *300* varieties, twenty of which are blue cheese? If you walk into a shop without a clue as to what you're looking for, the answer quite possibly is no. But for anyone who likes cheese (which presumably includes you if you are reading this book), the sights, the sounds, and the aromas add up to one fantastic sensory experience that makes the momentary discomfort worthwhile. In short, the cheese shop is the best and ultimately easiest place to buy cheese, despite the number of choices, because that is where you will get the most help. It helps to know what to ask, though.

You and the Cheesemonger

Obvious though this may be, it still bears stating: the best way to approach cheese buying is to engage in a dialog with the cheesemonger so he can help you select the right cheeses. You might be pleasantly surprised to find that you have more answers than you think. Here are a few basic questions to get you started:

- What are you using the cheese for? Cooking? Snacking? Entertaining?
- For a cheese course, when do you plan to serve it? Before dinner or after?
- How many people are you having?
- Are there any cheeses you know you do or do not like? If you know you dislike a certain cheese then state that right away. You will eliminate an entire group of cheeses and make your time at the cheese shop more efficient.

Based on your answers, the cheesemonger will guide you to different cheeses and to the number and quantity of cheeses you should serve.

Following are some specific situations, questions and tips that may be helpful when buying cheese.

If you are looking for something particular, say, a sheep's milk cheese that is not too strong:

- Do you like harder-style cheeses like Parmesan, softer-style ones like Monterey Jack or creamy ones like Brie? With this information the cheesemonger can determine your cheese preferences in general, regardless of the kind of milk they are made with.
- The retailer may tell you he has a very creamy and buttery Brie-like sheep's milk cheese and he also has a firm cheese that has nutty, buttery, and earthy flavors. Neither is strong or sheepy (reminiscent of the barnyard or of strong sheep or lamb aromas).

If you don't like a certain style of cheese (blue cheeses or goat cheeses, for example), but everyone else in your family does, you might ask the cheesemonger to let you taste some milder cheeses within that style. If you tend to like creamy cheeses in general, the cheesemonger might have you try some young blue cheeses—which are usually milder and almost always creamier—and point you toward some Brie-like blue cheeses such as Cambozola, Saga Blue, or a real crowd-pleaser called Montbriac. (See Chapter 8 for more on blue cheeses and page 205 for a recipe using Montbriac).

The same holds true with goat cheeses. Many people find they like goat cheese more than they thought after they taste one that isn't strong. Very often the goat cheeses they have tried in the past have been strong or goaty (reminiscent of the barn in which the animals live). One taste of a mild or even sweet goat cheese, such as goat gouda or a very popular cheese called Midnight Moon, will often convert even the most reluctant goat cheese eater.

If you have no idea what you want because you don't know much about cheese, the retailer will try to help narrow down your choices by ascertaining your basic preferences:

- Do you tend to like soft, creamy cheeses or firmer ones?
- Do you like mild and strong cheeses or just one or the other?
- Do you like salty cheeses?
- Do you like blue cheeses?

Tips

- **Never be afraid to ask for a taste no matter how busy the store might be.** Retailers are there to sell cheese, and they understand that you are much more likely to buy a cheese if you have tasted it.
- **If you don't have time to taste new cheeses, tell the retailer your very favorite cheese.** That provides a great starting point from which to select new cheeses. Or buy just a little of a few different cheeses and taste them at home. Don't forget to write down what you tasted!
- **If you feel like a deer in the headlights when terms like "nutty" and "earthy" are bandied about, don't be alarmed.** The only way you can possibly understand those terms is to taste a lot of cheese. It takes practice, but what a fun task that is.

You Are What You Eat

As I mentioned earlier, you can probably answer many of your cheese questions without the help of the retailer. While you cannot know the names of the cheeses to ask for, you can probably state your general preferences. You don't know your preferences? Think again.

Consider what you eat on a daily basis. You know whether or not you like strong, assertive flavors in the food you eat or milder, subtler flavors instead. Maybe you like both, depending on your mood or what the choices are at the moment. Still, there are ways to zero in on your preferences. Take a look at the following questions and then answer them. Believe it or not, you can apply your answers to cheese.

At a restaurant, are you more likely to order spice-crusted tuna or white fish in broth? If you chose the tuna, then chances are you gravitate toward assertive flavors. Naturally you might like both types of fish and simply have a preference for the tuna on a particular night, but that tells you something, too. It says you like a range of flavors. The cheese equivalents of the spiced tuna might range from a flavored cheese such as the pepper-studded Italian sheep's milk cheese called pecorino pepato to an aged cheese such as a 24-month Gouda or the classic Parmigiano-Reggiano. You might also like aged cheddar or Gruyère. On the other hand, the fish-in-broth lover might prefer younger, milder cheeses such as Havarti, Port-Salut, Monterey Jack, Colby, young Mahón, and young Gouda.

> BY IDENTIFYING YOUR GENERAL FOOD PREFERENCES YOU CAN GET CLOSER TO YOUR CHEESE PREFERENCES.

Do you gravitate toward silky, creamy, and buttery sauces or more intense meat reductions like a veal sauce? Creamy, buttery sauces are rich but generally mild. If that's your sauce preference, it is likely to be a style of cheese you like too. Think Brie, Camembert, Humboldt Fog, Pierre-Robert, Explorateur, and the like. (Never heard of those? Turn to the Soft-Ripened Cheeses chapter, page 88–111). If, however, you like sauce reductions, then that indicates you like a little punch, a little intensity, and rich flavors. In cheese, that might translate to aged Asiago, aged pecorino, a washed-rind cheese such as Munster or Reblochon, or a mountain cheese such as Comté, Gruyère, Abondance, or Emmentaler or an Italian toma.

When you order pasta, do you usually ask for extra Parmigiano-Reggiano grated on top or are you content with just a little? If you are in the more-is-better camp, then you probably like robust, salty flavors. Go for like cheeses. Parmigiano-Reggiano is an obvious choice. So is aged pecorino, often referred to as Pecorino Stagionato, (*stagionato* translates to aged), myzithra, cotija, and ricotta salata.

If just a little grated cheese suits you, then your obvious choice is to ask for less cheese. But the underlying question is whether you want less cheese because the flavor is too pungent for you? If so, then you might prefer full-flavored but less pungent aged cheeses such as aged Asiago, Piave Vecchio (aged) or Dry Jack.

Are you someone who prefers tangy, sour, and vinegarlike flavors or do you gravitate more toward honey, sugar, teriyaki, and dried fruit flavors in your food? If you're in the high-acid category, meaning you like lemony and tart flavors, then fresh goat cheese, ash-ripened goat cheeses (Pouligny-St.-Pierre, Selles-Sur-Cher, and Valençay), and cheeses that have a pronounced tangy quality such as Kirkham's Lancashire, Bellwether Farms' Carmody, or even a zingy blue cheese such as Point Reyes Farmstead Cheese Company's Original Blue will probably appeal to you. If you gravitate toward sweetness in your food, then do the same with cheese. Go for an aged Gouda, such as Old Amsterdam, the caramel-like Norwegian goat cheese called Gjetost, or Midnight Moon, an aged goat's milk Gouda.

 ### The Cost of Cheese Pleasure

Forget the cholesterol. It's often the price of cheese that can be heart-stopping. You can easily walk away with half a pound of cheese for which you might have paid somewhere between six and sixteen dollars. Why so much? There are myriad reasons for the high cost of cheese, and believe it or not, most of them are quite valid. In the United States, cheesemaking itself is very expensive, which means the product is too. Inspections, the cost of labor, the cost of equipment, milk, etc, and the extremely high cost of shipping keep the prices of American-made specialty and artisan cheese relatively high. (Factory-made cheeses are priced much more competitively because of the bulk nature of such operations.) In addition, cheese is expensive because much of what we get in specialty cheese shops is made in very small quantities and often by a small group of people, such as a co-op, or by just one person. In these cases, we are paying for highly specialized cheese and cheesemaking.

Yet another reason you leave a cheese shop with a lighter wallet is because of the very nature of cheese: it is perishable. A cheese shop has to cover its costs of storing and maintaining cheese, which means they have to buy it and tend to it before they sell it. They then have to cut and wrap the cheese, which involves still more labor. In the end, what you buy usually has been marked up by as much as 100 percent or even more. No question that's a huge markup, but most cheese shop owners will tell you they are not getting rich no matter how it may seem.

Finally, some countries subsidize their farmer's cheese, and that translates to cheaper prices on imported cheese for us. That, however, is dependent on the value of the foreign currency relative to the dollar. When the Euro or the English pound is high, so are the prices of cheese from those countries, which means that the subsidies don't always translate to cheaper prices on imports for us.

THE GROCERY STORE

Not all grocery stores are alike when it comes to cheese—many now have separate, staffed cheese departments, at others you're on your own. At a staffed cheese counter you have the opportunity to do exactly what you can do at a cheese store, ask questions and taste. Fortunately this type of grocery store setup is becoming more commonplace as store owners understand the importance of providing good cheese to the increasingly discriminating American cheese consumer.

If you shop at a store that has a separate cheese counter, take a cue from the hints in the cheese shop section and follow suit. Not to sound like a broken record, but the most important things you can do are to ask questions and taste.

Buying Cheese When There's No One Around to Help

Buying cheese at the grocery store unquestionably presents the greatest challenge. First, the types and variety of cheeses sold at grocery stores vary tremendously. Many stores offer fine cheese selections, even if nothing terribly unusual or exotic. Still, the offerings can be more than serviceable particularly when it comes to cooking with cheese. The problem is that in the case of most supermarkets, you are on your own to make your selections. Occasionally stores

 How to Read a Label

Cheese sold at grocery stores has labels that tell you the name of the cheese, the producer or manufacturer, the price per pound, the ingredients, nutritional information, possibly how long the cheese has been aged, and sometimes marketing tidbits such as whether the cheese is made with hormone-free (no rBST) milk. It might also contain information about how to serve the cheese and even sometimes wine- or beer-pairing suggestions. What is often missing from standard labels is the actual milk source — cow, goat, or sheep. If it does not say, that usually means it is made with cow's milk. "Usually" is the operative word. At times, I have found feta cheese that has

been made with sheep's milk (as it often is), but it does not say so on the label. Likewise, occasionally factory-made pecorino will not state that it is a sheep's milk cheese. I have yet to see a goat's milk cheese that wasn't labeled as such.

Cheese stores or supermarkets with staffed cheese counters usually cut and wrap their own cheese, so those labels most often contain the name of the cheese, the price per pound, the producer, whether or not the cheese is made with raw milk, and ususally the type of milk used. Since cheese labels don't usually give you flavor cues, either you have to be familiar with the cheese already or take your best guess by evaluating it based on what you know about the styles of cheese.

will have someone fairly knowledgeable about cheese on staff, but tracking that person down can be a challenge. In these situations, you, the cheese-buyer, must make choices about cheeses you may have never tasted. More important, you will not be able to taste them before buying. What do you do? We'll get to that shortly.

Cheese Word Tip-Offs

Whether a cheese label is made by the cheese store or the cheese manufacturer, usually it contains useful clues about the cheese. All you have to do is pay attention.

Here are just a few descriptors you might see:

- Creamy
- Soft
- Tangy
- Nutty
- Sharp
- Pungent
- Aged
- Extra-aged
- *Stagionato*
- *Vecchio*
- *Piccante*

The first three descriptors tell you the cheese is fairly young and mild. "Nutty," "sharp," and "pungent" tell you the cheese will be more assertive, while "aged" is a bit more nebulous. It might be a marketing ploy only because "aged" is seen as a value-added feature. Or it could actually be meaningful, indicating that the cheese has been brought to maturity and then to market at the optimum time. Very often a cheese labeled "aged" will be firmer in texture too. Extra-aged, *stagionato* and *vecchio*, all indicate hard chees-es. *Stagionato* means aged and *vecchio* literally means old. While old may not seem like a favorable term, when used as a modifier for certain types of cheese, it is intended to be a good thing. Literally "sharp," *piccante* is usually used to refer to a cheese that is both sharp and aged. The aged blue cheese called Gorgonzola Piccante is one of the most common examples.

Referring back to the styles of cheese, if you know the main characteristics of each style of cheese, you know what to expect when you see certain adjectives describing them.

BUYING CHEESE ONLINE

No matter where you live, good cheese can always be at your doorstep with the click of a mouse. Cheese buying on the Internet is a great way to go, although it has a few downsides: First, buying cheese this way is usually quite expensive. Although the cheese might be priced the same as it is in a cheese shop, the high cost enters in with the shipping. The perishability of cheese means that it must be shipped in either one or two days. This translates to the costliest means of ship-ping and therefore a very expensive product. It is not uncommon to find that a pound of cheese from an Internet site costs, say, $15, and then discover that the-cost of shipping is the same or much higher, thus doubling or tripling the cost. The good news is that the more cheese you order (up to a certain point), the less you are paying per ounce of cheese in shipping because the shipping costs are often the same whether you are buying a pound or three pounds of cheese.

Another issue in sourcing cheese over the Internet is that you cannot taste it, look at it, or smell it before buying. Instead, you must rely on the descriptions the site provides (these vary considerably in usefulness, although most are very good), and you also have to hope that the source of the cheese keeps it in top-notch condition. Most cheese sites care for their cheese, but because cheese is so perishable, you're at the mercy of the staff and their competence.

Overall, ordering cheese online is a good way to source cheeses you cannot get otherwise, but you must be prepared to pay a significant surcharge for the luxury of cheese at your doorstep. See page 265 for some online cheese sources.

 Perception Is Not Reality

If you were ever to linger around a cheese counter of any kind and take mental inventory of the cheeses being sold, you would be surprised by how many different kinds of the same cheeses there are. Usually there are at least two and often three or four fresh goat cheeses, several Brie-like cheeses, and a rainbow of blue cheeses. This means that while there might be 300 cheeses, there are not 300 *different* cheeses. See? Already the cheese aisle is more manageable. Still, knowing that does not help you know what the cheeses taste like; for that you need to learn the *eight styles of cheese.*

BECOMING CHEESE WISE

In order to be an informed cheese buyer and consumer, it helps to have some basic information about cheese. This section introduces you to the different styles of cheese and explains some other cheese essentials, such as the fundamentals of cheesemaking and cooking with cheese.

THE EIGHT STYLES OF CHEESE

Once you know something about the different styles of cheese, you will begin to be able to discern the basic flavor profiles of specific cheeses even if you have never tasted them. Really! From there, you will be able to make informed cheese-buying choices.

The eight styles are:
- Fresh cheeses
- Semi-soft cheeses
- Soft-ripened cheeses
- Surface-ripened cheeses
- Semi-hard cheeses
- Hard cheeses
- Blue cheeses
- Washed-rind cheeses

Terms like "semi-hard," "surface-ripened," and so on may not mean anything to you now, but I hope they will begin to make sense once you read more about them in the chapters to come. To give you a head start, here is a chart of the styles of cheese, a brief description, and a list of a few cheeses in each of the styles.

THE EIGHT STYLES OF CHEESE

	Flavors	How strong?	Examples
Fresh cheeses	mild, milky, tangy	mild	fresh goat cheese, ricotta, mozzarella
Semi-soft cheeses	milky, tangy, sweet	mild	Colby, Havarti, Port-Salut
Soft-ripened cheeses	buttery, creamy, mushroomy	mild to medium-strong	Brie, Camembert
Surface-ripened cheeses	creamy, earthy, mushroomy, tangy	mild to medium-strong	LaTur, Le Chevrot, St. Marcellin
Semi-hard cheeses	buttery, earthy, fruity, nutty	medium-strong	cheddar, Gouda, Gruyère
Hard cheeses	caramel candylike, salty, sweet, sharp	medium-strong to strong	Parmigiano-Reggiano, aged Asiago, pecorino
Blue cheeses	floral, musty, salty, pungent	medium-strong to very strong	Maytag Blue, Gorgonzola, Stilton
Washed-rind cheeses	beefy, creamy, gamy, nutty, salty	strong to very strong	aged brick, Epoisses, Munster, Taleggio

Texture Is Flavor

If you look closely at the list of the eight styles, you will see that most of them seem to be descriptions of texture rather than flavor. That is because *the texture of a cheese provides the single biggest clue as to how a cheese will taste.*

Let's take Parmigiano-Reggiano as an example. Just by virtue of its hard texture, you know the cheese has been aged for a long time. (Most cheese becomes harder over time in part because aging is a process of moisture loss.) In addition, the texture of a hard cheese will look and feel granular, not smooth. You know this because when you ask for grated cheese on your pasta, the cheese that is used is usually some type of Parmesan.

Because you've tasted Parmesan you already have a window into the texture of hard cheeses. As for the flavors in hard cheeses, you can count on the dominant flavors being just two things: salty and sweet. Of course, these are not the only flavors, but they are the ones that distinguish hard cheeses from the other cheese families. It's amazing how quickly you can become an expert in a style of cheese.

In addition, hard cheeses are very durable and don't need to be under constant refrigeration. This means that in a cheese shop or at a staffed supermarket cheese counter you will often find hard cheeses displayed on top of the counter rather than under refrigeration. This is another clue that you are in hard cheese territory. To test this, in your mind return to the supermarket cheese aisle where there is no one to help you. Find the section where most of the hard cheeses are located.

> KNOWING THE TEXTURE OF A CHEESE PROVIDES AN ESSENTIAL WINDOW INTO ITS FLAVOR.

The selection in most stores is usually fairly heavy on Italian cheeses because those are the hard cheeses most people are familiar with and use. (The other large subcategory of hard cheeses is aged Gouda, usually displayed separately from the Italian-style hard cheeses.) Once again, remind yourself of the key characteristics of hard cheeses (saltiness, sweetness, graininess, and it feels hard to the touch), and remember that most cheese displays include several variations of one main type of cheese. This means that there could be nine or ten different hard cheeses that are similar to Parmesan and will likely have the word "Parmesan" or, for the original, "Parmigiano-Reggiano," on their label. Now you are ready to pick out a hard cheese on your own even though no one has helped you. By understanding the main characteristics in each style, you have effectively reduced the 300 cheeses on display to just a fraction of that.

By connecting the dots—realizing that most hard cheeses are salty, grainy, and sweet—you have practically mastered a whole group of cheeses because you

Parmigiano-Reggiano

understand the main flavor components to expect in hard cheeses. How do you figure out which category a cheese falls into? That will be revealed in each of the style chapters that follows.

Needless to say, you cannot know exactly what a cheese tastes like until you've actually tasted it. The same is true for any food. If someone tries to describe what cabbage tastes like and they tell you it tastes a little like cauliflower, you may have some sense of what it is like (if you've tasted cauliflower), but you won't know until you try it. Another example is wine. If you are a wine drinker then you know that there are several styles of wines that are all made with the same grape. A Cabernet made by one winemaker in Napa will almost certainly taste different from the Cabernet made by the winemaker down the road, which is different still from a Cabernet made in Washington or France. So it is with cheese. Until you've actually tasted a particular cheesemaker's cheddar, you cannot know its exact flavors even though you may know generally what cheddar tastes like.

How Cheese Is Made

Although you don't necessarily need to know how cheese is made to be able to make good choices about which cheeses to buy, I believe it's important to have some understanding of how milk is transformed into the myriad cheeses that are before you in the cheese aisle.

The process of cheesemaking begins more or less the same, although innumerable decisions are made right from the start that will affect the outcome. The basic steps are:

1) Starter cultures are added to pasteurized or raw milk to start the acidification process or "souring" of the milk. (Alternatively, the milk is left to sour overnight on its own; this is called an acid-set cheese.)

2) Animal, microbial (vegetarian), or vegetable rennet (an enzyme) is added, which curdles the milk. When the curds (solids) are properly set, they look and feel very much like custard.

3) The curds are cut with knives called harps, which break the "custard" or curds into pieces and release the whey (liquid).

4) The whey is drained to varying degrees depending on the desired cheese.

5) The curds are put into molds of varying sizes and drained further. For harder cheeses, the curds may also be pressed with weights of some kind.

6) If the cheese is not going to be aged, it will be packaged and immediately sent to market. Otherwise, it is aged and tended to for a period of time that might extend from days to years.

Before coagulated curds are cut to expel the whey, their texture is like custard.

These steps are just the fundamentals of cheesemaking. They do not allow for the artistry that is also a significant part of the process. Almost anyone can follow the science of cheesemaking, but there are many other factors, including the milk quality, environment, diet of the animals, and what I call the "sixth sense" of the cheesemaker, which is that special ability to know how to finesse all of the factors to make one great cheese.

If I have fielded one particular question more than just about any other it is, "Should I eat the rind?" The answer is, it depends (unless the rind is waxed or has cheesecloth still clinging to it). Technically, most rinds are edible, but that doesn't necessarily mean you should eat them. Remember that the rind is part of the cheese, not something that is affixed later. It is there to protect and effectively nurture the cheese to maturity. Because of its exposure to air, it might become crusty or hard. It may be edible in the sense that it won't hurt you, but by eating it you are most likely detracting from the flavors and texture of the cheese itself because a crusty rind won't taste very good.

When it comes to eating the rind on soft-ripened cheeses like Brie, there is no "right" thing to do. That is to say, the white bloomy rind is an integral part of the cheese and as such, is intended for eating. In fact, to many it would be unthinkable to leave it behind, while to others, including the famed French cheesemonger, Pierre Androuët, it would be unthinkable *to* eat it. It provides a kind of chewy textural contrast to the creamy cheese beneath it, and although mild, has a distinct flavor all its own. Just know that if you decide not to eat the rind, you will not be committing a social faux pas, and vice-versa. Whether there is a rind or not, the interior, always edible portion of the cheese is called the paste or pâte. These words can be used interchangeably.

"Good Mold" is Not an Oxymoron

As a cheese's protector, think of the rind as a coat of armor. There are many types of rinds, including ones that are comprised of mold and bacteria. Sounds appetizing, doesn't it? But in the context of cheese, mold and bacteria are good things, or at least they can be. Each can also be destructive to a cheese, which the rind is there to buffer. Sometimes the rind will serve the dual function of keeping out the bad molds while facilitating the cheese-ripening process with good molds. On the other hand, a rind can be the first part of a cheese to deteriorate, as in the case of a soft-ripened (Brie-like) cheese, and will take the rest of the cheese with it. In any case, how can you tell whether the mold on a cheese—either at the store or at home—is edible or if it should be avoided?

Fresh Cheeses

As a general rule, the younger the cheese, the more important that it be free of mold. Put another way, a young cheese like mozzarella, crescenza, fresh Mexican cheeses such as panela, and many other fresh and some semi-soft cheeses should not have any mold because the whole raison d'être for that type of cheese is immediate consumption. If mold has developed, the cheese is almost certainly over the hill.

Semi-Soft Cheeses

Semi-soft cheeses have been aged for just a few weeks if at all, and should also be free of mold. Examples of these cheeses include waxed Goudas, Havarti, and Colby. The mold will not hurt you; it just tastes terrible.

Semi-Hard and Hard Cheeses

Cheeses with natural rinds such as farmhouse cheddar may very well develop a little mold on the rind and possibly in the paste (interior) of the cheese too, depending on its age. The older the cheese, the greater the chances are that blue mold will seep into the cracks of certain cheeses, particularly aged cheddar. It is up to you whether or not you choose to eat that part of the cheese. Some people treasure it, while others deride it.

Other semi-hard cheeses such as Gruyère, Comté, and Tomme de Savoie and hard cheeses such as Parmigiano-Reggiano should remain fairly mold-free. If the cut surface develops a little mold, simply cut off about ¼ inch of all cut surfaces of the rind, wiping the knife in between so as not to disperse mold spores, and go ahead and eat the cheese. If you don't like the way it tastes because it has become quite salty, then the cheese should probably be discarded.

Soft-Ripened, Surface-Ripened, and Washed-Rind Cheeses

Since mold is an integral part of these cheeses (these are cheeses with soft rinds that may be white, yellowish, or red-orange in color respectively), you cannot avoid mold unless you avoid those cheeses. This includes Brie and other similar cheeses. If, however, these cheeses look moldy, particularly if they have a black, kind of hairy mold on them, then do not buy them. This mold, called mucor, will not hurt you, but you can tell by the description alone that it may not be a mold you want to ingest.

Blue Cheeses

Like the three styles above, mold is an integral part of blue cheese. Usually you do not have to worry about other, unde-sirable molds colonizing blue cheeses. If anything, the mold that is there intentionally might continue to grow a little, which is fine.

Aroma Cues

Now that you know about rinds and about mold, it's time to stick your nose into it. Smelling cheese is an essential part of choosing and tasting it. Let's go back to the grocery store where there is no one to help you with the cheese. Not only can you look at the cheeses and visually evaluate their condition, sometimes you can smell them too. Granted, cheeses in a grocery store cheese display are sometimes too cold to smell or are packaged in such thick plastic that the only thing you can smell is the rotisserie chicken Ferris wheeling nearby. Still, many stores cut and wrap cheese themselves, which means it is usually wrapped in thinner plastic wrap, so you might be able to smell the aromas. A cheese's aroma can often tell you whether or not the cheese is in good condition.

If you are at a designated cheese shop as opposed to an unstaffed cheese display and are handed a piece of cheese to taste, be sure to breathe in the aromas before you take a bite. Smelling the cheese will give you a hint of what you're about to taste, and it actually prolongs the flavors you taste as well. That is because you taste with your entire olfactory system, which includes the nasal passage. No, you are not snorting the cheese, but separating your taste buds from your sense of smell is impossible. This is the same reason that the flavors in food are muted when we have a cold.

Although in the chapters to come you will learn what to look for (and what to avoid) when it comes to the aromas in the eight styles of cheese, for now just think about how a cheese should smell based on its age:

- Fresh cheeses should smell fresh, not like sour milk.

- Semi-soft cheeses will have very mild aromas. Sometimes they may have a vaguely tangy aroma, but mostly they should have fresh milk aromas.

- Soft-ripened and surface-ripened cheeses such as Brie and Robiola respectively should have clean or possibly mushroomy smells, but under no circumstances should they smell like ammonia.

- Semi-hard and hard cheeses might smell a little musty or possibly barnyardy, but for the most part, they should not have an overpowering musty or moldy smell like an old attic and instead should smell more like nuts, grass, and maybe hay among other aromas.

- Blue cheeses should not bowl you over with a strong smell; in fact, they might smell sweet or tangy. Stay away from blue cheeses that smell like ammonia.

- Washed-rind cheeses are distinctive *because* of their strong aromas. These strong-smelling cheeses have all kinds of character, and many people find their characteristic, sweaty gym-sock aroma completely off-putting. Others love it. Like soft-ripened and surface-ripened cheeses, washed-rind cheeses will start to smell like ammonia eventually. If the ammonia smell is strong, it's too late to eat them.

MILK DISTINCTIONS

You may or may not be able to tell the difference between a goat and a sheep (you'd be surprised how many people can't), but chances are if you were to taste their milk side by side, you'd notice the differences right away. A cow is a different animal altogether, and I'm not talking just her size. A cow's milk-fat globules are larger than those of her smaller four-legged counterparts, which does not translate to a more fattening cheese, just milk that presents particular challenges in cheesemaking. Also, a cow is a much more prolific milk-giver than the others. Still, the milk composition is for the cheesemakers to worry about. For you, the cheese eater, knowing the differences in flavor between cow, goat, and sheep milk is helpful when choosing cheeses.

Following are some general characterizations of the three main types of milk used for cheese. The fourth kind of milk comes from water buffaloes, whose milk has long been used to make cheese in southern Italy. Now there are thriving water buffalo dairies and water buffalo dairy product manufacturing in Vermont and California, with more getting started in other states. Buffalo milk is the main ingredient in the classic *mozzarella di bufala*, but it is also used to make yogurt and other cheeses.

Cow's milk:	Sweet, creamy, buttery
Goat's milk:	Lemony, tangy, earthy
Sheep's milk:	Buttery, nutty, oily, gamy
Water buffalo's milk:	Buttery, creamy, rich, tangy

Raw Versus Pasteurized Cheese

Not a week goes by that I am not asked about raw (unpasteurized) milk cheeses. Specifically, people want to know if they are legal in the United States. The answer is a qualified yes. Cheesemakers in the United States are allowed to make raw-milk cheeses just as European cheesemakers are allowed to make and sell them to us. The sole condition is that those cheeses must be aged for sixty days or more before they are sold.

To pasteurize milk, there are two legal methods in the U.S. Cheesemakers can either heat the milk for thirty minutes at a temperature of 145°F, or they can do so for fifteen seconds at a temperature of 160°F.

Are raw-milk cheeses better than pasteurized milk cheeses? Again, this has a qualified answer. Sometimes yes, sometimes no. I believe that the quality of the milk matters more than whether or not it is pasteurized, and the skill of the cheesemaker matters most of all. Still, there are certain cheeses, particularly younger ones, where the flavor nuances that are imparted by raw milk make the cheese unquestionably better than their pasteurized counterparts.

Orange Versus White Cheese

You have probably noticed that many cheeses are bright orange in color. Although unnatural looking, in fact, the dye used to color the cheese is entirely natural. It is called annatto and comes from the seed of a plant of the same name. In Spanish that plant is called achiote. Although we mostly associate orange cheese with American cheeses, annatto is also used in European cheeses such as France's Mimolette and England's Appleby's cheddar among others.

Remembering Your Cheeses

It is one thing to remember the eight styles of cheese (think fast: fresh, semi-soft, soft-ripened, surface-ripened, semi-hard, hard, blue, and washed-rind), but it's another to remember the names of specific cheeses. Unless you've got a photographic memory, the only way you can do it is to write them down. In particular, I like to encourage people to keep a cheese diary.

Below is a template to help get you started. Feel free to customize it to suit your particular needs.

Cheese Diary

- **Name of cheese**

- **Where and when you bought it**

- **Type of milk or milks it is made with**

- **Style of cheese** (fresh, semi-soft, soft-ripened, surface-ripened, semi-hard, hard, blue, or washed-rind)

- **How you used the cheese** (cheese board, cooking, etc.)

- **Flavor description**

- **Texture description**

- **The love factor:** Do you love, like, sort of like, do not like, loathe the cheese? Why?

Another way to remember cheeses is to eat them often, even daily. That doesn't mean that you should eat huge quantities every day. Instead, take a nibble here and there and believe me, you will begin to develop a taste memory very quickly because you will have tried familiar and new cheeses over and over.

Finally, use a variety of cheeses in cooking. The more you mix up your cheeses, the more likely you are not only to remember those you like but also to expand your cheese universe.

COOKING WITH CHEESE

When it comes to cooking, using a good cheese can transform a run-of-the-mill dish into a memorable one. Search out a full-flavored cheese at your local farmer's market or one that your cheese retailer recommends. Sometimes the cost of those cheeses may prevent you from cooking with them, but there are almost always acceptable less expensive variations of the expensive cheeses. Seeking out cheeses you may never have cooked with opens up a world of cheese recipe possibilities.

For example, let's say you've never had a washed-rind cheese. Maybe you don't know what "washed-rind" is. Once you read about that style of cheese, you can then use one of the cheeses listed to create the best potato gratin you've ever tasted by following the recipe on page 231. If you're used to using Swiss cheese to top your hamburgers, you'll be able to turn to the style chapter that includes Swiss cheese (semi-hard) and find a list of many other similar cheeses. The turkey burgers with Emmentaler on page 155 are delicious proof of how a slightly different cheese can improve a dish or bring new life to an old stand-by. Once you expand your cheese repertoire in the kitchen, I promise, you will never look back.

The Ooey-Gooey of Cheese—The Best Melting Cheeses

When it comes to making grilled cheese, pizza, omelets, or anything else in which you want the cheese to melt, there are certain cheeses that lend themselves to melting better than others. Following is a list of particularly good melters.

Appenzeller	Gouda (not aged)	Queso Oaxaca (nearly identical to mozzarella)
Asiago (fresh, not aged)	Gruyère	
Bel Paese	Havarti	Raclette
Brick	Iberico	Roncal
Brie	Jarlsberg	Swiss
Butterkäse	Mahón (not aged)	Teleme
Cantal	Manchego	Urgelia
Cheddar	Mimolette	
Cheshire	Monterey Jack	
Colby	Mozzarella	
Comté	Muenster	
Crescenza	Ossau-Iraty	
Double Gloucester	Pecorino (fresh, not aged)	
Edam	Port-Salut	
Fontina	Provolone	

Hard cheeses become toasty and nutty but not gooey when heated. That's why cheeses like Parmigiano-Reggiano and other aged cheeses are best used finely grated, as toppings rather than fillings.

Tips for Cooking with Cheese

Cooking with cheese is a cinch, although having a few tips in your back pocket never hurts. Here are some basics:

- 4 ounces of coarsely grated cheese is approximately 1¼ cups.
- 2 ounces of finely grated cheese is approximately 1 cup.
- 4 ounces of fresh cheese, such as ricotta, is approximately 1 cup.
- Grating your cheese for grilled cheese sandwiches makes the best sandwich. (It melts quicker, which means your bread won't burn before the cheese has become the molten texture you're looking for.)
- Cheese should be at room temperature for cooking (or eating).
- Cut the rind off soft-ripened and washed-rind cheeses when they are cold; bring them to room temperature before using.
- If melting a large quantity of cheese for fondue or a sauce, add a starch, such as flour, and an acid, such as lemon juice or wine, to prevent the cheese from curdling.

SAY *AMERICAN* CHEESE

Although American cuisine is no longer an oxymoron, the phrase "American cheese" has long conjured up an image of a strictly processed food not worthy of inclusion in a gourmet's vocabulary, let alone refrigerator. But thanks to a confluence of factors, the *new* American cheese has evolved, bumping its imported counterparts right off the shelves.

The shift started about fifteen years ago, when more Americans started traveling to Europe, where they had the opportunity to taste the types of cheeses that put France and Italy at the forefront of cheesemaking. They came home with an appetite for more of the same.

Fast-forward, and now it's easy to see that our interest in American cheese is being fueled by a variety of factors. We love farmers' markets, and because cheesemakers are part of most farmers' markets across the country, we get the chance to taste cheeses that might have been made just days before. Our skyrocketing interest and concern about where our food comes from dovetails with the opportunity to meet our local producers, including cheesemakers. Last but not least, the use of local cheeses by chefs has helped fuel the trend immeasurably. Ravioli might be ravioli, but when a chef creates pillows of pasta filled with ethereal ricotta made by the cheesemaker down the road, the humble dish takes on new meaning.

The evolution of American cheese is thrilling. No food trend has taken America by storm in quite the same way, possibly since the invention of fast food. While there are well-documented changes in the types and quality of the bread we eat, the coffee and wine we drink, and lately the chocolate we choose, it is cheese that has seized the American imagination in ways that other foods have not.

Consider that cheese factories have taken a nod from the artisan cheesemaking sector and have begun to convert entire plants into specialty cheesemaking facilities exclusively. Restaurant chains have begun to include specialty cheeses like Gruyère and Gorgonzola in their menu offerings, and now grocery stores are including American specialty cheeses instead of limiting the choices to generic bricks of cheese labeled "cheddar," "jack," and other vague descriptions.

The real trend in the growth of American cheese can best be seen through the viewfinder of the organization that is partly responsible for the trend—the American Cheese Society. In 2005, American cheesemakers submitted 715 cheeses for judging at the Society's annual cheese competition. In 2006, that number jumped to nearly a thousand, almost a 25 percent increase in the number of cheeses in just one year. And that number includes only cheesemakers that entered the competition. Imagine how many more there are quietly going about their way making and selling cheese, but who are not members of the organization.

Is all the cheese that's being made *good* cheese? Not necessarily. But the overall quality of cheese is astoundingly good, and it's getting even better. This is quite a feat considering we do not have the cheesemaking traditions in this country that the European cheesemakers have followed for centuries. Although our forebears brought cheesemaking with them and passed along the skill to subsequent generations, cheesemaking moved from the farm to the factory relatively early in our history.

Cheesemaking is now going in reverse, from factory to farm, and cheese-hungry Americans are clamoring for the results. Even those who, until recently, would not consider American cheese a phrase worth uttering, let alone a food worth eating, are now asking for it too. One of the best ways to look at the rise of American cheese is to look at the evolution of American wine. In its early days, American wine was mostly nondescript, mass-produced plonk. But a few individuals, particularly Robert Mondavi (someone we would probably now call an artisan), came along and began making excellent wines and, just as important, marketed them brilliantly. It didn't take long before American wine was respected rather than disparaged. The newfound respect for American cheese is evolving in a similar way, and most exciting of all, with approximately 150 cheesemakers in 2004 and at least 400 in 2006, the movement has clearly only just begun. (See Cheese Information Resources on page 255 for more information on American cheese and the American Cheese Society.)

Progressive Cheese List

Here is a guide to help you identify which cheeses are mild, medium, and strong in flavor.

Smooth and Mild

Burrata
Cotija
Cottage cheese
Cream cheese
Crescenza
Farmer's cheese
Feta
Fromage blanc
Goat cheese (also known as fresh chèvre or chèvre)
Halloumi
Manouri
Mascarpone
Mozzarella
Mozzarella di bufala
Neufchâtel
Oaxaca
Paneer
Panela
Pot cheese
Quark
Queso fresco
Requesón
Ricotta

Mild but Distinctive

Bel Paese (also made in the United States)
Brick (young)
Cheddar (young)
Cheshire
Colby
Crescenza
Edam
Fontal
Gaperon
Gloucester
Double Gloucester
Gouda (young)
Havarti
Iberico
Jarlsberg
Lancashire
Mahón (young)
Monterey Jack
Myzithra
Pecorino Fresco
Port-Salut
Queso Blanco
Ricotta Salata
Roomkaas
Saint-Paulin
St. Nectaire
Teleme
Wensleydale

Soft, Creamy, and Memorable

Banon
Brie
Brillat-Savarin
Camembert
Chaource
Cravanzina
L'Edel de Cleron
Explorateur
Fromager d'Affinois
Pave d'Affinois
Perail
Pierre Robert
Saint Albray
St. André
St. Maure
St. Simeon
St. Jean de Brie

Soft, Creamy, and Less Mild

Brin d'Amour
Chabichou de Poitou
Humboldt Fog
Monte Enebro
La Tur
Le Gariotin
Le Lingot
Robiola Bosina
Robiola Tre Latte
Rocchetta
St. Felicien
St. Marcellin
Selles-Sur-Cher
Valençay

Stand Up and Take Notice

Abbaye de Bellocq
Abondance
Appenzeller
Asiago
Beaufort
Cabécou
Cantal
Cheddar (farmhouse)
Chimay
Comté
Crottin de Chavignol
Dry Jack
Emmentaler
Fontina Val d'Aosta
Gjetost
Goat Gouda
Gouda (aged)
Graviera
Gruyère
Huntsman
Lagioule
Le Chevrot
L'Etivaz
Lincolnshire Poacher
Madrigal
Mahón (semi-hard)
Majorero
Manchego
Mimolette
Montasio
Monte Veronese
Murcia al Vino
Oka
Ossau-Iraty
Pecorino Sardo
Pecorino Toscana
Piave Mezzano
P'tit Basque
Prima Donna
Red Leicester
Rembrandt
Roncal
Sage Derby
São Jorge
Tête de Moine
Tomme de Savoie
Ubriaco
Vacherin Fribourgeois
Zamorano

Bites the Tongue (but delicious)

Asiago (aged)
Beemster Classic Extra-Aged
Beemster XO
Bra Tenero
Cotija
Fiore Sardo
Mahón (aged)
Mimolette (aged)
Montasio
Old Amsterdam
Parmigiano-Reggiano
Parrano
Pecorino Romano
Pecorino Stagionato
Pecorino Toscano
Piave Vecchio
Prima Donna (aged)
Provolone (*piccante* or sharp)

What's That I Smell?

Affedelice
Brescianella
Brescianella Stagionato
Brick (aged)
Epoisses
Esrom
Limburger
Livarot
Mariolles
Morbier
Munster
Pont-l'Evêque
Port-Salut
Raclette
Reblochon
Schlosskäse
Soumatrain
Taleggio
Tilsiter
Tomme du Berger
Vacherin Mont d'Or

There's Blue

Bleu d'Auvergne
Blue Castello
Cambozola
Cashel Blue
Crozier Blue
Fourme d'Ambert
Gorgonzola Dolce
Maytag Blue
Monte Enebro
Original Blue
Picon
Roaring Forties Blue
St. Agur
Windsor Blue

And There's Really Blue

Cabrales
Gorgonzola Piccante
Peñazul
Shropshire
Stilton
Valdeon

Clockwise from top: feta, mozzarella, fromage blanc

CHAPTER 2

FRESH

CHEESES

Use Fresh Cheeses for

- Casseroles
- Desserts
- Eggs
- Stuffed meat and poultry
- Salads
- Pasta
- Pizza
- Polenta
- Vegetables

What Are They?

Note: There are six categories of fresh cheese: soft, pasta filata, brined, pressed, whey, and nonmelters.

Soft Cheeses

France
Chèvre (goat cheese)
Fromage blanc
Neufchâtel

Germany
Quark (soft cheese)

United States
Cottage cheese
Cream cheese
Fromage blanc
Goat cheese (also called chèvre)
Herbed goat cheese (also known as chèvre)
Mascarpone
Quark

Pasta Filata Cheeses

Greece
Kasseri (sheep and goat's milk)

Italy
Burrata
Mascarpone

United States
Mozzarella
Mozzarella di bufala (water buffalo mozzarella)
Oaxaca

Brined Cheeses

Greece
Feta (sheep, goat, cow, or mixed milk)

United States
Feta (sheep, goat, cow, or mixed milk)

Pressed Cheeses

Mexico
Cotija

United States
Cotija
Farmer's cheese
Pot cheese

Whey Cheeses

Greece
Manouri (sheep and goat)
Myzithra (sheep and goat; *see also* hard cheeses)

Italy
Ricotta
Ricotta Salata (sheep's milk)

Mexico
Requesón

Norway
Gjetost

United States
Requesón
Ricotta

Nonmelters
Greece
Halloumi (sheep, sheep and goat's, and/or
  cow's milk)

India
Paneer

Mexico
Oaxaca
Queso fresco

United States
Farmer's cheese
Paneer
Panela
Pot cheese
Queso fresco

You know it's a Fresh Cheese when...

Soft Cheese

- It is bright white, off-white, or light ivory
- It is loose and fluffy or very creamy and smooth

Pasta Filata Cheese

- It is white to light ivory
- It is vacuum-sealed or packed in water

Brined Cheese

- It is white to off-white
- It is shiny and either crumbly or grainy
- It is grainy or crumbly
- It is packed in brine

Pressed Cheese

- It is white to off-white
- It is crumbly or grainy, smooth and silken, or pockmarked and crumbly

Whey Cheese

- It is bright white to off-white
- It is smooth-looking, almost silken (ricotta salata, myzithra, manouri) or pillowy and/or creamy (ricotta and requesón)
- It is firmly packed (ricotta salata, myzithra, manouri)

Nonmelter

- It is white to off-white
- It is mild
- It is milky
- It is shiny
- It is crumbly or smooth
- It is custardlike

The Explanation

Just looking at the list of fresh cheeses, you can probably surmise that this is a diverse group of cheeses. But by subdividing them you can easily get a handle on the differences between the categories and ultimately choose the cheese you're looking for *even if you've never tasted it before*. The following list tells you what texture you can expect from each type of fresh cheese. I will explain more about these later on, but for now this is the simplest means of understanding fresh cheeses.

Soft cheese = milky cheese, whether made from whole milk or whey

Pasta filata cheese = mild and stretchy

Brined cheese = crumbly cheese

Pressed cheese = dry, meant for grating or crumbling, whether made from whole milk or from whey

Whey cheese = pillowy and creamy or smooth and dry

Nonmelter = either crumbly or custardlike

Think of all fresh cheeses as having two dominant flavor characteristics: milky or salty and sometimes both. Some also have a tangy quality reflective of the milk itself as well as, in some cases, the lactic acid in the cheese. After that, subtler flavors will emerge.

> THE WORD "FRESH" IN THE PHRASE "FRESH CHEESES" DOES NOT MEAN THE OPPOSITE OF SPOILED. INSTEAD, IT MEANS THE OPPOSITE OF AGED.

Fresh cheeses run the gamut in texture and, to some degree, color. But the phrase "fresh cheese" simply refers to cheeses that are not aged and are instead, made and sent to market quickly. However, there are a couple of exceptions to this rule as you will see.

One of the hallmarks of a fresh cheese is its color. Because it has not been aged, it retains the color of the milk from which it was made. Fresh goat cheese is the best example of this. Because goats and sheep don't process beta-carotene (the natural chemical responsible for giving vegatables their orange or yellow colors) the way that cows do, their milk remains white.

Also, because goat's milk cheese and other soft fresh cheeses are usually sold within the course of three or four days, and because of the method by which they are made, they do not take on the slightly darker hues that older, aged cheeses do. Consequently, even cow's milk cheeses remain quite light in color when fresh. But as I said, not all fresh cheeses end up the same. They do, however, start off similarly with the exception of whey cheeses.

Soft Cheeses

The first subcategory of fresh cheese is soft cheeses. These are fresh cheeses that are fluffy, light, creamy, and delicate, often requiring a spoon or fork to eat because of their, well, spoonable texture. Like other fresh cheeses, they are terrific for cooking because of their creaminess. In addition, they are spreadable, making great options for toast or bagels. The best known of the soft cheeses are fresh goat cheese (also referred to as chèvre), cream cheese, cottage cheese, and the lesser-known but delicious fromage blanc, usually made from cow's milk. (See page 64 for a recipe using fromage blanc).

Soft cheeses are mild and should not be excessively salty. Instead they should taste most like the milk from which they are made. As a reminder, the distinguish-

 Are Mascarpone and Cream Cheese One and the Same?

Mascarpone is often called Italian cream cheese, yet placed side by side with American cream cheese, you can see they are entirely different. Mascarpone has a much smoother texture, almost like thick cream, while cream cheese has a denser, sometimes even chunky, texture. Mascarpone is made entirely with cream, while cream cheese is most often made with a combination of cream and milk.

To make mascarpone, tartaric acid is added to bring the cream from its natural liquid state to a thicker yet still creamy texture. This is basically all that is done to turn cream into mascarpone. Cream cheese starts off like most cheeses. A starter culture is added, followed by a coagulant. The curds are cut and then drained in cheesecloth for a few hours or overnight. For artisan-made cream cheese, the drained curds

are lightly salted, packaged, and sent to market. Industrial cream cheese often has gums and thickeners added. It is processed to become either a smooth block or whipped, while most small-production cream cheese is packaged in a plastic container in its natural loose form.

While we're on the subject of cream, I should mention crème fraîche. While it is often characterized as a cheese, it really is not. This is mainly because to make it, heavy cream is acidified, with either cultured buttermilk or sour cream (my preference), the mixture thickens and voilà, you've got crème fraîche. No curd separation, no draining. Crème fraîche is a runny product—not nearly as thick as mascarpone—similar in texture to sour cream or yogurt. It is often sweetened and whipped (instead of cream) to top desserts, or it might be drizzled over a vegetable soup puree, or spiced and spooned over a quesadilla.

ing characteristic of goat's milk will be its tangy quality; cow's milk will also be tangy yet sweet too; and sheep's milk will be buttery and tangy as well.

Cottage cheese is considered a fresh cheese. While most cheeses made in America got their start in other countries, cottage cheese is essentially an American creation even though it is thought to have been derived from a German spreadable cheese called Schmierkäse. Originally called "cottager's cheese" because it was made by people who lived in cottages (appropriately enough), it was usually smeared on bread. Then as now, the curds were made from skimmed milk.

The component in cottage cheese that distinguishes one brand from another is the dressing. This is the milky substance you find in all cottage cheese. The dressing determines both the flavor and texture of the final product and is made up of milk, sometimes cream, and salt. Large manufacturers often add stabilizers and possibly sugar to the dressing as well. However, the government has specific guidelines about the amount of milk fat that can be added to cottage cheese—it can range from as much as 4 percent to zero. This makes even the highest fat cottage cheese a fairly lowfat product.

In the same family as cottage cheese are pot cheese and farmer's cheese. While not significantly different from each other, pot cheese is the moister of the two, with farmer's cheese being extremely dry. In fact, farmer's cheese is sold in loaf form and pot cheese is usually sold in containers. Both are drained cheeses, and both are lightly salted. Each is essentially a form of cottage cheese, just drained to different degrees. Farmer's cheese is often used in cheese blintzes, and pot cheese is used interchangeably with cottage cheese or as a substitute for farmer's cheese.

Pasta Filata Cheeses

You may not know the term *"pasta filata,"* but you do know the cheeses that fall within this category. Mozzarella and string cheese are the best known *pasta filata* cheeses, but others include Provolone, scamorza, and the more unusual southern Italian cheese called caciocavallo.

Pasta filata or "stretched-curd" cheeses take their name from the method used to make them. Unlike most cheeses in which the whey is drained shortly after the curds have reached the desired texture and acidity, stretched-curd cheeses bathe in the whey for quite a long time, sometimes overnight, to increase the acidity in the cheese significantly. This, in turn, sets them up for the next step in the cheese-making process, which is the stretching.

Once they reach the desired level of acidity, the curds are immersed in hot water to make them pliable. They are then pulled and stretched, much like saltwater taffy, and formed into the desired shape. Scamorza is pear-shaped, while provolone is round, cylindrical or sausagelike, and caciocavallo looks similar to a gourd or a jug. Mozzarella is made in many forms. Small balls are called bocconcini, while the most common shape is orblike or globular. As you already know from firsthand experience, fresh *pasta filata* cheeses make the world's best melters.

 Provolone May Start Out Like a Fresh Cheese, but Doesn't End Up That Way

Remember what I said about how certain cheeses start out like fresh cheeses, but are then aged instead? Provolone and caciocavallo are two such cheeses. Like mozzarella and scamorza, these cheeses are in the *pasta filata* family, which means they start out by being pulled and stretched just like their unaged cousins, but they are brined and coated with a light wax to set them up for long-term aging, perhaps as long as years. Sometimes they are smoked.

There are two kinds of provolone. The young version is referred to as *dolce*, which is aged a short period, usually two to three months. The longer-aged provolone is called *piccante* or "sharp," and is usually aged much longer, from a few months to well over a year.

After it is molded into the desired shape, provolone is tied with rope. You will often see it hanging from the ceiling,

usually in an Italian delicatessen or certain cheese shops in America or in any number of shops in Italy. Likewise, if you come upon caciocavallo (it is relatively scarce in the United States), you will see it in pairs tied together with rope. This method of tying two cheeses together is traced to the cheese's origins, although there are various explanations for its name. The most popular explanation has the cheese's name stemming from the means by which it was transported — slung over the saddle of a horse (the word *cacio* translates to "cheese" and *cavallo* to "horse"). Another account says that the cheese was once made with mare's milk although that seems to have been discounted, and yet another explanation is that it is derived from a Turkish cheese called qasqawal. Whatever the origin of the nomenclature, caciocavallo is typically aged longer than provolone *dolce*, about three to four months, and like provolone, might be smoked.

Brined Cheeses

Although some *pasta filata* cheeses are brined, that is, immersed in a saltwater bath, that is usually just one step in the production and is not necessarily their defining feature. Distinct from those cheeses are brined fresh cheeses. These are cheeses that develop their unique characteristics, the most prominent being saltiness, *because* they are brined. The best-known example of this style is feta, a cheese made with each of the three milk types and sometimes a mixture of sheep and goat's milk. While not all feta is packaged and sold in brine, it always spends some time in it, from a few days to several months.

To make feta, the curds and whey are separated. The curds are then pressed, drained, and sliced (feta means "slice" in Greek), and placed in brine. If following the traditional method, the feta will be brined in barrels, but some industrial methods simply brine the cheese in tanks.

Pressed Cheeses

Cotija, cotija añejo, and ricotta salata are examples of fresh cheeses that are pressed. In the case of cotija, the curds are cut into tiny pieces, much the same way a semi-hard or hard cheese is made, salted generously, and then pressed to extract as much moisture as possible. Its shape is rectangular, and the resulting cheese is quite salty. In fact, cotija añejo is often referred to as Mexican Parmesan. Añejo translates to "aged."

Ricotta salata and myzithra, made from sheep's milk whey, are also pressed cheeses, but the curds are not cut into tiny pieces. The result is a cheese with a pillow-soft silken texture yet also one that lends itself to grating. Generally, it is easier to shave ricotta salata instead of finely grate it, but it will work both ways. Myzithra and cotija añejo are defined as fresh cheeses because of how they are made, yet paradoxically, because of their high salt content and the fact they are pressed, they are most often used the same way hard cheeses are—grated over finished dishes rather than eaten as whole chunks.

Whey Cheeses

As the description suggests, these cheeses are made from the whey, which is the liquid by-product of cheesemaking. Most cheesemakers either throw out the whey or, if they have animals, they may capture it and feed the high-protein "drink" to their animals. In some parts of the world, the whey is used to make cheese and butter.

The best known whey cheese is ricotta, which means "recooked" in Italian. The fluffy cheese is so named because it originally came about as a by-product of making mozzarella. To make ricotta, then as now, the whey is literally recooked after it goes through the initial heating phase to create mozzarella and other cheeses. Because not all of the milk solids make their way into the curds, there are always some remaining in the whey. Along with the whey proteins, these milk solids are heated at a high temperature, acidified usually with citric acid or vinegar, and become a creamy, somewhat liquidy, mixture. The resulting cheese is drained and then packaged. Many cheesemakers hand-ladle the ricotta into draining baskets or molds, treating the soft cheese with delicate hands. Manufactured ricotta is just that, and does not have the fresh, milky flavors nor the lighter, almost ethereal, texture that handmade ricotta does.

Manouri, another whey cheese, is a mixed sheep and goat's milk cheese to which a little sheep's cream may have been added. Manouri is made somewhat similarly to a fresh goat cheese in that the nascent curds are put in bags that are pulled taut, drained, and finally packaged. The texture is creamy like a soft fresh cheese.

A completely different whey cheese is Gjetost (also spelled Gietost), which is a Norwegian goat's milk cheese. However, the end result is a semi-hard cheese (not a fresh one) that tastes like caramel but has a toasted and somewhat animal-like flavor. Still, because it is a whey cheese, it deserves inclusion here. For the final part of your Norwegian lesson, the word *mysost* refers to a similar cheese made entirely of cow's milk whey.

Nonmelters

Although different from each other in texture, the cheeses in this subcategory share a rather distinctive characteristic: they do not melt when exposed to heat. They soften, but that is their only concession to heat. Panela, queso blanco, and Indian paneer are three such cheeses.

When whole, panela is shaped like the basket in which it is drained, and it quivers like a big wheel of pudding. When cut, it resembles a light custard. Queso blanco is very different—crumbly and a little salty—and because of its texture, is usually used for sprinkling over dishes like salads, beans, and enchiladas. Cotija straddles the line between nonmelters and pressed fresh cheeses because it does not melt *and* it is a pressed cheese. It has the salty component that other pressed cheeses have and it will not melt, only soften.

From the opposite side of the world comes Indian paneer. Very similar to queso blanco, paneer is made from milk and usually vinegar. Unlike queso blanco, however, salt is not usually added. It is a firm cheese, very similar in texture to tofu, and can be used in many different ways. Like its fellow nonmelters, it holds its shape when heated and its mildness provides a textural addition to cooked dishes rather than added flavor. Continuing the 'round-the-world nonmelting cheese journey, halloumi, a sheep, goat, and/or cow's milk cheese fits the bill. This cheese hails from Cyprus and is often grilled or sautéed.

Nonmelters may be made from any milk, though the majority are made from cow's milk. With nonmelters the milk source is less important to the final product than the acidity level of the milk during cheesemaking. This is the factor that separates nonmelters from all other fresh cheeses.

💡 Why Don't Certain Cheeses Melt?

If you've ever put a cheese under the broiler only to find it wouldn't melt, blame it on two factors: acidity and calcium. In nonmelters, either the acidity is quite low or, illogical as it sounds, very high. In both cases, cheese will not melt because of the effects on the calcium.

In low-acid cheeses like queso fresco, calcium, a mineral, acts as a sort of straitjacket around the proteins because there isn't enough acidity to dissolve the calcium. When these so-called calcium crosslinks are abundant, the proteins are kept apart. This means they cannot melt in the presence of heat. Guess what that means for the cheese?

Conversely, a high-acid cheese such as feta won't melt either, but for an entirely different reason. In high-acid cheeses the crosslinks become soluble and wash out with the whey. So you would think that without those crosslinks, the proteins would be free to roam and ultimately melt. *Au contraire*. It turns out that the proteins that are left behind contain equal numbers of positive and negative charges. This results in a protein matrix that is stubbornly bonded. Call it a protein standoff. When this happens, the cheese softens when heated, but this standoff between proteins keeps the cheese stubbornly firm instead of breaking loose and melting.

The Bottom Line

Fresh cheeses have a variety of applications, from cooking to eating out of hand, although their primary use is in cooking. Despite their differences, the cheeses within each subcategory have a lot in common, making substitutions a cinch. Soft goat cheese can be substituted for fromage blanc or ricotta; ricotta salata can be substituted for myzithra; mozzarella can be substituted for scamorza, and so it goes. If you're in the mood for fresh, clean, and straightforward flavors, then there's no question that this category of cheeses is for you.

Cheesemaker Liam Callahan of California's Bellwether Farms checks the ricotta.

WHAT TO LOOK FOR WHEN BUYING FRESH CHEESES

By definition, fresh cheeses are intended for purchase and consumption within a few days. For that reason, you're best off buying no more than what you need for the next day or two.

VISUAL CUES

Because fresh cheeses are not aged, their color should look like the fresh milk from which they were made. Goat and sheep's milk fresh cheeses will be white, and fresh cow's milk cheeses will be off-white. Fresh cheeses should not have any yellowish tinges or mold. Since these are rindless, they should look uniform throughout.

Soft Cheeses	*Pasta Filata* Cheeses	Brined Cheeses
• Bright white, off-white, or light ivory • Loose and fluffy • Packaged either in plastic cups, vacuum-sealed packaging, or bulk tubs or crocks	• White to light ivory • Vacuum-sealed or packed in water • Compact yet come apart in onionlike layers or "strings"	• White to off-white • Shiny and either crumbly or grainy • Appear pockmarked • Will often be packed in brine
Pressed Cheeses	Whey Cheeses	Nonmelters
• Bright white to off-white • Crumbly or grainy • Vacuum-sealed • Either smooth and silken or pockmarked and crumbly	• Bright white (or caramel-colored in the case of Gjetost) • Smooth, silken texture or pillowy	• White to off-white • Glistening, smooth, or custardlike

TEXTURAL CUES

Most fresh cheeses are not about feel and are instead about appearance. Consequently, there is really no touch test for fresh cheeses except for *pasta filata* cheeses.

Soft Cheeses	*Pasta Filata* Cheeses	Brined Cheeses
• Billowy, possibly a little grainy, and light but firm like beaten egg whites	• Firm yet feel a little spongy when lightly pressed • Toothsome and possibly squeaky when chewed	• Grainy or crumbly
Pressed Cheeses	**Whey Cheeses**	**Nonmelters**
• Compact, usually cut in a rectangular shape • Firmly packed, smooth, and silken (ricotta salata, myzithra, manouri) or pockmarked and crumbly (cotija, cotija añejo)	• Either velvety-looking or like thick whipped cream • Smooth and silken	• Either smooth and glistening or loose textured

AROMA CUES

All fresh cheeses should smell clean with very little aroma.

• Creamlike
• Fresh milk
• Scalded milk
• Do *not* buy if it smells like sour milk

FLAVOR CUES

The flavors in fresh cheeses differ far less than the textures.
Overall flavor characteristics are:

• Acidic	• Gamy	• Scalded milk
• Buttery	• Green apple	• Sour
• Citrusy	• Lemony	• Sweet
• Crème fraîche-like	• Mild	• Tart
• Earthy	• Milky	

Some distinctive flavor characteristics for the subcategories
of fresh cheeses are:

Soft Cheeses	*Pasta Filata* Cheeses	Brined Cheeses
• Mild and milky	• Mild	• Salty
• Tangy	• Milky (fresh mozzarella)	• Tangy
• Creamy	• Sweet milk	• Earthy

Pressed Cheeses	Whey Cheeses	Nonmelters
• Buttery	• Sweet (soft whey cheeses)	• Fresh milk
• Gamy	• Salty (pressed whey cheeses)	• Mild
• Salty	• Tangy	• Sweet
• Tangy		

MOUTHFEEL

Because fresh cheeses are all about texture, their mouthfeel is determined
by the type of fresh cheese you are eating.

Soft Cheeses	*Pasta Filata* Cheeses	Brined Cheeses
Creamy, soft, like billowy clouds	Stretchy, chewy, toothsome, squeaky	Rough, gritty, crumbly

Pressed Cheeses	Whey Cheeses	Nonmelters
Silken and creamy or crumbly, sandy, or gritty	Creamy (soft whey cheeses), silken (pressed whey cheeses), possibly chalky	Smooth, slightly resistant to the bite, possibly spongy

<table>
<tr><th colspan="3" align="center">FINISH</th></tr>
<tr><th>Soft Cheeses</th><th>*Pasta Filata* Cheeses</th><th>Brined Cheeses</th></tr>
<tr>
<td>Because of their creaminess, the texture and sometimes the flavors in soft cheeses tend to last a surprisingly long time in the mouth. This is assuming the cheese is made with an excellent milk source, a gentle handling of the curds, and that it has not been over salted.</td>
<td>Fresh mozzarella will have a nice, long finish, particularly if the cheese has been made with water buffalo milk, which is more fatty and rich.</td>
<td>Brined cheeses leave a lingering saltiness in the mouth. Some brined cheese like feta, particularly when it is made with sheep's and/or goat's milk, has lingering buttery flavors too.</td>
</tr>
<tr><th>Pressed Cheeses</th><th>Whey Cheeses</th><th>Nonmelters</th></tr>
<tr>
<td>These cheeses don't have a terribly long finish, nor are they really meant to. Instead, the dominant flavor is salt, which is why these cheeses are primarily used to sprinkle on vegetable and bean dishes and salads.</td>
<td>Soft whey cheeses are quite sweet and mild, and those that are artisan-made leave a lasting impression because of the good milk source that is usually used. Pressed whey cheeses vary in their finish, but most tend to be mild but leave lingering saltiness.</td>
<td>Most of these cheeses are very simple. Consequently, their finish is simple too. You will probably remember the fresh milk flavor characteristics of these cheeses.</td>
</tr>
</table>

A FEW NOTEWORTHY FRESH CHEESES

UNITED STATES

California

Bubalus Bubalis: Mozzarella

To the uninitiated, the words Bubalus Bubalis might sound more like a term of endearment than the Latin term that it is. Meaning "water buffalo," Bubalus Bubalis is also the name of the California company that makes mozzarella and other products from the milk of water buffaloes. A long-standing cheesemaking tradition in Italy, water buffalo milk mozzarella production is rare in this country. But company president Hanns Heick and Grazia Perrella, his southern Italian wife who hails from a cheesemaking family, are doing their part to remedy that. (Another company —Woodstock Water Buffalo in Vermont—is also doing so with their cheese as well as their excellent buffalo milk yogurt.)

Water buffaloes, although formidable looking, are surprisingly docile. (They are not the same animals as American bison, which are indeed fierce.) Water buffaloes are also stingy milk-givers. But the snow-white milk that emerges from them is very high in fat, about twice that of cow's milk, so most of the milk can be transformed into cheese since there's very little water content. The result is cheese that is as rich as the milk it is made from.

Water buffalo mozzarella, or *mozzarella di bufala* as it is called in Italy, is highly prized because of its soft, almost pillowlike texture and abundant richness. A little goes a long way, which is why something acidic, such as tomato, is often paired with it.

Cowgirl Creamery: Cottage Cheese

Although there are just a handful of artisan-made cottage cheeses in the United States, Cowgirl Creamery in California and Washington, DC, makes an exemplary organic cottage cheese. Much drier than most other cheeses, Cowgirl Creamery's product is also a bit richer owing to the small amount of crème fraîche they put in their dressing. Although it is very different from commercial brand cottage cheese, one taste of it and you will likely be hooked.

Texas

Pure Luck Grade A Goat Dairy: Fresh Chèvre

You might not expect to find a goat dairy thirty minutes from Austin. But for Austinites and beyond, it's a welcome treasure. Begun by Sara Bolton, who tragically passed away in 2006, and now run by her daughter, Amelia Sweethardt, Pure Luck Dairy makes a fresh goat cheese that puts almost all others to shame. The artisan nature of it is apparent long before you take a bite. Rather than being scooped into plastic containers or extruded into vacuum-sealed packaging, Pure Luck's fresh goat cheese is drained in basket molds and sold in its round, flat Camembert-like shape. The texture is pure silk, and its flavor is fresh and sweet. It is as delicate as a thin sheet of glass, but its mild flavors belie its power to mesmerize.

 **If you can't find**

Myzithra, use **ricotta salata** or **Pecorino Romano**

Fromage blanc, use **ricotta** or **fresh goat cheese (chèvre)**

Brined feta, use regular **feta**, **cotija** or **cotija añejo**

Pot cheese, use **slightly drained cottage cheese**

STORING FRESH CHEESES

Because fresh cheeses vary, their storing methods do too, at least a little. Follow these guidelines for each style.

Soft Cheeses

If the cheese has been packaged in an airtight plastic container, then just leave it in that. If not, transfer it to one.

Pasta Filata Cheeses

If the cheese is packed in water, leave it that way. That said, these cheeses are meant to be eaten right away, so don't keep the water-packed version for more than about a week.

If the cheese is vacuum-sealed, transfer it to an airtight container after you've opened it. For storing aged *pasta filata* cheeses like provolone, wrap them in waxed paper followed by a layer of plastic wrap.

Brined Cheeses

If packaged in brine, keep the cheese in the brine unless you find the cheese is too salty. If that is the case, then repack the cheese in plain water with a tiny amount of salt. If the salt is just right (remember, feta is supposed to be on the salty side), be sure to change the brine if it begins to look especially cloudy, usually after a few weeks or a month. To do this, make a saltwater solution of 1 tablespoon kosher salt and 2 cups water. Your cheese should keep for another two to three weeks.

If the cheese is vacuum-sealed instead of brine-packed, then transfer it to an airtight container. You can even immerse it in a brine solution if you wish.

Pressed Cheeses

These cheeses mimic semi-hard cheeses and should therefore be stored the same way. Wrap them first in waxed paper followed by a layer of plastic wrap.

Whey Cheeses

Store as you would soft cheese.

Nonmelters

These cheeses typically come wrapped in plastic. Remove the plastic and place the cheese in an airtight container.

As with all cheeses, keep fresh cheeses in the drawer of your refrigerator.

 Fresh Cheese and Wine Pairing ☆☆

Because fresh cheeses are not usually eaten by themselves and instead lend their flavors and textures to cooked dishes, salads, and desserts, it would be a little unusual to pair wines with these cheeses. That said, brined and pressed cheeses lend themselves to white wines. Look for lighter white wines. Pinot Grigio, Falanghina, or Vernaccia di San Gimignano from Italy, Moschofilero from Greece (a great grape making its way into wine stores) and Sancerre (Sauvignon Blanc) or a dry Chenin Blanc from the Loire Valley in France would be my choices for wine pairing in this category. Otherwise, you're best off looking at the other ingredients in the dish and pairing wine accordingly.

TAKE-HOME TEST
GETTING TO KNOW FRESH CHEESES

Because fresh cheeses share common characteristics yet at the same time differ from one another, it takes direct exposure to the various styles to really "get" what they're all about. One common bond is their tanginess, as you will see.

THE ASSIGNMENTS

Assignment #1

Buy

• 2 to 4 ounces fresh goat cheese (chèvre)

• 2 to 4 ounces cow's milk ricotta

• 2 to 4 ounces sheep and/or goat's milk feta, (not cow's milk)

• 2 to 4 ounces ricotta salata (don't worry if you can't find it, although it has become fairly readily available)

• 1 bagel, cut in half and toasted (or use two pieces of white, sourdough, or wheat bread, toasted)

• 1 lemon, cut in wedges

• ½ cup whole or lowfat milk (do not use nonfat)

• ¼ cup honey

Have a few spoons and forks available

Put the cheeses in the following order on a plate, being sure to mark each one so that you know which is which. Arranging them clockwise is usually helpful, placing the first cheese, in this case the chèvre, at 12 o'clock and progressing from there.

– Chèvre
– Feta
– Ricotta
– Ricotta salata

1) Take a taste of the fresh chèvre, paying attention to both its flavor and its texture. It will be smooth and creamy in the mouth, possibly ever-so-slightly gritty like fine sand, and will have tangy and mild to moderate salty flavors. Notice how the cheese lingers in your mouth.

2) Take a lemon wedge and lightly bite into it to extract a small amount of juice. Naturally, it will be very sour, but that's the point. Take another taste of the chèvre. Do you see how similar the goat's milk cheese and sour lemon are? While the lemon will be more sour than the cheese, this demonstrates just how tangy fresh goat cheese really is.

3) Now, dip your spoon into the honey and taste a small amount followed by a taste of goat cheese. In this case, you have an example of contrasting flavors—sweet and tart. If you never really noticed how tangy goat cheese really is, now you know.

4) Repeat this exercise substituting feta for the goat cheese. Sheep's milk feta in particular will have a more buttery flavor than goat's milk, but it will still taste tangy. The feta's distinct salty feature leaves a tangy impression too. In this case, the lemon will mitigate the salt but it will also accentuate the cheese's tangy quality. Although sweet, the honey will have the same effect.

5) Let's move on to the two ricotta cheeses. Start with the soft cow's milk ricotta. Take a bite of the ricotta and concentrate on its flavors and textures. Presumably it is mild and milky and once again tangy too. Depending on your ricotta, it will range in texture from soft and pillowy to more dense and relatively firm. Do the lemon test again. Notice how the lemon brings out the lemony quality in the cheese once again. Yet the cheese also becomes sweet and reminiscent of fresh milk. This shows that ricotta magically embodies both a tangy quality and a fresh milk quality at the same time.

6) Just as in the dessert recipe (or cheese course, depending how you serve it) on page 68, ricotta and honey are made for each other. Give the combo a go. Not only are you experiencing a textural symphony from the smoothness of the honey and the creamy quality of the ricotta, you can also experience another sweet-tart sensation by combining the two. The honey will also bring out a somewhat earthy quality in the cheese you may not have noticed before.

7) The minute you take a taste of the ricotta salata, you will see how very different it is from the ricotta you just ate. Being salted and pressed, ricotta salata is a very firm and salty product. Also, it is made from sheep's milk rather than cow's milk, which means it has a more assertive flavor. (Creamy ricotta can be made from sheep's milk too, but it is relatively rare in the United States). Time for the lemon test again. Just as with feta, the lemon will soften the saltiness. However, the cheese will taste a bit more sour because of the sheep's milk base of the ricotta salata, which is inherently richer and less tangy.

THE LESSON

Because this was a multipronged exercise, there are a few lessons to be gleaned.

First, by sampling goat cheese with lemon juice, you can see just how tangy goat's milk is. This is particularly helpful when you are cooking with goat cheese, but it is equally useful just knowing what to expect when you open a package of goat cheese.

The same is true with feta cheese, except that you learned that the lemon mitigates the saltiness of the cheese. Once again, you can apply this discovery to cooking. If you're using feta, you might want to include a splash of vinegar or citrus juice to neutralize the salt (unless, of course, you're using feta deliberately for its salty feature).

Unlike fresh goat cheese, ricotta—a whey cheese often with whole milk added—is much richer even though it has a tangy quality too. However, when matched with the lemon, you can see that the ricotta seems sweet, with almost a caramel-like note. This is the result of the milk proteins being exposed to high heat.

That same caramel note was accented by honey, which is why ricotta alone lends itself to a cheese course or dessert when paired with honey and a few other simple ingredients (or none at all!).

Ricotta salata is smooth textured because it is pressed. So while you might consider stuffing pasta with the "fluffy" style of ricotta, you are best off topping that pasta with grated ricotta salata. This is to say, ricotta and ricotta salata share the same "recooked" moniker, but they are two entirely different cheeses. Their common bonds are that each is traditionally made with whey, and in some cases, ricotta is made with sheep's milk while ricotta salata always is.

Assignment #2

Just in case you don't know quite understand what a melting cheese is and what it is not, I hope this exercise will enlighten you.

Buy

- 4 ounces halloumi or panela or queso fresco or paneer
- 1 tablespoon olive oil

In a small sauté pan, heat 1 tablespoon of olive oil over medium high heat. Add the cheese and cook on one side until it turns golden, similar to the white of a fried egg. Turn the cheese and cook until the other side looks the same as the first side. As you can see, the cheese has softened but it has not melted. When you taste it (after it has cooled, of course), you will also notice that the cheese is more toothsome —possibly even spongy—than gooey.

The Lesson

By understanding what it means for a cheese to resist melting you can also see how to use these cheeses in cooking. Because they don't change in texture but do become richer when they are exposed to heat, nonmelters, whether heated or at room temperature, make great centerpieces on a cheese board surrounded by hearty bread, olives, and perhaps oven-roasted tomatoes. Also, because they are mild, think about them as the "tofu" of cheese—they take on the flavors they are surrounded by. If you cook panela in a tomatillo sauce, it will take on the tangy tomatillo flavors, but the cheese will provide a welcome toothsome texture and will also mitigate the acidity in the dish.

GRILLED SHRIMP WITH MANGO-ORANGE QUINOA AND COTIJA

I first made this dish for my book group, which weighed in with a unanimous thumbs-up. I like it because the quinoa, a grain that can be traced back thousands of years, can be made a day ahead with just a couple of ingredients added at the last minute. Most of all, I like the citrusy flavors in this dish combined with the salty, crumbly cheese.

For the shrimp

Juice of one lime, to make about ¼ cup

2 tablespoons peanut oil

2½ teaspoons ground cumin

1 teaspoon kosher salt

24 large (16–20 count) shrimp (about 1¼ pounds), peeled and deveined

For the quinoa

2 cups low-sodium chicken stock or water

1 cup quinoa, rinsed in cold water and drained

1 teaspoon kosher salt

½ cup canned black beans, drained

½ cup fresh or frozen corn kernels

2 jalapeño chiles, seeds removed and very finely chopped

2 teaspoons finely grated orange zest

½ teaspoon cumin

1 medium mango (about ½ pound) cut into ½-inch dice

¼ cup finely chopped cilantro plus whole stems for garnish

4 ounces cotija cheese, coarsely crumbled (or use feta)

To prepare the shrimp: In a large bowl, mix together the lime juice, peanut oil, cumin, and salt. Set aside.

Put the shrimp in a glass dish and pour the lime juice mixture over the shrimp, being sure to coat both sides. Let sit for 30 minutes at room temperature.

Preheat a gas grill to medium high. Alternatively, set a rack in the broiler about six inches below the heating element and preheat.

To make the quinoa: In a medium pot, bring the stock to a boil. Reduce the heat to medium-low and add the

quinoa and salt. Cover and let cook for 10 minutes. Add the beans, corn, jalapeño, orange zest, and cumin and cook for 10 more minutes, or until most of the liquid has been absorbed. Turn off the heat and leave the pot covered. (Note: The quinoa can be made 1 day ahead up to this point and refrigerated. Bring to room temperature and add the mango and cilantro just before serving.)

To grill the shrimp: Place the shrimp on the grill. Cook for 2 minutes. Turn the shrimp and cook for 1 to 2 more minutes, or until they are just pink and feel firm but not hard to the touch. Overcooking will make the shrimp tough and dry.

To broil the shrimp: Transfer the shrimp to a broiler pan. Broil for 2 to 3 minutes, or until the shrimp have turned light pink and feel firm but a tad springy to the touch. Overcooking will make the shrimp tough and dry. (Note: No need to turn the shrimp.)

To assemble: Gently mix the mango and cilantro into the quinoa. Transfer to individual plates or a large platter. Lay the shrimp on top, and sprinkle the cheese over the shrimp and quinoa. Garnish with cilantro and serve.

Serves 4

WATERMELON, RICOTTA SALATA, AND FRESH HERB SALAD

This salad is as refreshing as a not-too-hot summer day and evokes images of the same with its mixture of herbs and the light citrus dressing. The cheese adds the salt component and dense texture to the otherwise ethereal salad.

2 tablespoons plus 2 teaspoons lime juice	4 ounces ricotta salata cheese, cut into ¼-inch dice (or use feta or myzithra cheese)
2 teaspoons lime zest	¼ cup julienned fresh mint plus extra mint sprigs
½ teaspoon kosher salt (or to taste)	¼ cup julienned fresh basil
¼ cup extra-virgin olive oil	¼ cup coarsely chopped fresh Italian parsley
6 cups watermelon, (about a 6-pound piece) preferably seedless, cut into ¾-inch chunks (or use pre-cut watermelon)	Salt

In a small bowl, whisk together the lime juice, zest, and salt. Add the oil slowly and whisk until incorporated. Set aside. (You can make the dressing up to 1 day ahead. Cover and refrigerate. Bring to room temperature before using.)

Drain the pre-cut watermelon, if using.

To assemble: Toss the watermelon with the cheese. Add the dressing and herbs. Taste and depending on the saltiness of the cheese, add salt a little at a time to bring out the full flavors of the salad. Garnish with mint sprigs and serve right away.

Serves 8

FROMAGE BLANC–STUFFED
PORK LOIN ROAST

Fromage blanc is a simple cheese that looks a lot like ricotta but is a little less sweet. It is delectable when sweetened with honey and raisins, and equally good in a savory context. In this recipe, the cheese creates a textural foil for the broccoli rabe (also called rapini), a bitter green, and is a host for the flavorful lemon peel and garlic. The filling picks up the flavors of the prosciutto-lined pork loin and at the same time acts as a warm blanket around the leafy greens. Because of its ease and its visual appeal, this dish would make a particularly good main course at your next holiday dinner.

1 boneless center-cut pork loin roast, about 3 pounds (make sure loin is one piece, not two tied together)	3 tablespoons olive oil
	6 ounces broccoli rabe, stems trimmed, bunches separated into individual long strands (or use baby broccoli, chard, or kale)
Salt and freshly ground pepper	
6 ounces (about ¾ cup), fromage blanc (or use ricotta)	¼ teaspoon crushed red pepper flakes
3 cloves garlic, minced	3 ounces prosciutto, sliced paper-thin
1 tablespoon plus 1 teaspoon finely grated lemon zest	Kitchen string

Butterfly the pork: Place the roast on your work surface with one long side facing you. Using a sharp knife, make a horizontal cut in the roast lengthwise one-third down from the top and all the way from end to end. Do not cut all the way through to the other side; cut only to within ½ inch of the other side. You have just created a flap like the cover of a book. Open that flap.

To make the next cut, press the flat side of your knife against the inside of that flap. Using the tip of the knife, make a 2-inch downward cut along the entire length of the roast. Now place your knife, blade down, into the cut you

have just made. Create your second "book cover" by cutting back through the remaining thick part of the meat with a horizontal cut just like the first cut you made, to within ½ inch of the side. Open that flap. You should have one flat piece of meat about 1 inch thick.

Place plastic wrap or butcher paper over the meat and gently pound it with a meat pounder or other heavy object such as canned tomatoes, to a thickness of about ½ inch. The meat should be one relatively flat piece. If it does not lay flat, make small cuts in the

continued

thickest parts; this will help. Salt and pepper both sides of the meat. Cover and refrigerate for at least 1 hour and up to 8 hours.

Prepare the cheese mixture: In a small bowl, mix together the fromage blanc, garlic, and lemon zest. Set aside. (You can make this up to 24 hours ahead of time. Cover and refrigerate.)

To prepare the broccoli rabe: Heat 1 tablespoon of the oil in a large sauté pan over medium heat. Add the broccoli rabe, cover and cook, stirring occasionally, until it is tender but still firm to the bite, about 10 minutes (if it is sticking to the pan, add a little water). Add the pepper flakes and salt to taste. Set aside to cool.

Preheat the oven to 375°F.

To assemble: Place the roast on your work surface with one long side closest to you. Lay the slices of prosciutto on the meat to cover most of the surface. Carefully spread the fromage blanc mixture over the prosciutto, leaving a 1-inch border around the roast. Lay the broccoli rabe lengthwise down the center of the cheese mixture.

Starting at the side of the meat closest to you, gently roll the meat away from you to enclose the filling. Using kitchen string, tie the roast about every 1½ inches to make sure it stays closed. (Note: If the meat is quite difficult to roll, simply remove 1 or 2 stems of the broccoli rabe.)

In an ovenproof sauté pan large enough to hold the meat, warm the remaining 2 tablespoons oil over medium-high heat. Add the roast and, using tongs, turn constantly to brown it evenly on all sides. This will take about 10 minutes. Once the outside of the meat is light brown, transfer the pan to the oven.

Cook for 40 to 45 minutes or until the meat measures between 148°F and 153°F on a meat thermometer and the meat feels firm but not stiff. Remove the meat from the oven, and let it rest for about 10 minutes. Slice and serve.

Serves 6 to 8

FLO'S COTTAGE CHEESE RUGELACH

Flo Braker is indisputably one of the most skilled bakers (and baking book authors) in this country. She graciously agreed to let me use her unusual and delicious recipe for rugelach in this book. Rugelach is traditionally made with a cream cheese dough, but drained cottage cheese turns out to be a lighter yet no less flavorful alternative, demonstrating how versatile cottage cheese really is. I find that draining the cottage cheese and assembling the easy-to-make dough the day before baking is easiest. These taste best after a few hours or even the next day when the flavors have had a chance to meld and fully develop.

For the dough

16 ounces small-curd cottage cheese (4 percent milk fat)

2 cups flour

¼ teaspoon salt

1 cup (2 sticks) unsalted butter, cut into ¼-inch slices

For the filling

½ cup sugar

1 teaspoon ground cinnamon

4 tablespoons apricot jam, strained

1 cup finely chopped walnuts

Spoon the cottage cheese into a sieve over a bowl. Drain for at least 2 hours, mixing occasionally with a rubber spatula. Remove 1 cup of the cottage cheese for the dough, and reserve the rest for another use.

To make the dough: In a food processor, pulse the flour and salt just to combine. Scatter the butter over the flour. Pulse on and off until the butter seems to disappear into the mixture. Scatter the cottage cheese, in bits, over the mixture; pulse on and off just until a cohesive ball is formed (this will take several pulses). Divide the dough into quarters. Shape each into a flat disc and wrap in plastic wrap. Refrigerate at least 4 hours or overnight.

When ready to bake, place a rack in the lower third of the oven. Preheat to 350°F. Line a large baking sheet with a silicone mat, such as Silpat, or with foil.

In a small bowl, combine the sugar and cinnamon.

To assemble the cookies: Remove 1 dough disc from the refrigerator and let sit for 10 minutes. On a lightly floured surface, roll the dough into a 10- to 11-inch circle about ⅛-inch thick. Spread 1 tablespoon of the jam evenly over the dough. Sprinkle with 2 tablespoons of cinnamon sugar followed by ¼ cup of the walnuts. With a rolling pin, lightly press the filling into the dough.

continued

Using a sharp knife, cut the circle into 16 equal-size pie-shaped pieces. Starting with the wide end, roll up each piece. Place 1 inch apart, point down, on the baking sheet. Bake for 17 to 23 minutes, or until the rugelach are golden brown. Cool pan on a wire rack 5 to 10 minutes, then transfer cookies to the rack to cool completely. Repeat with the remaining dough and filling, wiping off the Silpat or using fresh aluminum foil. Cooled cookies will keep in an airtight container for 2 to 3 days or frozen for 3 months.

Variation: For a sweeter cookie, increase the sugar by ¼ cup and the cinnamon by ½ teaspoon. After you have assembled the cookies, roll them in the extra cinnamon sugar mixture. Bake as directed.

Makes about 5 dozen cookies

RICOTTA WITH HONEY AND FRUIT BREAD

Although simple, this cheese dessert is deeply satisfying providing you use the freshest ricotta you can find and a high-quality, flavorful honey. Sheep's milk ricotta is particularly good, but if you can't find it look for a local source of fresh-made cow's milk ricotta. Your farmer's market is a great place to start (for the honey too).

- 12 ounces fresh ricotta, cow's or sheep's milk
- ¼ cup flavorful honey, such as chestnut
- ½ cup walnuts, lightly toasted and coarsely chopped
- 8 slices panettone (see note) or any dried fruit bread, such as raisin (preferably without cinnamon) cut into 3-inch wide and ¼-inch thick slices and lightly toasted

Using an ice cream scoop, divide the ricotta among 4 small bowls. Drizzle the honey over the ricotta and top with the walnuts. Serve with the bread slices on the side.

Serves 4

Note: Originally from Milan, panettone ("big bread") is a sweet bread that is now made throughout Italy and sold at Christmas time there as well as in the United States. It is light in texture and studded with dried fruit, usually raisins, and citrus peel.

CHOCOLATE–GOAT CHEESE FONDUE
WITH FRESH FRUIT

When I first made this, people said "chocolate with goat cheese?" Then they tasted it. The tanginess of the cheese brings startling intensity to the chocolate —not a cheesy flavor. Although I suggest strawberries and bananas as dippers for the fondue, feel free to use any fruit. I like to serve coconut shortbread cookies (see next recipe) with this—they further intensify the chocolate.

16 ounces bittersweet chocolate, coarsely chopped

8 ounces semisweet chocolate, coarsely chopped

½ cup plus 2 tablespoons heavy cream

8 ounces fresh goat cheese

8 ripe but firm bananas cut into 2-inch slices

1 basket of strawberries, washed, dried, and hulled

Coconut Shortbread Cookies (see following recipe)

Combine the chocolates, cream, and cheese in a medium-size heavy saucepan. Cook over low heat, stirring constantly until chocolate has melted.

Transfer to a fondue pot and serve with fruit and cookies.

Makes 2 cups, serves 8 to 10

COCONUT SHORTBREAD COOKIES

The lacy edges of these buttery make-ahead cookies are created by the coconut, which adds a welcome crunch and a tropical flavor when dipped in the Chocolate–Goat Cheese Fondue (see preceding recipe). No time to make fondue? Don't worry, these cookies are great anytime, and best of all they freeze especially well.

---

1 cup (2 sticks) unsalted butter, at room temperature

½ cup granulated sugar

½ cup confectioners' sugar

1 teaspoon vanilla extract

½ teaspoon salt

2 cups flour

½ cup coconut, toasted

Using a stand or hand-held mixer, cream the butter and sugars. Add the vanilla and salt and mix. Turn the mixer on low and add the flour. Mix just until the flour is incorporated.

Turn half the dough out onto a piece of plastic measuring about 18 inches. Roll into a log measuring about 12 inches long. Gently press half the coconut onto the entire surface of the log. Repeat with the remaining dough and coconut. Refrigerate for a minimum of 1 hour and up to 1 day.

Preheat the oven to 350°F.

Cut the dough logs into ½-inch slices. Place on 2 baking sheets 1 inch apart. (If you have only one baking sheet or room for just one in your oven, keep one log refrigerated until ready to cut and bake). Bake for 12 to 15 minutes, alternating baking sheets halfway through, until cookies are light brown on the edges. Let cool completely.

Store any extra cookies in an airtight container for up to 1 week. You can also freeze the cookies for up to 3 months.

Makes about 48 cookies

Clockwise from top:
St. Nectaire, brick, Havarti

CHAPTER 3

SEMI-SOFT

CHEESES

USE SEMI-SOFT CHEESES FOR

- Burgers
- Casseroles/vegetable dishes
- Eggs
- Entertaining
- Grilled cheese sandwiches
- Pizzas
- Quesadillas
- Sandwiches
- Snacks

WHAT ARE THEY?

Denmark

Esrom (*See also* washed-rind cheeses)

Fontina

Havarti

Tilsit (*See also* washed-rind cheeses)

France

Etorki (sheep's milk)

St. Nectaire

Port-Salut (*See also* washed-rind cheeses)

Saint-Paulin

Tomme de Savoie

Holland

Edam

Gouda (*See also* semi-hard and hard cheeses)

Roomkaas (double-cream)

Italy

Asiago Fresco

Bel Paese (also made in the United States)

Crescenza (*See also* fresh cheeses)

Fontal

Montasio (*See also* semi-hard and hard cheeses)

Monte Veronese (*See also* semi-hard and hard cheeses)

Pecorino Fresco

Pecorino Toscano (*See also* semi-hard cheeses)

Spain

Iberico (cow, goat, and sometimes sheep's milk)

Mahón (*See also* semi-hard and hard cheeses)

Tetilla

Switzerland

Tilsiter (*See also* washed-rind cheeses)

United States

Asadero

Bel Paese (also made in Italy)

Brick (*See also* washed-rind cheeses)

Butterkäse

Chihuahua

Colby (*See also* semi-hard cheeses)

Crescenza

Gouda

Havarti

Monterey Jack

Queso blanco

Teleme

Wales

Caerphilly

England
Ticklemore (goat's milk)

France
Brin d'Amour (sheep's milk)
Fleur du Maquis (sheep's milk)
Gaperon
Tomme Crayeuse

Italy
Bra Tenero
Cacio di Roma (sheep's milk)
Crucolo
Marzolino (young pecorino)

Morlacco
Raschera (*See also* semi-hard cheeses)

Spain
Ibores (goat's milk)

United States
Connecticut
Cato Corner Farm: Bridgid's Abbey

Georgia
Sweet Grass Dairy: Holly Springs (goat's milk), Thomasville Tomme

Louisiana
Bittersweet Plantation Dairy: Kashkeval

Vermont
Crowley Cheese: Mild Crowley

 You know it's a semi-soft cheese when . . .

- You see tiny holes, or the texture does NOT have holes but is perfectly smooth and looks plump and youthful

- It is springy to the touch

- The paste (interior) is pale white to light ivory or orange

The Explanation

Like all cheeses, semi-soft cheeses may be made with cow, sheep, or goat's milk or a combination of milks. Next to fresh cheeses, semi-soft cheeses are the mildest, but that doesn't mean they are boring. In fact, cheeses like Iberico from Spain (the cheese that outsells all others in that country, even more than Manchego), and Tomme Crayeuse from France are among the world's best cheeses because of their complexity and sublime texture.

Other cheeses like Havarti, Colby, and Asiago Fresco may be milder, but like most of the other semi-soft cheeses, they are stellar melting cheeses. This is why these cheeses are used most often in cooking.

To create the semi-soft texture, a cheesemaker will leave the curds larger to retain more moisture. The nascent cheese is usually left to drain on its own rather than being pressed, which also helps to keep in the moisture, and the cheeses are most often aged just a few days up to a couple of months. The result is a cheese that remains fairly elastic.

Semi-soft cheeses almost always have tiny holes or eyes, called mechanical eyes, which form when a cheese is not pressed or pressed only lightly during the early phase of cheesemaking. Through gravity-draining rather than pressing, a cheese will retain quite a bit of moisture and the curds do not knit, or come together, as tightly, leaving behind eyes. These eyes along with a higher moisture content help define this style of cheese. That said, not all semi-soft cheeses end up having eyes. They might be perfectly smooth, but in either case the cheese will feel springy to the touch.

The Bottom Line

Semi-soft cheeses are mild but not uninteresting. They are simply subtler and tend to make their loudest statement with their supple texture. As a result, it is that texture—whether completely smooth or dotted with tiny eyes—that you should seek out when buying semi-soft cheeses. These cheeses are not aged for long, usually less than two months. This allows them to retain their moisture and therefore creaminess, and it also keeps them from developing the deeper colors associated with longer-aged cheeses. As a result the color is almost always off-white to light ivory.

WHAT TO LOOK FOR WHEN BUYING SEMI-SOFT CHEESES

VISUAL CUES

• Light ivory to pale white color or orange • Tiny eyes (usually) • Soft and/or supple-looking	• Do not buy if the cheese has visible mold on the cut surface or if the edges of non-rinded cheeses look dry or discolored

TEXTURAL CUES

- Pliable texture; elastic
- Firm but still gives to the touch. It will return to its original shape even after being poked with your finger.

- When pressed, certain semi-soft cheeses such as crescenza or a ripe Teleme are softer and maintain the impression long after you've pulled away your finger

AROMA CUES

The cheese should smell clean with very little aroma.

- Earthy
- Floral
- Milky

- If a rindless semi-soft cheese smells musty, like mold, do not buy it

FLAVOR CUES

The range of flavors in semi-soft cheeses is a little narrower than other styles. Generally these cheeses are mild but melt really well.

- Buttery
- Mild
- Mildly earthy
- Milky

- Sweet
- Sweet butter
- Tangy

MOUTHFEEL

Initially somewhat firm, then creamy. It will be a little like the texture of a cheese omelet, where the first bite of egg is firm, even a little spongy, but the melted cheese inside overtakes the texture of the egg, leaving you with a creamy impression overall.

FINISH

Medium, with tangy or milky overtones

A Few Noteworthy
Semi-Soft Cheeses

France

Brin d'Amour
From the French island of Corsica, Brin d'Amour cheese is distinguished by its herb-covered surface. It is usually made from unpasteurized sheep's milk (although sometimes it is made of goat's milk). Its texture is moist and creamy when young, about one month, runny as it gets a little older, and then finally semi-hard as it ages further. The herb coating may be comprised of rosemary, thyme, savory, juniper berries, possibly dried peppers, and other herbs found in the region. Although the herbs are a big flavor component in the cheese, they do not overwhelm it. Instead, they complement the sweet yet tangy sheep's milk as well as the luscious texture of the cheese in its semi-soft stage and deeper, earthier flavors when it ages. This cheese may also be marketed as Fleur du Maquis. Maquis is the brambly groundcover for which this island is known.

Port-Salut
This is a very mild cheese and because of its lack of assertive flavors is very popular among Americans. Although technically Port-Salut is a washed-rind cheese, its rind is actually dyed orange to look like the type of washed-rind cheese made by the Trappist monks, who invented it. But unlike those washed-rind cheeses, which are typically strong, this one is mild in both flavor and aroma. Overall it is a better cooking cheese than a simple eating cheese, though for those who prefer mild cheeses, this unquestionably fits the bill.

United States

California

Peluso Teleme
This square-shaped pasteurized cow's milk cheese has been around since the 1930s and remains unique in its style despite other cheeses that have come along with the same name. Peluso Teleme was created in northern California by Giovanni Peluso and may have been his attempt to make the Italian cheese Stracchino. Giovanni's grandson, Franklin Peluso, carries on the tradition of making this very creamy pasteurized cheese. Peluso Teleme is mild but distinctive, not only because of its oozy texture, which develops when it's about two months old, but also because of its milky and somewhat buttery flavors. The cheese is dusted with rice flour, which further distinguishes it aesthetically but does not affect its flavor.

Crowley Cheese

Claiming to be the oldest continuously operating cheese producer in the United States, the Crowley Cheese company, located in Healdville, Vermont has always made just one cheese, appropriately named Crowley after the company's founder. Crowley cheese is officially categorized as a Colby, but the company proudly makes the claim that their cheese long preceded the Wisconsin version. This American original is distinguished by its white color (no annatto is added), but its flavor is the real stand-out. Where Colby is a rather unexciting cheese, the unpasteurized Crowley has real complexity and interesting texture, depending on its age. The cheese is aged to varying stages ranging from mild to extra-sharp, and ranges in flavor from straightforward to complex. The medium and sharp strike the best balance of moisture and complexity. Crowley also makes flavored cheeses, including smoked, muffaletta, dill, and sage.

WALES

Caerphilly

This cheese is named after the Welsh town where it was first made, Gorwydd (pronounced *GOR-wyth*). It is made with raw milk and has an inedible rind around the creamy, milky, ivory-colored paste. While the cheese is pronounced *care-PHIL-y*, there is no need to eat it carefully. It's a hearty yet delectable and creamy cheese that gets softer underneath the rind just as a soft-ripened cheese does.

 Semi-Soft Cheese and Wine Pairing ☆☆

I find most cheeses in this category only marginally compatible with wine. Their fresh-milk flavor and creamy consistency tend to take the fruit in wine and transform it into something bitter. All is not lost, though. White wines without oak or with nice fruit, such as Chenin Blanc, Spanish Verdejo, Pinot Grigio, Austrian Grüner Veltliner, and Sauvignon Blanc will all be fine with most semi-soft cheeses. If you're a red wine–only person, then choose the lightest red wine you can find, such as a light-style Pinot Noir or a Gamay. If you are interested in tasting beer with these cheeses instead, then opt for a light beer, such as a lager.

 **If you can't find**

Brick, use **Butterkäse, Limburger,** or **Munster** (Alsatian)

Caerphilly, use **Tomme de Savoie** or **Tomme Crayeuse**

Danish Fontina, use **Danish** or **American Havarti**

Tilsit, use **Danish Fontina, Esrom** or **brick**

Mahón, use **Port-Salut, St. Nectaire,** or **fresh Asiago**

Port-Salut, use **St. Paulin, American Muenster,** or **Bel Paese**

Teleme, use **Crescenza, Monterey Jack,** or **mozzarella**

Brin d'Amour, use **herb-coated fresh goat cheese** or **Pecorino fresco**

Crowley, use **Colby**

St. Nectaire, use **Port-Salut, Esrom, Butterkäse,** or **Urgelia**

Etorki, use **Ossau-Iraty, Pecorino Fresco,** or **St. Nectaire**

STORING SEMI-SOFT CHEESES

Like washed-rind cheeses, semi-soft cheeses have a high degree of moisture. That means that they also have more potential for premature spoilage if they can't breathe. To store semi-soft cheeses, you can either wrap them lightly in waxed paper and then place them in an airtight container, or you can wrap them in waxed (or parchment) paper and then wrap them loosely with a piece of plastic wrap. The plastic will help seal in the moisture but the waxed paper will let the cheese breathe. As with all other cheese, store semi-soft cheeses in the drawer of your refrigerator.

TAKE-HOME TEST
GETTING TO KNOW SEMI-SOFT CHEESES

Because most semi-soft cheeses are mild, sometimes it takes a few extra ingredients or even a little heat to bring out the distinguishing features in this family of cheeses.

THE ASSIGNMENT

Buy

- 4 ounces Mahón cheese (as young as possible)

- 4 ounces Port-Salut cheese

- 4 dried apple slices (found in the bulk bin section or dried fruit section)

- 4 raw almonds

- 2 slices white bread, crusts removed, lightly toasted on one side

Cut each cheese into 8 equal slices. Place 4 slices of each cheese on a plate along with the apples and almonds.

1) Take a bite of each cheese by itself. What do you taste? What kind of texture do you detect? You will probably find that the Port-Salut is mild with a creamy mouthfeel and a milklike flavor. Although semi-soft cheeses are generally mild, they will likely have a pleasant finish or aftertaste though not a lingering one.

2) Taste a dried apple with each cheese. Does that make the cheese taste a bit more savory? Do you detect more depth in the cheese than you noticed before? It not only does that, but it also makes the cheese taste heartier.

3) Taste an almond with another small piece of each cheese. You will probably find the cheese tastes a little milder, yet the semi-soft texture is exaggerated when contrasted with the crunchy nut.

4) Make an open-face toasted cheese sandwich by putting the remaining slices of each cheese on the untoasted sides of the bread. Place in the broiler or toaster oven and cook until the cheese is golden, bubbly, and melted entirely. Let cool about 3 minutes.

Taste the cheese toast. You will discover that the cheese has developed a brown butter and saltier flavor that was not apparent in its uncooked form. The flavors in your mouth last a tad longer, and although the cheese is not particularly strong, its flavors are more pronounced when the cheese is melted.

THE LESSON

In their uncooked form, semi-soft cheeses are primarily mild. Therefore, to bring out the best in them, think about enhancing them with dried fruits and raw almonds or walnuts (toasted nuts overwhelm the flavors in this style of cheese). Alternatively, cook with these cheeses to bring out their marvelous silken texture and magical buttery flavors that shine in their melted form.

GRILLED MAHÓN AND OLIVE
SANDWICH

As a huge grilled cheese sandwich fan and someone who even wrote a book on the subject, I was excited to create yet another grilled cheese recipe. I took a nod from Spanish cuisine to develop this sandwich, which is my current favorite. I love the crunchy almonds, salty olives, and the tangy yet sweet orange peel. Bathing these textural and flavorful ingredients in a creamy cheese makes everything right with the world in one bite.

½ cup green olives, pitted and finely chopped

3 tablespoons whole almonds, toasted and finely chopped

1 tablespoon plus 1 teaspoon finely grated orange zest

Freshly ground pepper

8 slices sourdough bread

¼ cup mayonnaise (use lowfat if you prefer)

8 ounces young Mahón cheese, coarsely grated (or use Port-Salut, St. Nectaire, or Manchego)

In a small bowl, mix together the olives, almonds, orange zest, and pepper. Set aside.

To assemble: Spread the mayonnaise on one side of each slice of bread. Put 4 slices on your work surface, mayonnaise side down. Distribute the olive mixture then the cheese evenly over them. Place the remaining 4 bread slices on top, mayonnaise side up.

Place the sandwiches in a large sauté pan, preferably nonstick, over medium heat. (Do this in batches if necessary.)

Cover and cook for 4 to 6 minutes, or until the bread is golden brown and the cheese has begun to melt. Uncover and turn the sandwiches with a spatula, pressing firmly to flatten them slightly. Cook uncovered, for 3 to 4 more minutes, or until the undersides are golden brown. Turn the sandwiches again, press with the spatula, and cook for 30 seconds to 1 minute, or until the cheese has melted completely. Let sit for 3 to 5 minutes, then cut and serve.

Serves 4 as a main course; 16 appetizer portions

HAVARTI DILL DIP WITH
PARMESAN TOASTS

Hot Swiss-Parmesan dip with artichoke hearts instantly became my favorite dip the first time I tasted it as a teenager. Two melted cheeses in one dish was all it took to hook me. This recipe is a variation on that dish. Instead of using the traditional Swiss cheese, I decided to use Havarti because of its fantastic melting qualities, and I use dill because it is a frequent Havarti companion. Finally, I deconstructed the original dip by putting the Parmesan on the toasts instead of in the dip. The result is my favorite dip all over again.

1 long baguette, about 2 feet long, cut into about 48 half-inch thick slices

⅓ cup olive oil

2 ounces Parmesan cheese, finely grated

⅔ cup mayonnaise

12 ounces Havarti cheese, coarsely grated (or use Monterey Jack)

One 14-ounce can artichoke hearts, drained well and coarsely chopped

2 bunches scallions (about 10) white and light green parts only, finely chopped

2 tablespoons finely chopped fresh dill

Freshly ground pepper

Preheat the oven to 350°F.

To make the toasts: Brush both sides of each slice of bread with the oil. Place on a baking sheet and toast in the oven on one side until lightly browned, about 5 minutes. Turn and distribute the Parmesan on the bread slices. Toast until the Parmesan turns a nutty brown color, 5 to 7 minutes. Let cool.

To make the dip: In a medium bowl, mix together the mayonnaise, Havarti, artichoke hearts, scallions, dill, and pepper to taste. Transfer to an oven-proof ceramic dish just large enough to hold the dip. Bake until heated through and bubbly, about 20 minutes. Let cool for about 20 minutes. (The dip is very hot and tastes best when it has a little time to cool.) Serve with the Parmesan toasts.

Serves 10 to 12; makes about 3 cups

MONTEREY JACK, BACON, AND AVOCADO "FLATBREAD"

The contrast of crispy tortillas with this classic California cheese is not only delicious, but it also brings the magnificent melting qualities of Monterey Jack into full focus. This recipe couldn't be simpler and works equally well as an appetizer or as a light main course with a salad alongside.

4 slices bacon, coarsely chopped

4 large (9-inch) flour tortillas

1½ tablespoons vegetable oil

1 medium avocado (about 8 ounces), preferably Hass, peeled and cut into ¼-inch thick slices

8 ounces Monterey Jack cheese, coarsely grated

½ teaspoon crushed red pepper flakes

Preheat the oven to 500°F.

In a medium sauté pan, fry the bacon over medium-high heat, stirring occasionally, until it is crisp and brown, about 10 minutes. Transfer to a paper towel-lined plate to drain.

Place tortillas on a baking sheet and brush with oil. Arrange the avocado slices in a spokelike pattern on each tortilla. Top with the cheese and bacon. Bake for 8 to 10 minutes, or until the edges of the tortillas are browned and the cheese is golden and bubbly. Drizzle the flatbreads with crème fraîche and serve.

Serves 4 as a light entrée; 8 as an appetizer

ALL AMERICAN CHEESE STRATA

A cheese strata is a casserole consisting of layers of cheese and bread with a little milk to moisten it and egg to lift it. When I was growing up, my mother referred to it as mock cheese soufflé. Strata plays an equally good role at the brunch, lunch, or dinner table because of its focus on cheese yet its relative lightness, and you can assemble it up to one day ahead. The cheeses here are American originals, both created in Wisconsin, and make a great combination in this classic recipe.

1 teaspoon butter, at room temperature

2½ cups whole or lowfat (2%) milk

6 large eggs, lightly beaten

¾ teaspoon salt

¼ teaspoon freshly ground pepper

Five 1-inch thick slices French bread, crusts removed

4 ounces brick cheese, coarsely grated (or use Butterkäse or Havarti)

4 ounces Colby cheese, coarsely grated (or use Crowley or mild cheddar)

Preheat the oven to 375°F. Butter an 8 x 8-inch glass pan. Set aside.

In a large bowl, mix together the milk, eggs, salt, and pepper. In a medium-size bowl, toss the cheeses together.

Place 2 pieces of bread on the bottom of the prepared pan. The bread should cover most of the bottom. If it does not, add another piece of bread or part of one to fill in the gap. Sprinkle with one-third of the cheese. Place the second layer of bread over the cheese and again, fill in any large gaps with extra bread. Carefully pour the milk and egg mixture over the entire casserole. It will seem like a lot, but the bread will soak it up as it cooks. Top with the remaining cheese. (At this point you can cover and refrigerate the strata for up to 24 hours before baking.)

Bake for 45 to 50 minutes. or until the casserole is very puffy and the cheese is golden brown on top. Let sit for about 10 minutes before cutting and serving. (Note: Because this is a soufflé-like dish, it will deflate a few minutes after you take it out of the oven. It may not look as spectacular, but it tastes great!)

Serves 6 as a main course; 10 to 12 as a side dish

Note: If you want to use thinner, presliced bread, use 2 or 3 extra slices

Humboldt Fog from
Cypress Grove Chèvre

CHAPTER 4

SOFT-RIPENED

CHEESES

USE SOFT-RIPENED CHEESES FOR

- Cheese courses
- Entertaining
- Pasta
- Quesadillas
- Salads
- Sandwiches and panini
- Sauces
- Tarts and pizzas
- Vegetable dishes

WHAT ARE THEY?

France

Brie

Brillat-Savarin

Bucheron

Camembert

Chaource

Coulommiers

L'Edel de Cleron (*See also* washed-rind cheeses)

Explorateur

Fromager d'Affinois Florette (goat's milk)

Montbriac (*See also* blue cheeses)

Pave d'Affinois

Pierre Robert

Saint Albray

St. André

St. Jean de Brie

St. Simeon

Germany

Cambozola (Germany, U.S.; see also blue cheeses)

Champignon (with mushrooms)

Mirabo (with walnuts)

Ireland

Cooleeny

Italy

Brinata (sheep's milk)

Robiola Bosina

Spain

Nevat (goat's milk)

United States

Brie

Camembert

Cambozola

California

Cowgirl Creamery: Mt. Tam, Pierce Point, St. Pat (organic)

Cypress Grove Chèvre: Humboldt Fog (goat's milk)

Marin French Cheese Company: Rouge et Noir Brie, Camembert

Redwood Hill Farm: Camellia, Bucheret (goat's milk)

Colorado

Haystack Mountain Goat Dairy: Haystack Peak, Snow Drop (goat's milk)

MouCo Cheese Company: Blü (*See also* Blue Cheeses), Camembert

Massachusetts

Westfield Farm: Hubbardston (cow's milk) and Classic Blue Log (goat's milk; *see also* blue cheeses)

New York

Old Chatham Sheepherding Company: Hudson Valley Camembert (cow and sheep's milk), Shepherd's Wheel (sheep's milk)

Oregon

Juniper Grove Farm: Pyramid

Off the Beaten Path

France
Gratte-Paille

United States

California

Andante Dairy: Acapella, Adagio, Melange, Metronome, Minuet (goat's milk); Cadenza, Largo, Nocturne, Piccolo, Rondo (mixed milk)

Cypress Grove Chèvre: Fog Lights, Mad River Roll (goat's milk)

Elk Creamery: Black Gold

Goat's Leap: Eclipse, Hyku (goat's milk)

Marin French Cheese Company: Yellow Buck Camembert, La Petite Crème, Le Petit Bleu (*See also* blue cheeses)

Georgia

Sweet Grass Dairy: Green Hill (cow's milk), Lumiere (goat's milk)

Indiana

Capriole Goat Cheese: Wabash Cannonball, Sofia, and Crocodile Tear (goat's milk)

Louisiana

Bittersweet Plantation Dairy: Feliciana Nevat (cow and goat), Evangeline, Gabriel (goat's milk), Holy Cow — Vache Santé (cow's milk)

North Carolina

Spinning Spider Creamery: Camille, Stackhouse (goat's milk)

Oregon

Ancient Heritage Dairy: Valentine (sheep's milk)

Pennsylvania

Hendricks Farms & Dairy: Cow Pie

Texas

Pure Luck Goat Dairy: Del Cielo (goat's milk)

Vermont

Blue Ledge Farm: Lake's Edge

Blythedale Farm: Brie and Camembert

Doe's Leap: Caprella (goat's milk)

Jasper Hill Farm: Constant Bliss

Lazy Lady Farm: Valençay, Les Pyramids

Willow Hill Farm: Fernwood, La Fleurie (cow's milk), Alderbrook, Cobble Hill (sheep's milk)

Woodcock Farms: Summer Snow (sheep's milk)

Virginia

Oak Spring Dairy: Camembert

Washington

Mt. Townsend Creamery: Cirrus, Seastack

Port Madison Farm: Baby Brie (goat's milk)

 You know it's a soft-ripened cheese when . . .

- It has a bright white rind, often referred to as a bloomy rind
- The inside of the cheese has a softer, creamier-looking texture than the outside and when made with cow's milk, is much more yellow compared to the rind
- The area just beneath the rind looks practically translucent while the rest of the interior of the cheese looks relatively firm

Soft-ripened cheeses, also called bloomy-rind cheeses, are possibly the most fundamentally appealing food, not just cheese, in existence. They are creamy, generally mild, and so viscerally appealing that they can supplant rational thought with reverie in an instant. While other cheeses can be deeply satisfying, soft-ripened cheeses tend to be the stuff of dreams.

One of the best features of soft-ripened cheeses is that they are like two cheeses in one. The rind, although an integral part of the cheese, has a texture and flavor all its own. While not everyone likes that texture or flavor even though it is generally mild, it is also the element that gives the cheese added character because of the tension that exists between the toothsome quality of the rind and the creaminess of the paste, or pâte, as it is also called.

Soft-ripened cheeses are made with all three milks, although most often with cow's milk. Sometimes cheesemakers choose to mix milks, but generally the cheeses are made from just one milk. Regardless of the milk source, the method for making these cheeses is mostly the same. Along with the milk and starter cultures goes a mold called *Penicillium candidum*. This is the component in soft-ripened cheeses that gives them their distinctive white, so-called bloomy rind. Sometimes the *candidum* is added to the milk at the beginning of cheesemaking and other times it is sprayed onto the cheeses at the start of the aging phase. Either way, the end result is a mold that serves to ripen the cheese and also protect it from unwanted molds and bacteria during the ripening process.

You might think that ingesting mold and bacteria sounds pretty unappetizing, but remember that all cheese is the result of the interactions of certain bacteria and possibly molds both within the milk and in the air along with myriad other elements.

When you watch soft-ripened cheeses develop, they seem like nothing short of a minor miracle. The moist curds are placed in the round (usually) molds that form them into the shape in which you will ultimately buy them. The curds are either hand-ladled or molded mechanically. Once they drain and dry for a day or two, they are surprisingly firm. They are also naked because the mold has not yet begun to form. After a few days, the downy white mold will start forming and eventually cover the entire cheese.

The reason these cheeses are called soft ripened is because unlike most other cheeses, these cheeses literally get softer as they age. This is unusual because ripening (aging) is a process of moisture loss, which naturally results in a cheese getting harder over time. But with soft-ripened cheeses, the mold serves to break the cheese down and soften it over time. Those same molds will also create a reaction that results in a cheese smelling and ultimately tasting of ammonia. This is the telltale sign that a soft-ripened cheese is over the hill and ready for nothing but the garbage disposal.

The ripening of soft-ripened cheese starts just under the rind and eventually makes its way toward the center. The visual manifestation of this ripening is a translucent and very creamy thin layer just under the rind, which gives way to a firmer center . Some soft-ripened cheeses never become completely soupy in the center, but most will at least soften. That said, many of the industrially made bries and camemberts will never soften. They start out and remain as close to rubber, not to mention as tasteless, as something edible can be.

 Brie versus Camembert

Very often you will see the terms Brie and Camembert used interchangeably. You will also see the names of these cheeses capitalized as often as you will find them in small letters. You'll sometimes find Camembert in a large disk and Brie in a small size despite the fact that neither is traditional. This can be rather confusing for the cheese buyer.

Authentic Brie and Camembert—those cheeses made in the French towns where they have official designations—are capitalized because they are named after the towns in which they were invented and are still made. The official name of Brie is actually Brie de Meaux or Brie de Melun (Meaux and Melun being the names of the towns). You will see Brie de Meaux in cheese shops around the United States, but since that is a raw milk cheese and might not be aged the required sixty days, you will sometimes see it as Fromage de Meaux instead. This is the pasteurized version of the original cheese. Perhaps the most prevalent Brie is Brie de Nangis.

Authentic Brie is made in large wheels, over a foot in diameter, and can weigh more than 6 pounds. Copycat brie (note I have not capitalized this because I am no longer referring to the cheese made in Meaux or Melun) is made in varying sizes, some as small as 4 or 5 ounces. Sometimes this is referred to as "baby brie."

Camembert is a town in the Normandy area of northern France. Camembert is made in a much smaller format than Brie, about 5-ounce wheels, and is actually made a bit differently. While Brie curds are barely cut, Camembert curds are cut several times, which encourages more drainage early on in the cheesemaking process. Because Brie is made in such a large format, curds that are too dry can lead to cracked cheese. The cultures used to make Brie and Camembert (or brie and camembert) are similar, but in general I find Camembert to be a stronger, more aromatic cheese than most Bries.

Triple-Crème Cheeses

There is a subcategory of soft-ripened cheeses that may be single-handedly responsible for their popularity: triple-crème cheeses. These are cheeses to which cream has been added to the milk at the beginning of the cheesemaking process. The cream boosts the amount of fat in the cheese to 75 percent or above. These include St. André, Explorateur, Pierre-Robert, and Brillat-Savarin. Cheeses with fat levels below 75 percent but above 60 percent are called double-crèmes. These include some Bries, such as Fromager d'Affinois, and are certainly delicious even with "less" cream.

The Bottom Line

Remembering the meaning of the term "soft ripened" is simple since it is literal. Simply put, a soft-ripened cheese softens as it ripens (ages). This is the reason these cheeses are so fundamentally appealing. First, you can see them develop practically before your eyes because they change so rapidly. Second, in the course of ripening, they become creamy. While not everyone likes a creamy cheese, from what I've seen, I'd say this style of cheese is the most popular overall. Most people are familiar with Brie or other soft-ripened cheeses, and familiarity breeds anything *but* contempt when it comes to cheese. The more familiar we become with a cheese (assuming we like it), the more likely we are to buy it repeatedly.

Most soft-ripened cheeses are aged a short time, from two to eight weeks, and will always be white on the outside with possible splotches of yellow or light red. The pâte (interior) will range from off-white to yellow and will become soft and creamy just under the rind and creamier toward the center as it ages.

WHAT TO LOOK FOR WHEN BUYING SOFT-RIPENED CHEESES

Soft-ripened cheeses are delicate, which means their shelf life is limited. Usually this style of cheese does not last longer than about ten days, depending how ripe it was when you bought it and the method by which it was made. Some last up to four weeks if you buy the cheese at the beginning of its life, which you can tell by looking and feeling.

VISUAL CUES

- White, velvety rind
- Off-white to ivory to golden paste
- Possible yellowish or very light red coloring on rind, particularly on Camembert
- Smooth and creamy just under the rind and somewhat firmer toward the center
- Do not buy if the cheese has a lot of dark gray striations or rust-colored edges

TEXTURAL CUES

- Young cheeses give a little when gently pressed in the middle but the finger depression does not usually last
- More mature cheeses feel soft and creamy the minute you touch them. If it this is the case *and* the rind is still mostly white, the cheese is most likely at its peak
- Smooth (no cracks) on the rind
- Varying states of creaminess, from soft to soupy

AROMA CUES

The cheese should smell clean with very little aroma. If it smells a little like mushrooms, as many Camemberts do, then that's natural and, in fact, optimal. Of the soft-ripened cheeses, Camemberts tend to be the strongest-smelling ones.

- Buttery
- Floral
- Gamy
- Milky
- Mushroomy
- Do *not* buy if it smells pungent or like ammonia

FLAVOR CUES

Think butter and you'll have a head start in knowing what to expect from soft-ripened cheeses.

- Buttery
- Citrus
- Creamlike
- Earthy
- Floral
- Gamy
- Grassy
- Mushroomy
- Rich
- Salty

A FEW NOTEWORTHY SOFT-RIPENED CHEESES

FRANCE

St. Simeon

St. Simeon is one of those cheeses that is immediately pleasing and yet somewhat unusual. The bright orange dye on the surface that peeks through the snowy white rind is the first indication that it is a different type of cheese. Most bloomy-rind cheeses do not look like washed-rind wannabes. Nor do they taste like them. St. Simeon doesn't either. Instead, this double-crème cheese, which has been made in the heart of Brie country in France since 1929, is mild yet totally engaging because of its discernible acidity, which keeps the rich cheese from being cloying. Looking positively fetching in its see-through container, the cheese made by the Brie Dairy Company is becoming increasingly available as word spreads about the easy-to-love cheese.

ITALY

Robiola Bosina

Made from cow and sheep's milk, Robiola Bosina is usually square shaped and downright creamy. Hailing from the Langhe area in Italy's Piemonte region, Robiola Bosina is as comfortable on a plate of sweets as it is with savory accompaniments. Although it is mild, it is not boring. In fact, the older and consequently creamier it gets, the more interesting it becomes. Although you will find the word "robiola" as part of the names of several cheeses, including Robiola di Roccaverano and sometimes Robiola Rocchetta, those cheeses fall more neatly in the surface-ripened cheese category because of their wrinkly, yellowish, and generally thinner rinds. Those cheeses also tend to be a little stronger as well. The word "robiola" refers to a small cheese, about 4 ounces, that is not aged very long.

United States

California

Elk Creamery: Black Gold
As California's only certified organic goat dairy, Elk Creamery was in a position to distinguish itself the minute it began operations. But that alone would not have been enough to sustain it. Instead, they figured out how to make great cheese, including their cheese called Black Gold. A light coating of ash covers the 8-ounce wheel, and its downy white rind completes its aesthetic beauty. The cheese is made with pasteurized milk and is aged two to three weeks before it is sold. Like most soft-ripened cheeses, Black Gold becomes creamy just under the rind, but unlike the cow's milk versions of this cheese, the goat's milk provides a welcome tang in contrast with the creamy paste. The result is a cheese reflective of the rugged northern California coast on which it is made—dramatic and memorable.

Washington

Mt. Townsend Creamery: Seastack
What do you get when you have three ambitious young guys from three different businesses coming together to form a cheese company? The answer: Mt. Townsend Creamery in Port Townsend, Washington, and unbelievably delicious cheese. Seastack is an ash-covered, sea salt-dusted gem of a small wheel. About 3 inches tall, the pasteurized primarily Jersey milk cheese is creamy yet has a pleasant chalkiness toward the center. Modeled loosely after France's Chaource from the region of Champagne, Seastack's ash coating distinguishes it from its French counterpart. Unlike Chaource, Seastack—named for the rock formations along the Pacific Northwest coast—is less salty. Like other soft-ripened cheeses, Seastack becomes molten just under the rind as it ages. The excellent milk used to make all Mt. Townsend Creamery cheeses really shines through, in part because of the gentle handling of the milk and also because of owners Will, Matt, and Ryan's skill in matching the milk with the particular cheeses they have chosen to make.

 **If you can't find**

Brillat-Savarin, use **Pierre-Robert**, **St. André**, **Explorateur**, or **Fleur de Lis**

Nevat, use **Haystack Peak** or **Humboldt Fog**

Camembert, use **Brie** or **Fromager d'Affinois**

St. Simeon, use **St. André** or **Fromager d'Affinois**

STORING SOFT-RIPENED CHEESES

Like other mold-ripened cheeses, soft-ripened cheeses need to breathe. This is best accomplished by putting them in a (mostly) airtight container with a few holes poked in it. Place the unwrapped cheese in the container and put the whole thing in the drawer of your refrigerator. Alternatively, if your cheese has come packaged in a wooden box, leave it in that. If it was also wrapped in paper, then you should probably change that paper about every three days, using waxed paper instead. Finally, if you do not have the appropriate airtight container, then place the cheese on a plate, cover it with waxed or parchment paper followed by plastic wrap. Poke a few holes in the wrapping and keep the plate in the drawer or on the bottom shelf of the refrigerator.

Soft-Ripened Cheese and Wine Pairing ☆☆☆

Although the rinds of soft-ripened cheeses often interfere with the flavors in wine, these cheeses make good wine partners nevertheless. I tend to remove the rind when I am focusing on wine pairing because I find it makes the wine taste "off."

For a memorable experience, enjoy triple-crème cheeses with Champagne or other sparkling wines. The bubbles and acidity of the wine offset the richness and saltiness in this style of cheese.

For Brie or Camembert, which are slightly less rich but still creamy, a not-too-oaky Chardonnay is a good match, as is an earthy Pinot Noir.

TAKE-HOME TEST: GETTING TO KNOW SOFT-RIPENED CHEESES

This is a two-part exercise. First, I would like you to become familiar with the differences between Brie and Camembert. To do this, you need to do your best to get authentic Camembert, such as Le Chatelain, and Brie labeled Fromage de Meaux, Brie de Meaux, or Brie de Nangis at a well-stocked local store or by mail order. Second, you will taste a triple-crème soft-ripened cheese next to a soft-ripened cheese that has not been enriched. If you thought regular Brie was rich before, just wait.

THE ASSIGNMENT

Buy

- 4 ounces Brie de Meaux, Fromage de Meaux, or other high-quality authentic French Brie, at room temperature

- 4 ounces Camembert, such as Le Chatelain or Isigny, at room temperature

- 4 ounces St. André or Explorateur, at room temperature

- 4 ounces dried apricots

Put the cheeses on separate plates so that if they are runny they will not run into each other to become a muddled mess.

1) Take a taste of the Brie *without* the rind. Notice it is fairly mild and milky, with lingering buttery and mushroomy flavors and an "outdoor" quality like grass. The deeper, earthier flavors sneak up on you more slowly. Now try it with the rind. Notice the textural contrast between the more toothsome rind and the creamy center. Eat an apricot to cleanse your palate.

2) Taste the Camembert without the rind. Do you notice how much more mushroomy this cheese is? It may also smell stronger than the Brie. Its flavors are a bit more concentrated and earthy. Now try it with the rind. This will make the cheese taste stronger, and create a textural contrast. Eat another apricot.

3) Taste the triple-crème without the rind. Does the word butter ring a bell? Triple-crème cheeses appeal to most people because of that pronounced buttery quality. That stands to reason since it's about as close to butter as a cheese can be. Now try it with the rind—you can sense the notable textural difference. Take another apricot.

4) Finally, go back to the Brie. Taste it with or without the rind. Take another taste of the triple-crème. Chances are you can tell the difference, both because of the differences in the weight of the two cheeses in the mouth (the triple-crème is heavier, more mouth-filling) and also the difference in the richness. You may have thought the Brie was rich until you tasted it next

to the triple-crème. The Brie will have a much earthier flavor than the triple-crème.

THE LESSON

Brie and Camembert, while often mentioned in the same sentence, have their own distinct tastes. This is important to know when serving or cooking with them. If you're looking for buttery flavors, then Brie is your best choice, and if you're looking for earthier notes, then choose Camembert. As for triple-crème cheeses, because they are so rich, they are best served in small amounts with a sweet-tart accompaniment just like the dried apricots in this exercise or incorporated in a sauce (without the rind).

CAMEMBERT, HAM, AND CARAMELIZED ONION SANDWICHES

This sandwich couldn't be easier, yet its elegance betrays its simplicity. The onions take a little bit of time, but if you'd like to prepare them in advance, rewarm them when you're ready to assemble the sandwiches. These make great picnic fare but are good just about any place or time.

¼ cup currants

½ cup very hot water

1 tablespoon butter

1 medium red onion (about 8 ounces), peeled and thinly sliced

2 teaspoons red wine vinegar

½ teaspoon kosher salt

Freshly ground pepper

1 long baguette cut into 5-to 6-inch pieces, then halved lengthwise (or use 4 individual mini-baguettes or long rolls)

8 thin slices Black Forest ham (about ¼ pound)

8 ounces Camembert cut into ¼-inch-thick slices (or use Brie)

Put the currants and hot water in a small heat-proof bowl. Let sit for at least 15 minutes or as long as 1 hour, then drain. Set aside.

In a medium-size sauté pan, melt the butter over low heat. Add the onions and cook, stirring occasionally, for about 30 minutes, or until soft. Add the vinegar, currants, salt, and pepper to taste and cook for 10 more minutes. Let cool.

To assemble: place a few onions and some currants on the bottom half of the bread. Top with the ham, cheese, and other bread half. Serve right away.

Serves 4

Note: It is easiest to cut this cheese when it is cold. Bring to room temperature before using.

BRIE TOASTS WITH CHARDONNAY-SOAKED GOLDEN RAISINS

Some of the characteristics of a classic American Chardonnay are vanilla, butter, and if it has been aged in oak, a toasty quality as well. Because Brie and Chardonnay typically go well together, I decided to deconstruct some of the elements in Chardonnay to create this hors d'oeuvre. The result is both sweet and savory and a great showcase for the buttery cheese. To get the full flavor from the raisins, it is best to prepare them the day before. Note that it's easiest to cut this type of cheese when it is cold. Bring to room temperature before serving.

1½ cups water

1 cup Chardonnay

¼ cup plus 2 tablespoons sugar

1 vanilla bean, split in half vertically

1 cup golden raisins

12 ounces Fromager d'Affinois cheese sliced into 24 pieces (or use any double-crème brie)

24 slices baguette cut ¼ inch thick

4 tablespoons (½ stick) unsalted butter, melted

In a medium-size saucepan, combine the water, wine, and sugar. Bring to a simmer over medium-high heat until the sugar is dissolved. Reduce heat to medium and simmer for 5 minutes. Turn off the heat. Scrape the insides of the vanilla bean into the liquid and add the remaining bean. Add the raisins. Let steep uncovered for at least 1 hour at room temperature. Refrigerate overnight.

Drain the raisins, reserving the liquid. Discard the vanilla bean. Put the liquid back in the saucepan and bring to a boil. Reduce to about ⅓ cup, or until the syrup turns a deep golden color, 10 to 15 minutes. Watch carefully so the syrup doesn't burn. If it starts to foam, remove from heat immediately. The syrup will continue to thicken as it cools, and have a texture similar to light maple syrup. Cool completely.

Preheat the oven to 400°F.

Brush butter onto both sides of the bread slices. Bake for 8 to 10 minutes or until golden brown. Let cool completely.

To assemble: Put a slice of cheese on each toast. Sprinkle with a few raisins and drizzle syrup over the top.

Makes 24

Note: If you have any raisins and syrup left over, combine them and refrigerate in an airtight container. They will keep for 2 weeks.

VALENÇAY WITH CHERRIES AND PLUMS

I have read that cherries grow in the Loire Valley, where the ash-covered goat cheese Valençay is made, so I made the assumption that cherries and the local cheese would probably go well together. It turns out they do. But rather than creating something sweet with the cherries, I decided to give them a savory slant instead. The result is a salad course with sweet, tangy, and earthy flavors all in one bite. Don't worry if you can't find Valençay; other goat cheeses work just as well.

½ pound fresh Bing cherries, pitted and cut in quarters (or use a combination of cherries that are in season in your area)

1 pound purple plums, pitted and cut into ¼-inch slices (or use a variety of plums such as Elephant Heart, Green Gage, or whatever is in season)

¼ cup finely chopped fresh basil

1 tablespoon plus 1 teaspoon extra-virgin olive oil

2 teaspoons fresh lemon juice

¼ teaspoon kosher salt (or more to taste)

1 piece Valençay cheese, about 7 ounces (or use Humboldt Fog or other soft-ripened or fresh goat cheese)

In a medium-size bowl, mix together all of the ingredients except the cheese. Let sit at room temperature for at least 15 minutes and up to 1 hour, stirring occasionally. Alternatively, you can refrigerate the mixture for up to 6 hours, but do not add the basil until you're ready to serve.

To cut the cheese: If using Valençay, cut the cheese horizontally two-thirds of the way down. Cut both pieces into quarters by criss-crossing to make a total of 8 triangular pieces. If using a different cheese, cut into 8 equal pieces.

To serve, distribute the cherry mixture on 8 small plates. Lay a piece of cheese next to the mixture and serve.

Serves 8

GOAT CHEESE AND LENTIL SALAD

I created this recipe in Colorado, where I had ready access to that state's Haystack Mountain Goat Dairy's sublime cheese called Haystack Peak. If you can get that cheese for this or any other dish, do it! The vinegar and the creaminess of the lentils are a perfect match for a creamy goat cheese. Ideally, your cheese should be at the perfect ripeness, where the cheese just under the rind has become creamy and the rest of the cheese *tastes* creamy and yet is still firm.

For the lentils

1 cup dried lentils

1 large clove garlic, peeled

For the dressing

2 tablespoons plus 2 teaspoons red wine vinegar

2 teaspoons balsamic vinegar

1½ teaspoons Dijon mustard

2 tablespoons chopped fresh dill plus whole sprigs for garnish

¼ teaspoon kosher salt

Freshly ground pepper

3 tablespoons plus 2 teaspoons extra-virgin olive oil

For the salad

4 scallions, finely chopped

1 medium carrot, peeled and cut into 1/8-inch dice

1 large celery stalk, cut into 1/8-inch dice

About 1 cup peeled, finely diced English cucumber

1 whole Haystack Peak cheese, about 8 ounces (or any soft-ripened goat cheese, preferably with ash, such as Humboldt Fog)

To prepare the lentils: Fill a 2-quart saucepan about halfway with water. Add the lentils and garlic. Bring to a boil, then reduce the heat to a simmer. Cook, uncovered, until the lentils are tender but not mushy, 15 to 20 minutes. Drain in a strainer or small holed colander. Remove and discard the garlic and let cool to room temperature.

To make the dressing: In a small bowl, whisk together the vinegars, mustard, dill, salt, and pepper to taste. Slowly add the oil in a steady stream, whisking constantly to emulsify the dressing. Set aside. (You can make this 1 day ahead. Cover and refrigerate, but bring to room temperature before using.)

To make the salad: In a medium-size bowl, mix the lentils with the scallions, carrots, celery, and cucumber. Add the

dressing and mix gently. Add a little salt, then taste and adjust the seasoning if necessary. Let sit for at least 15 minutes and preferably up to 1 hour at room temperature.

To prepare the cheese: Cut the cheese horizontally two-thirds of the way down. Cut the two pieces into quarters by criss-crossing to make 8 triangular pieces. If you're not using a pyramid-shape cheese, then simply cut cheese into 1-ounce portions.

To assemble: Put about ¼ cup lentils on each of 8 salad plates. Lay a piece of cheese on the side of the salad (rather than directly in the center) but still touching the beans. Garnish each plate with a dill sprig.

Serves 8

CHICKEN "PICCATA" WITH GOAT CHEESE

This dish may look complicated because of the number of steps, but most of the elements can be prepared ahead of time. If you are in a time pinch, the chicken alone is terrific and can be made fairly quickly. The goat cheese contributes a silken element, and its bright white color makes the dish look springy and refreshing. Why call it "piccata"? Chalk it up to my imagination and the presence of the classic piccata duo of capers and lemon.

For the chicken

4   boneless chicken thighs with skin, about 1¾ pounds (Note: If you cannot find boneless chicken thighs, use boneless, skin-on chicken breasts)

2   teaspoons herbes de Provence (or use chopped fresh thyme or ¾ tablespoon dried)

2   teaspoons finely grated lemon zest

½   teaspoon salt

Freshly ground pepper

8   ounces Bucheron cheese or use other soft-ripened goat cheese such as goat brie, cut into 16 slices or use fresh goat cheese

For the marinade/dressing

½   cup olive oil

¼   cup plus 2 tablespoons fresh lemon juice

1   teaspoon kosher salt

Freshly ground pepper

2   tablespoons capers, drained

For the salad

4   slices bacon, coarsely chopped

1   small red onion (about 6 ounces) cut lengthwise into ⅛-inch slices

Salt

½   pound spinach leaves, washed and dried well

2   medium tomatoes (about ¾ pound), coarsely chopped then lightly salted

To prepare the chicken: Place the chicken, skin side up, in a glass dish just large enough to hold it. In a small bowl, mix together the herbes de Provence, lemon zest, ½ teaspoon salt, and pepper (and fresh goat cheese, if using). Carefully slip the herb mixture under the skin of each thigh, distributing it as evenly as possible. If using slices of cheese, place 2 slices side by side under the skin. If the skin tears, secure it with 1 or 2 toothpicks.

To make the marinade: In the same bowl you used to mix the herbs, mix together 2 tablespoons of the olive oil and the 2 tablespoons lemon juice. Pour over the chicken. Salt and pepper both sides of the thighs. Let sit at room temperature at least 30 minutes, or up to 2 hours, refrigerated.

When ready to cook, place an oven rack 6 inches below the heating element and preheat the broiler.

continued

When ready to cook, place an oven rack 6 inches below the heating element and preheat the broiler.

To make the dressing: Using the same bowl you used to make the marinade, mix together remaining 6 tablespoons olive oil and ¼ cup lemon juice. Add the capers and 1 teaspoon salt. Set aside. (Dressing can be made 1 day ahead and refrigerated).

To prepare the salad: Cook the bacon until crisp in a medium-size skillet over medium heat, about 6 minutes. Transfer the bacon to a paper towel-lined plate. Drain all but 2 tablespoons of the bacon fat. To the same pan, add the onion slices and cook over medium heat until the onions are limp, about 5 minutes. Add a touch of salt, and set aside.

To cook the chicken: Place the chicken in a shallow broiler-proof pan, skin side down. Broil the chicken until it is slightly dark around the edges, tan in the center, and feels firm yet slightly springy to the touch, 8 to 10 minutes. Turn and cook until the skin is very crisp and the chicken feels firm but still gives slightly when touched, about 8 minutes. (Note: If using chicken breasts, cook about 1 minute less on each side so they will not dry out.)

To assemble: Place the spinach, bacon, and onions in a large bowl. Toss with the dressing. Put one piece of chicken on each of 4 dinner plates. Distribute the spinach salad on top of each thigh, and sprinkle with chopped tomatoes. Place 2 slices of cheese on top of the tomatoes, give a couple of twists of pepper, and serve.

Serves 4

ROASTED VEGETABLE PASTA WITH TRIPLE-CRÈME CHEESE

This recipe is admittedly a cross-cultural affair (you'll rarely see cumin, Pecorino Romano, and a triple-crème cheese in the same dish), but because creaminess soothes spiciness, I thought that the triple-crème cheese would be the perfect antidote to the spicy chiles. The corn adds a welcome sweet element, the squash mirrors the cheese in its creamy texture, and the Pecorino Romano adds just the right amount of salt.

1 medium white or yellow onion

2 tablespoons vegetable oil

8-10 tomatillos (about ¾ pound), quartered

1 pound pattypan squash cut into ½-inch pieces (or use other summer squash such as yellow or zucchini)

3 small jalapeños, stemmed, seeded, and cut crosswise into ¼-inch pieces

1 tablespoon plus 2 teaspoons kosher salt

2 teaspoons ground cumin

1 cup fresh corn (1 to 2 medium cobs), or 1 cup frozen corn, thawed

1 wheel or 1 piece St. André cheese, about 7 ounces (or use Explorateur, or other triple-crème cheese)

½ pound fusilli pasta

¾ cup finely chopped cilantro plus whole sprigs for garnish

½ cup finely grated Pecorino Romano cheese (or use aged cotija, aged Asiago, or other hard cheese)

Preheat the oven to 400°F. Line a baking sheet with foil and lightly oil the foil.

Cut the onion in half crosswise, then cut lengthwise into ½-inch chunks. Separate the chunks into pieces.

In a large bowl, mix together the oil, onions, tomatillos, squash, jalapeños, 2 teaspoons of the salt, and 1 teaspoon cumin. Spread the vegetables on the foil and roast for 15 minutes. Add the corn and cook, stirring occasionally, for about 15 more minutes or until vegetables are soft and caramelized around the edges.

Remove the rind from the cheese and cut cheese into ½-inch pieces. It is easiest to cut this style of cheese when it is cold; bring to room temperature before using.

Meanwhile, in a large (4-quart) pot, bring 2 quarts of water and the remaining tablespoon of salt to a boil. Add the pasta and cook 8 to 10 minutes, or until the pasta is tender but still slightly firm to the bite. Ladle out 1 cup of the pasta water and drain the rest.

Put the pasta in a large bowl along with the vegetables, St. André, the remaining 1 teaspoon cumin, and ¼ cup of pasta water. Working quickly, mix all the ingredients together until most of the cheese has softened. Add the cilantro and mix again. If the mixture seems dry, add more pasta water 2 tablespoons at a time. Transfer to a platter or individual plates. Top with the grated cheese and garnish with cilantro sprigs.

Serves 4

Clockwise from left: St. Marcellin,
St. Maure, Pointe de Brique

CHAPTER 5

SURFACE-RIPENED

CHEESES

Use Surface-Ripened Cheeses for

- Cheese courses
- Entertaining
- Salads
- Vegetable dishes

What Are They?

France

Banon (goat's milk sometimes mixed with cow's milk)

Brebiou

Cabécou (*See also* Rocamadour)

Chabichou de Poitou

Crottin de Chavignol

Le Chevrot

Le Gariotin

Le Lingot

Pérail (sheep's milk)

Picodon

Pointe de Brique

Pouligny-St.-Pierre

St. Félicien

St. Maure

St. Marcellin

Selles-Sur-Cher

Rocamadour (*See also* Cabécou)

Valençay

Italy

Cravanzina (cow and sheep's milk)

Robiola di Roccaverano (goat's and/or mixed milk)

Robiola Tre Latte (sheep, goat, and cow's milk)

Rocchetta (sheep, cow, and goat's milk)

La Tur (sheep, cow, and goat's milk)

Off the Beaten Path

Spain

Queso de la Serena (sheep's milk)

Torta del Casar (sheep's milk)

United States

California

Marin French Cheese Company: Le Petite Camembert

Pug's Leap Farm: Buche (goat's milk)

Redwood Hill Farm: California Crottin (goat's milk)

Indiana

Capriole Goat Cheese: Wabash Cannonball, Crocodile Tear, Piper's Pyramid

Louisiana

Bittersweet Plantation Dairy: Fleur de Lis, Fleur de Teche

Oregon

Juniper Grove Farm: Buche, Dutchman's Flat, Otentique, Pyramid (goat's milk)

Texas

Pure Luck Goat Dairy: Sainte Maure

Vermont

Blue Ledge Farm: Crottina (goat's milk)

Vermont Butter & Cheese Company: Bijou, Bonne Bouche, Coupole (goat's milk)

You know it's a surface-ripened cheese when . . .

- It has a wrinkled rind
- It has a paper-thin rind with tinges of white, possibly a little pink, or maybe a straw color
- It has a yellowish hue interspersed with splotches of white mold on the rind
- It is either firm to the touch *or* molten and gooey
- The color of the paste is white to light ivory
- It is tall and cylindrical in shape

THE EXPLANATION

If you think wrinkly, then you'll immediately understand surface-ripened cheeses or at least the ones I discuss here. Technically, soft-ripened cheeses and washed-rind cheeses are also surface-ripened cheeses. The difference in the cheeses I refer to here is that these have either a wrinkly rind or a very thin, delicate rind. But don't judge a cheese on looks alone. These cheeses taste different too.

Surface-ripened cheeses tend to fall into two subcategories: **firm**—which may be chalky and possibly a little dry and flaky—or very **creamy**. The firm ones are most often goat cheeses, while the creamy ones could be any one of the three milks or a combination of milks.

The main constituent that distinguishes these cheeses is the predominance of a yeast called *Geotrichum candidum*. Sometimes this yeast is introduced into the milk during cheesemaking, and other times it exists in the ambient air of the cheesemaking or aging facility. This yeast is found in many places, including our own bodies. *G. candidum* has a variety of purposes in cheese including the contribution of certain key enzymes, which help in flavor development, aging, and the reduction of bitterness. It also affects the texture and thickness of the rind.

Firm Style

In the firm goat cheeses, the visible result of the presence of *G. candidum* is a surface that looks kind of "brainy." Once you see this type of cheese, you'll know why I use this description. This type of rind is most often found on the goat cheeses of France's Loire Valley. Many American cheesemakers are now making similar cheeses. These cheeses are a little chalky, yet also creamy, and almost all are tangy and earthy.

Creamy Style

The creamy type of surface-ripened cheese looks a little like a hybrid between a soft-ripened cheese and a surface-ripened cheese. The gooey cheese called St. Marcellin is a perfect example. It too is exposed to G. candidum, but its rind is paper-thin and becomes almost indistinguishable from the paste the minute you cut into it. But since the rind is not snow-white like, say, Brie (that is, it does not have Penicillium candidum), and because it does have G. candidum, it belongs in this style. (Not to confuse you, but I have to acknowledge the fact the G. candidum is also found in soft-ripened cheeses. The difference is that in soft-ripened cheeses, the mold responsible for creating the velvety white rind, the Penicillium candidum, dominates and grows over the G. candidum making its effects less obvious.)

Although not exactly scientific, another way you can tell the difference between a soft-ripened and surface-ripened cheese is that generally, the surface-ripened cheeses are: small (2 to 4 ounces), slightly flattened rounds; tall and cylindrical; or pyramid-shaped, while soft-ripened cheeses like Brie and Camembert will be wheel-shaped with a flat surface.

One telltale difference between the firm style of surface-ripened cheese and soft-ripened cheese is that the former can become hard over time, to the point where you can grate it over salads, pastas, and the like, while soft-ripened cheese always gets increasingly soft as it ages.

Most surface-ripened cheeses are not usually aged for long, on average about 3 to 10 weeks, although you can keep the firm style for months because it eventually becomes a grating cheese. The relatively short aging time for most of these cheeses belies their full flavor and complexity. A surface-ripened goat cheese is infinitely more interesting than a young goat cheese, and a surface-ripened creamy cheese has surprising complexity as compared with some of its soft-ripened counterparts.

The Difference in Flavor

The two types of surface-ripened cheeses share some flavor characteristics but diverge on others. The firmer style goat cheeses have the characteristic goat's milk tanginess, but they also have grassy, earthy, possibly sulfur-like and light cream flavors too. The creamy style may also have these characteristics, but more likely the flavors will seem sweeter and more floral, or conversely, like mushrooms. Although the creamy style is more delicate in texture, it is not always more delicate in flavor. These cheeses are not strong, but neither are they wimpy. They are mild-looking on the surface, but they have plenty of character beneath the thin rinds.

The Bottom Line

Although used as a broad term to represent any cheese that is ripened by surface molds and yeasts, in this context surface-ripened cheeses are those that have a wrinkly rind, such as many French and American goat cheeses, or whose rinds are thin and barely contain the runny cheese within.

WHAT TO LOOK FOR WHEN BUYING SURFACE-RIPENED CHEESES

VISUAL CUES

The firm style of surface-ripened cheeses, such as many of the goat cheeses that come from France's Loire Valley, have very firm, solid rinds that look as though they have a matrix of curly wires running all over the surface (this is a good thing). The creamy style is much more delicate and should look vibrant and youthful.

Firm Style	Creamy Style
• Wrinkled rind • Ivory to yellowish or even brown-colored rind • Bright white to light ivory paste • Possible blue mold spots or mold covering the cheese entirely in longer-aged cheeses • Somewhat dry-looking rind but not dried out and cracking	• Paper-thin rind ranging in color from white to yellowish to pinkish or faint orange • Slightly wrinkled but delicate rind • Delicate and possibly oozy • Surface mold looks vibrant and uniform

TEXTURAL CUES

Firm Style	Creamy Style
• Firm and somewhat dry (mostly applies to surface-ripened goat cheeses) • Initially chalky but then creamy • Will not give when touched; feels a little rough, like textured paper	• Extremely creamy, possibly even soupy • Will give instantly and possibly even tear when gently touched • Might feel as if it has liquid inside

AROMA CUES

The firm style should smell earthy and maybe musty, but should not smell strong. The creamy style should smell clean with very little aroma.

• Barnyard	• Grassy	• Truffle
• Blue mold-like	• Lemony	• Do *not* buy if it smells like ammonia
• Crème fraîche-like (creamy style)	• Milky	
• Earthy	• Mushroomy	
	• Musty	

FLAVOR CUES

Both categories of surface-ripened cheeses have many of flavors ranging from mild and tangy to strong and mushroomy. Many of these cheeses may be small, but they pack a punch.

• Buttery	• Earthy	• Musty
• Chalky	• Floral	• Sulfury
• Creamy (like fresh cream)	• Grassy	• Sweet
• Crème fraîche-like	• Lemony	• Tangy
	• Mushroomy	• Truffly

MOUTHFEEL

The mouthfeel of the firm style is chalky, then creamy (it may also be a little flaky yet mouth-coating). The creamy style will be just that—creamy.

Firm Style

The flavors will linger for what seems like forever, partly due to the textural changes that happen once you bite into one of these cheeses. The rind is firm, even a little rough or chewy, and the paste ranges from downright creamy to chalky.

Creamy Style

The flavors are long-lasting because these cheeses tend to embody more of the mushroomy qualities inherent in some surface-ripened cheeses. This pleasant flavor gives way to the fresh cream like flavors also found in this style of cheese. The creamy texture itself will coat the mouth, making for a cheese with a long and enjoyable finish.

A FEW NOTEWORTHY SURFACE-RIPENED CHEESES

FRANCE

Pouligny-St.-Pierre

Often referred to as the "Eiffel Tower" because of its tower or pyramid-like shape, Pouligny-St.-Pierre from the Loire Valley unquestionably rises to the top of excellent surface-ripened goat cheeses. The Loire Valley, located southwest of Paris, is famous for goat cheese, and although the cheeses there differ, they typically are the surface-ripened style. In the case of Pouligny-St.-Pierre, the cheese sent to the United States is made with pasteurized goat's milk and has the signature wrinkly rind, which ranges in color from light beige to orangish with gray and white mold spots. Aged about 4 or 5 weeks, the paste of the cheese ranges from chalky to creamy and its flavors are tangy, earthy, herbaceous, and nutty.

La Tur

If Nat King Cole had been singing about a cheese in his classic song "Unforget-table," La Tur would almost certainly have been the object of his affection. Made in the wine-rich region of Alba, in northern Italy's Piemonte region, this blend of pasteurized cow, goat, and sheep's milk is practically sinful in its creaminess and perfect combination of buttery tang. The rind is wrinkled with a tinge of yellow, and the cheese is so creamy and delicate that it is packaged on a paper doily inside individual plastic cups. The cellophane "lid" allows you to see the cheese from the top down. La Tur is aged a short ten days and flown across the Atlantic to arrive in the United States in perfect shape. Plan to cut it with a knife but eat it with a spoon so that all that is left is the memory of one very excellent cheese.

UNITED STATES

Vermont

Vermont Butter & Cheese Company: Bijou

This little 2-ounce gem deserves its name. Bijou, or "jewel" is a crottin that becomes creamier over time, although it is versatile enough that it will become a grating cheese in just a day or two if you take it out of its wrapping and leave it ex-posed in the refrigerator. Bijou is one of the newest cheeses from the twenty-three year-old Vermont Butter & Cheese Company in Websterville, Vermont, having debuted in 2006. One of three aged goat's milk cheeses made by the company, Bijou may be small but it packs a lot of flavor. The use of *Geotrichum candidum* is obvious in its coral-like surface but also in its yeasty aromas and flavors. The cheese starts out mild and while it never gets strong, the tangy yet nutty flavors become more pronounced, giving this small jewel of a cheese a big bang for its bite.

 If you can't find

Crottin de Chavignol, use **Le Chevrot, Redwood Hill California Crottin,** or **Chabichou de Poitou**

Cravanzina, use **St. Marcellin, Pérail,** or **Robiola Bossina**

La Tur, use **Rocchetta** or **St. André**

Valençay, use **Selles-Sur-Cher, Vermont Butter & Cheese Company Bonne Bouche,** or **Humboldt Fog**

STORING SURFACE-RIPENED CHEESES

Firm Style

Get out your airtight plastic container, poke a few holes in it, and put a small, slightly damp piece of wadded-up paper towel in the container to maintain a little humidity. Put the unwrapped cheese in the container and close it. Place it in the refrigerator drawer. Change the paper every couple of days.

Creamy Style

An airtight container with a few holes is also good for the creamy style of surface-ripened cheeses. Take the cheese out of its packaging (except St. Marcellin and St. Felicien, which come in their own ceramic or plastic crock), and put it in the container. Shut the lid and store it in the refrigerator drawer. No airtight containers on hand? Then put the cheese on a plate, wrap it in waxed paper followed by plastic wrap placed around it, and poke a few holes in it. Again, keep it in the drawer of your fridge or on the bottom shelf.

 Surface-Ripened Cheese and Wine Pairing ☆☆½

Because so much of the complexity of surface-ripened cheeses is in the rind, it is harder to pair these cheeses with wine because the rinds almost always create bitterness in the wine. You should choose wines with little to no tannins (the astringent compounds that come from red grape skins and oak). Instead, choose white wines like Pinot Grigio, Sauvignon Blanc, or Chenin Blanc. If you want to drink a red wine, then look for a Cabernet Franc or Pinot Noir from the Loire Valley or a Barbera from the Piemonte in Italy.

TAKE-HOME TEST: GETTING TO KNOW SURFACE-RIPENED CHEESES

Since many cheesemongers will not distinguish between surface-ripened cheeses and soft-ripened cheeses, I thought it might be helpful for you to be able to make the distinction yourself. That way you won't be in for any surprises when you bring home a St. Marcellin, expecting it to taste like Brie.

THE ASSIGNMENT

Buy

- 1 California Crottin, Le Chevrot, Crottin de Chavignol or other "wrinkly" goat cheese, at room temperature

- 1 wheel St. Marcellin, at room temperature

- 2 to 4 ounces Fromager d'Affinois or any double-crème Brie, at room temperature

- 2 to 4 ounces Taleggio, Epoisses, Reblochon, Red Hawk, or other washed-rind cheese, at room temperature

- 1 baguette, sliced (optional)

Because all of these cheeses except the crottin are runny, you might choose to use spoons instead of knives to portion out the cheeses. The bread is part of the assignment because it is a convenient host for these cheeses, but to get the most from this assignment you would be better off eating the cheese right off the spoon rather than putting it on bread; it gives you a better sense of the flavor and texture of the cheese.

One social note: unless you are doing this exercise by yourself, you might want to avoid double-dipping so as to avoid the scorn of friends or family. To do this, put a spoon in or next to each of the runny cheeses, and use that to scoop the cheese onto your own spoon.

You probably noticed that you bought cheeses belonging to three of the cheese styles—surface ripened, soft ripened, and washed rind. Technically each of these is a surface-ripened cheese. But you're about to find out how they differ.

1) First, take a taste of the crottin (make sure to eat the rind too). I want you to experience its many textures. It will be firm on the outside, maybe even a little rough, and then the inside might be creamy just under the rind and definitely chalky toward the center. Or, depending on your particular cheese, it might simply be dry and chalky. This is the quintessential firm category of surface-ripened cheese. In fact, as time goes on and it continues to lose its moisture, it will actually become a grating cheese.

2) Moving on to the creamy style, take a taste of the St. Marcellin including the rind (even if you wanted to eat this cheese without the rind, it would be very hard to avoid because of how thin it is). Notice how it starts off mild but then becomes

a little mushroomy as it lingers in your mouth. Also notice how the rind is delicate, almost ethereal. A delicate rind is fairly common in this category of surface-ripened cheeses.

3) Now taste the Fromager d'Affinois. Like the St. Marcellin, it is creamy although probably not quite as soupy. Relatively speaking, the rind of the Brie-like cheese is thicker and more toothsome. The soft-ripened cheese is probably milder too, with little to no mushroomy flavor.

4) Next, taste the washed-rind cheese. Compared with the St. Marcellin and Brie, it will be much stronger and, depending which cheese you purchased, the rind will be thicker, possibly even a little crunchy in places, or at the least, much stronger in flavor than the St. Marcellin and Brie. While the washed-rind cheese starts off similarly to other surface-ripened cheeses it parts ways during the aging process and results in stronger flavors and aromas.

THE LESSON

While there are many cheeses that are referred to as surface-ripened cheeses, the ones highlighted in this chapter are significantly different and are the only ones to really be referred to as surface-ripened cheeses (the others are almost always referred to as either soft-ripened or washed-rind cheeses, at least in retail settings). The firm surface-ripened cheeses have a firm, hearty rind—not a soft one—and a texture that ranges from creamy to chalky. With this assignment, I hope you noticed both the textural and distinct flavor differences among the styles of cheese.

MUSHROOM TOASTS WITH ROCCHETTA

One of the telltale signs that you are eating a surface-ripened cheese is when it tastes mushroomy. That's why I combined cheese with mushrooms to create this recipe. Although it calls for the Italian cheese Rocchetta, you can choose from a number of different surface-ripened cheeses. You want a cheese that will soften on contact with the hot mushrooms and stand up to their earthy flavors.

6 slices sourdough bread (crusts removed) cut in half crosswise

4 tablespoons (½ stick) unsalted butter, at room temperature

1 small shallot, minced

1½ pounds assorted mushrooms, stemmed and cut into 1/2-inch pieces

½ teaspoon kosher or coarse sea salt, or more to taste

½ teaspoon freshly ground pepper

2 tablespoons sherry vinegar

¼ cup heavy cream

1 half wheel of Rocchetta cheese, about 4.5 ounces, cut into 6 equal-size pieces (or use La Tur, Perail, St. Andre or any double- or triple-crème Brie, rind removed)

2 tablespoons finely chopped fresh parsley

Place an oven rack 6 inches below the heating element and preheat the broiler.

Put the bread slices on a baking sheet. Broil until golden brown, about 45 seconds. Watch to make sure the bread doesn't burn. Turn the bread and spread with 2 tablespoons of the butter. Broil until the bread has a few little brown spots and is a half-shade darker, about 45 seconds to 1 minute. Do not toast too much. Set aside.

In a large sauté pan, melt the remaining 2 tablespoons butter over medium-high heat. Add the shallot and cook for 2 minutes. Add the mushrooms and cook, stirring occasionally, until they are soft and have released most but not all their juices, about 10 minutes. Add the salt and pepper.

Turn the heat to high and add the vinegar. Cook for 1 minute. Reduce the heat to medium, add the cream, and cook until the sauce has thickened slightly and the mushroom mixture looks creamy but not soupy, about 1 to 2 minutes. Taste and adjust seasoning if necessary. (Note: You can prepare the mushrooms up to 2 hours ahead. Cover and keep at room temperature. Reheat to piping hot.)

To assemble, place 2 pices of toast on individual serving plates. Distribute the mushrooms on top of the toast. Place the cheese on top, sprinkle with parsley, and serve right away.

Serves 6

Sweet-Tart Goat Cheese Salad

While goat cheese with beets is a well-loved combination, the addition of apples and raspberry vinegar enhances the sweetness of the beets by adding a sweet-tart element. I have my loyal recipe tester Sheri Castle to thank for suggesting these ingredients and for helping to make what was a good recipe into one that is memorable—and pretty too.

For the walnuts

¼ cup confectioners' sugar

⅛ teaspoon cayenne pepper

½ teaspoon salt plus more to taste

1 heaping cup walnut halves and pieces (about 4 ounces)

For the salad

2 large beets (about 1 pound) around 2½ inches in diameter or the approximate diameter of the cheese, scrubbed and stemmed but not peeled

¼ cup raspberry vinegar (or use cider vinegar)

⅓ cup best-quality extra-virgin olive oil

Salt

1 small fennel bulb (about ¼ pound)

1 small Granny Smith apple, cored, seeded, and sliced paper-thin

1 round (about 6 ounces) Crottin de Chavignol, Le Chevrot, or other crottin

¼ teaspoon freshly ground pepper

Preheat the oven to 350°F.

To prepare the walnuts: In a medium-sized bowl, mix together the sugar, cayenne, and salt.

Bring a small saucepan of water to a boil. Add the walnuts and blanch them for 3 minutes. Drain well and immediately roll the walnuts in the sugar mixture until thoroughly coated. The sugar will melt slightly.

Transfer the walnuts to a baking sheet or pan and bake, stirring occasionally, until they are a deep golden-brown, about 12 to 15 minutes. Watch carefully the sugar can burn easily. Let cool completely before serving. Makes 1 cup walnuts.

To make the salad: Place a steamer basket in a medium (3- or 4-quart) pot. Add the beets and fill pot with water to 1 inch above the beets. Cook for about 40 minutes or until the beets feel soft when poked with the tip of a knife. Peel while still warm yet cool enough to handle. Cut the beets horizontally into ¼-inch thick slices to get 12 slices. Sprinkle with 2 tablespoons of the vinegar. Set aside.

In a small bowl, whisk together the oil and remaining tablespoon vinegar for the dressing. Add salt to taste. Set aside.

Cut the fennel in quarters lengthwise. Remove the core and then slice each piece crosswise into paper-thin slices. (A mandoline works well for this.) In a medium bowl, toss the fennel and apple with ¼ cup of the dressing. Taste and add salt if necessary. Let rest about 30 minutes to allow the flavors to meld.

Cut ⅛ inch off the top of the crottin horizontally and discard. Cut the remainder of the cheese into ⅛ inch-thick slices. You should have 12 slices.

To assemble: Make a bed of fennel and apple on each of 4 salad plates. Try to make sure the mixture lies relatively flat. Beginning with 1 slice of cheese, lay it on top of the fennel-apple mixture toward the center of the plate. Place a slice of beet underneath the cheese followed by another slice of beet and so on to create a pinwheel pattern on top of the fennel and apple. Drizzle with a little more dressing. Give it a twist of black pepper, and sprinkle with about 2 tablespoons of walnuts per serving. (Save extra walnuts for another use, such as an accompaniment for a cheese course.) Serve right away.

Serves 4

ROASTED CAULIFLOWER WITH CREAMY ST. MARCELLIN

St. Marcellin is the embodiment of creamy decadence. The tiniest prick of a knife, and off it runs. In fact, it's so delicate and creamy that it is sold in either a ceramic or plastic container just large enough to contain it. While tiny, about 4 ounces, St. Marcellin and its counterpart St. Félicien pack a ton of flavor. As a result, the cheese holds its own against an assertive vegetable like roasted cauliflower. This dish is rich, which is why I call for several vinegary ingredients that cut the richness yet do not detract from it.

For the cauliflower

1   medium cauliflower (about 1¼ pounds), broken into small florets about ½ inch wide and 1 inch long

2   tablespoons olive oil

1   teaspoon kosher salt

For the vinaigrette

1   teaspoon Dijon mustard

1   tablespoon red wine vinegar

¼   teaspoon kosher salt

3   tablespoons extra-virgin olive oil

2   rounds of St. Marcellin cheese (about 8 ounces) or use any type of Robiola or Camembert

12 cornichons

¼   cup cocktail onions, drained

Preheat the oven to 400°F.

On a large baking sheet, mix together all the cauliflower ingredients. Roast for 20 to 25 minutes, or until the edges of the cauliflower have browned and it is tender but not soft. Let cool for 15 minutes. Leave the oven on.

Meanwhile, make the vinaigrette. In a small bowl, mix together the mustard, vinegar, and salt. Slowly whisk in the olive oil until the mixture becomes thick.

If the cheese has not come packaged in ceramic crocks, transfer to ramekins or another type of ovenproof dish. Put the containers of cheese in the oven and bake for 8 to 10 minutes, or until the cheese becomes warm and soupy.

To assemble: In a large bowl, toss the cauliflower with the vinaigrette. Place the cheese in their containers on a platter. Scatter the cauliflower around the containers of cheese. Put the cornichons and onions into separate small bowls and place the bowls on the table. Instruct each person to take a little cauliflower, a few cornichons and onions, and spoon as much cheese as they like over the cauliflower. Enjoy right away.

Serves 4

ITALIAN-STYLE GRAPE COMPOTE WITH LA TUR

When I visited the Piemonte region in northern Italy, I was introduced to a local cheese accompaniment called *cogna* (pronounced *CONE-yah*). It is made from the skins and seeds left over from winemaking (called grape must), as well as pears, hazelnuts, figs, and sometimes spices. I loved this runny mixture with the local cheeses and thought it would be fun to try to re-create it. Since grape must is not readily available, I adjusted the recipe to use fresh grapes and wine instead. You can enjoy the compote with all kinds of cheeses. Although the mixture takes a while to cook, it is quite simple to make and will last for at least a month in the refrigerator.

---

1 cup dry red wine

¼ cup sugar

2 cups (about ⅔ pound), seedless red grapes

1 medium pear, preferably Bosc, peeled, cored, and cut into ½-inch chunks

2 tablespoons whole hazelnuts

1 whole piece of La Tur cheese (about 8 ounces)

French baguette slices

Combine the wine and sugar in a medium-size saucepan over medium-high heat. Cook, stirring constantly, just until a few bubbles break the surface and the sugar has dissolved. Reduce the heat to medium-low and add the grapes, pears, and nuts. Cook, stirring occasionally, until the grapes are shriveled and the pears are very soft, about 1 to 1¼ hours.

Transfer the mixture to a blender or food processor and blend until very smooth. The mixture will be very runny. Let cool completely.

To serve, place the compote in a small bowl and the whole cheese and bread slices on a separate plate. Alternatively, slice the cheese into individual portions and place on individual plates along with the bread. Pass the compote separately.

Makes about 1¼ cups compote

Note: The compote will serve about 20 people, so if you are serving that many, plan to buy two pieces of La Tur or about 1 pound of cheese.

HAROLD'S STRAWBERRIES AND CREAM
WITH BUTTERY BASIL COOKIES

In the debut season of Bravo TV's hit show, *Top Chef*, I was lucky enough to be a guest on one of the segments. I got to eat food that was prepared by the chef contestants, including Harold Dieterle—who was voted the Top Chef at the end of the season. Receiving that honor was no easy feat, but it shows what a great chef Harold is. He is also a cheese fan, and told me he particularly likes creating accompaniments to cheese. I asked him to create one for this book, and this is what he came up with. Not only is it beautiful, it is easy to make and absolutely delicious.

For the cookies

2 egg whites

⅓ cup sugar

3 tablespoons unsalted butter, melted

⅓ cup flour

2 teaspoons julienned fresh basil plus whole sprigs for garnish

2 tablespoons sliced almonds, lightly toasted

For the strawberries

¾ cup water

⅓ cup sugar

2 cups strawberries (about 8 ounces), stems removed and berries quartered

1 teaspoon vanilla extract

8 ounces La Tur cheese, cut into 8 slices (or use Robiola Bosina)

To make the cookies: Preheat the oven to 350°F.

In the bowl of a stand mixer, using the whisk attachment, beat the egg whites until frothy, about 2 minutes (a hand mixer works fine too). Slowly add the sugar and beat until soft peaks form, 5 to 10 minutes. Slowly drizzle the butter into the egg white mixture and mix for 1 minute. Turn the mixer to low speed and add the flour and basil. Mix just until incorporated.

Line a baking sheet with a silicone mat such as Silpat (or use parchment paper). Mound tablespoons of the batter 2 inches apart on the sheet. Place about 3 almonds on each cookie. Bake until golden brown, 10 to 12 minutes. Let cool to room temperature. (Cookies are best eaten the same day, but you can store them in an airtight container for up to 2 days. The texture may become a little chewy.)

To prepare the strawberries: In a medium-size saucepan, combine the water and sugar over high heat. Cook, stirring constantly, until the mixture comes to a boil. Let cook 1 more minute. Turn off heat and let cool to room temperature, about 45 minutes.

Measure out $1/3$ cup of simple syrup. Reserve the rest for another use. Put the strawberries, simple syrup, and vanilla into the saucepan you used to make the simple syrup. Bring to a simmer and cook for 2 minutes. Turn off heat and let cool to room temperature. The strawberries will continue to release liquid as they cool.

To assemble: Place two cookies on either side of 8 dessert plates. Place a slice of cheese in the middle of the plate. Using a slotted spoon, put a few strawberries next to the cheese. Garnish with a sprig or two of basil on each plate. Serve right away.

Serves 8; makes about 16 cookies

Clockwise from top: Bellwether Farms San
Andreas, Montgomery Cheddar, Zamorano,
Comté, Fiscalini Farms San Joaquin Gold

CHAPTER 6

SEMI-HARD

CHEESES

USE SEMI-HARD CHEESES FOR

- Burgers
- Cheese courses
- Eggs
- Entertaining
- Fondue
- Gratins and vegetable casseroles
- Grilled cheese
- Quesadillas
- Sandwiches
- Savory tarts
- Vegetables

WHAT ARE THEY?

England
Cheddar
Cheshire
Gloucester
Double Gloucester
Huntsman (*See also* blue cheeses)
Lancashire
Red Leicester
Sage Derby
Wensleydale
Westcombe Red

France
Abbaye de Bellocq (sheep)
Abondance (*See also* washed-rind cheeses)
Beaufort
Brin d'Amour (*See also* semi-soft cheeses)
Cantal
Comté
Istara (sheep's milk)
Lagioule
Madrigal
Mimolette (*See also* hard cheeses)
Ossau-Iraty (sheep's milk)
Raclette (*See also* washed-rind cheeses)
Petit Agour (sheep's milk)
P'tit Basque (sheep's milk)

Greece
Graviera (sheep's milk)
Kasseri (sheep and goat's milk; see also fresh cheeses)

Holland
Beemster Classic (*See also* hard cheeses)
Boerenkaas (farmhouse gouda)
Goat Gouda
Gouda
Leerdamer
Leyden
Parrano (*See also* hard cheeses)
Prima Donna (*See also* hard cheeses)
Rembrandt
Van Kaas
Vincent

Italy
Asiago
Boschetto al Tartufo Bianchetto (cow's and sheep's milk)
Bra Tenero (*See also* hard cheeses)
Caciocavallo
Caciotta (sheep's milk)
Fiore Sardo (sheep's milk; see also hard cheeses)
Fontina Val d'Aosta
Montasio (*See also* semi-soft and hard cheeses)
Monte Veronese (*See also* semi-soft and hard cheeses)
Pecorino Romano (sheep's milk; see also hard cheeses)
Pecorino Toscano (sheep's milk; see also semi-soft cheeses)
Piave Mezzano
Provolone (*See also* hard cheeses)
Sottocenere al Tartufo
Ubriaco

Norway

Gjetost (also spelled Gietost; goat's milk whey cheese)

Jarlsberg

Portugal

São Jorge

Spain

Garrotxa (goat's milk)

Ibores (goat's milk)

Idiazabal (sheep's milk; lightly smoked)

Mahón (See also semi-soft and hard cheeses)

Majorero (goat's milk)

Manchego (sheep's milk)

Murcia al Vino

Roncal

San Simon

Zamorano (sheep's milk; see also hard cheeses)

Switzerland

Appenzeller (See also washed-rind cheeses)

Emmentaler

Gruyère

United States

Beecher's Handmade Cheese: Flagship

Cheddar (farmhouse styles: Cabot, Grafton, Shelburne Farms, Fiscalini Farms)

Colby (See also semi-soft cheeses)

Emmentaler

Fontina

Gouda

Gruyère

Monterey Jack (See also semi-soft cheeses)

Provolone (See also hard cheeses)

Raclette (See also washed-rind cheeses)

Romano

Swiss

OFF THE BEATEN PATH

England

Berkswell

Doddington

Lincolnshire Poacher

Ireland

Coolea

Gubbeen

Italy

Bitto

Bra Duro

Caprino (goat and cow's milk)
  Monte Veronese

Piacentinu (Sardinian sheep's milk peppercorn and saffron cheese)

Raschera (See also semi-soft cheeses)

Sora

Toma Piemontese

Testun

Vento d'Estate

Scotland

Isle of Mull

Switzerland

Hoch Ybrig

L'Etivaz

Le Marechal

Raclette

Vacherin Fribourgeois (See also washed-rind cheeses)

United States

California

Bellwether Farms: Carmody; San Andreas (sheep's milk)

Bravo Farms: Silver Mountain

Cypress Grove: Creamline Midnight Moon (goat's milk), Lambchopper (sheep's milk), goat's milk cheddar

Matos Cheese Factory: Pedrozo Dairy, Northern Gold St. George

Pug's Leap Farm: Pavé

Rinconada Dairy: Pozo Tomme, Chapparal (sheep's milk)

Three Sisters Farmstead Cheese Company: Serenita

Vella Cheese Company: Mezzo Secco

Winchester Cheese Company: Sharp Gouda

Off the Beaten Path (cont'd)

Colorado

Haystack Mountain Goat Dairy: Queso de Mano (goat's milk)

Connecticut

Cato Corner: Womanchego

Georgia

Sweet Grass Dairy: Holly Springs (goat's milk), Georgia Gouda

Indiana

Capriole Goat Cheese: Old Kentucky Tomme

Louisiana

Bittersweet Plantation Dairy: Kashkaval

Michigan

Leelanau Cheese Company: Raclette (*See also* washed-rind cheeses)

New York

Sprout Creek Farm: Ouray

Oregon

Juniper Grove Tumalo Tomme (goat's milk)
Willamette Valley Cheese Company: Brindisi

Texas

Pure Luck Goat Dairy: Claire de Lune

Vermont

Blue Ledge Farm: La Luna

Cobb Hill Cheese: Ascutney Mountain

Dancing Cow Farm: Menuet

Major Farms: Vermont Shepherd (sheep's milk)

Orb Weaver Farm: Orb Weaver Farmhouse Cheese

Taylor Farm: Gouda

Thistle Hill Farm: Tarentaise

Twig Farm Goat: Tomme (goat's milk)

Willow Hill Farm: Mountain Tomme (cow's milk), Autumn Oak (sheep's milk)

Virginia

Everona Dairy: Piedmont (sheep's milk)

Meadow Creek Dairy: Appalachian, Mountaineer

Washington

Estrella Family Creamery: Black Creek Buttery, Grisdale Goat

Mount Townsend Creamery: Trailhead

Washington State University Creamery: Cougar Gold

Wisconsin

Carr Valley Cheese Company: Benedictine (mixed milk), Cave-Aged Marisa (sheep's milk), Cocoa Cardona (goat's milk), Gran Canaria (mixed milk)

Natural Valley Cheese: Petenwell Reserve (goat's milk), Twin Bluff Select

Upland's Cheese Company: Pleasant Ridge Reserve (*See also* washed-rind cheeses)

 You know it's a semi-hard cheese when . . .

- The color ranges from ivory to deep ivory to tan to light gold to bright yellow (or orange)
- It says "aged" but not "extra-aged," "*stagionato*," or "*vecchio*"
- the surface of the interior is fairly smooth, with few, if any, eyes (except Swiss-style cheeses)
- You see tiny eyes, but you know it isn't a semi-soft cheese because the interior of the cheese barely gives when you press it
- There are more types of this style of cheese than any other in the store

The Explanation

As you can see by the long list of cheeses, the selection of semi-hard cheeses you are likely to encounter on the cheese aisle is extensive. Not surprisingly, the flavors of these cheeses run the gamut too, but not just because of the sheer number. Each producer has his or her own "recipe" for making cheese: one person's cheddar is going to be different from another's. Then how does knowing the basic flavor components in this style provide a window into the flavors of all semi-hard cheeses? Because just like the other styles, if you know a few basic common traits of semi-hard cheeses as well as the particular flavor profiles of some of the subcategories, you won't find any huge surprises when you taste a cheese you've never tried before.

 It's a Verb, It's a Place, It's a Noun — It's cheddar/Cheddar!

The term "cheddar" is confusing because it is, in fact, a noun, a verb, and a place. The noun refers to the cheese called cheddar, the verb refers to the process by which cheddar cheese is made, and the place is the location where the cheese is believed to have originated. To be called cheddar in England today, the cheese must be made according to traditional methods for cheddar-making, and it must be made in Somerset County, which includes the town of Cheddar.

Wherever it is made, two distinct steps in the cheesemaking method distinguish cheddar cheese. The first is that once the whey has been drained, the curds are gathered and piled to form sheets of curds. These sheets are stacked on top of each other to facilitate further whey drainage. While the stacks are draining, the acidity is rising. This contributes to cheddar's distinct spicy and sometimes sharp flavor. Once the desired level of acidity is reached, the sheets of curds are cut into smaller strips, which are put through a mill and cut into tiny pieces. This aids in further expulsion of the whey and sets the cheese up for long-term aging. After milling, the cheese is salted, which halts the rise in acidity. At this point, cheesemaking resumes in the same way it does for many other types of semi-hard and hard cheeses.

Most of the traditional farmhouse cheddars are made in England, but cheesemakers in the United States are following suit. In 2006, Cabot Clothbound Cheddar, a joint effort between Cabot Creamery and Jasper Hill Farms, both in Vermont, won the Best of Show award from the American Cheese Society. The cheese is made by Cabot and aged by Jasper Hill Farms, and emulates the English farmhouse cheesemaking and aging methods.

When buying cheddar, you may notice that some farmhouse cheeses may have cracks with blue mold running through. That is not a defect and by many is considered a prized feature. It is entirely up to you if you want the musty flavors that accompany that type of blueing or not, but know that it is probably not a defect.

Semi-hard cheese achieves its texture a number of ways, but there are two stages in the cheesemaking process that are particularly important. First, the curds are heated, in some cases at very high temperatures. Second, the wheels or blocks of cheese are pressed to expel the whey. When either or both of these processes are employed, moisture is extracted from the curds, creating a low-moisture cheese. The result: a semi-hard cheese.

A by-product of this cheesemaking method is usually a cheese with a smooth rather than "holey" paste or interior. Such holes, or "eyes" as they are called, are more common in semi-soft cheeses such as Havarti, but they do occur in semi-hard cheeses too because of certain bacteria that are added to the milk at the beginning of cheesemaking. As a cheese ages, it is constantly changing and evolving. Part of that evolution might be eye formation. Eyes may also occur as a result of long-term aging as in the case of an older Beaufort, owing to the micro-biological process, and of course, in Swiss-style cheeses.

Although varied in style and flavor, semi-hard cheeses have the greatest balance between protein, fat, and salt, inherent nutty and buttery qualities, and the way they linger in your mouth and on your taste buds. You will not find any especially strong cheeses in this category nor will you find excessively salty cheeses (unless they are aged too long, causing the salt in the cheese to concentrate, or if they were ill-conceived in the first place). Salty cheeses are found primarily in the hard, blue, and washed-rind styles, and in all those cases the pronounced salt is deliber-ate. Semi-hard cheeses are made with all three main types of milk and sometimes a combination of two or three.

 Eye Insight

The large holes or eyes you find in Swiss-style and some Dutch cheeses are entirely different from the minuscule holes you find in other types of cheese. The large holes, or eyes, are the result of propionic bacteria that are added to the milk during cheesemaking. These bacteria produce carbon dioxide as the cheese ages, which create bubbles that eventually burst and leave behind the familiar holes. When you see these large holes in a cheese, you are assured that the cheese belongs in the family of semi-hard cheeses because that is the only style where you will find the big eyes.

The Bottom Line

A semi-hard cheese is an aged cheese that might spend just a couple of months on the aging shelf, a couple of years, or even more. This translates to cheeses whose interior is usually smooth-looking. If you bend the paste of a semi-hard cheese, it will make a clean break—not a crumbly one. The flavors within this style range from mild to assertive, but the main constituents—protein, fat, and salt—will be very balanced.

WHAT TO LOOK FOR WHEN BUYING SEMI-HARD CHEESES

Semi-hard cheeses earned this moniker because they are not quite as malleable as a firm pillow, but neither are they hard like a handball. They fall in between, which means you should be able to press them and feel some resistance, but not to the point where the cheese won't budge.

VISUAL CUES

Semi-hard cheeses will last a long time, and for that reason they might also remain on store shelves for quite a while.

- Ivory to deep ivory; tan, light gold, bright gold, or orange
- Smooth surface; few if any holes (other than for some Swiss-and Dutch-style cheeses)

- Sturdy and firm looking, as if you could make a nice, neat slice without losing much (if anything) to crumbles
- Do *not* buy if there is a thin layer of white mold on the cut surface

TEXTURAL CUES

If you were to make a fairly tight fist and press the spot between your thumb and forefinger, much the way one does when testing the doneness of a steak, you will know what most semi-hard cheeses feel like.

- Firm, not very pliable, and will usually break, though not crumble, when bent

- Texture ranges from holey to smooth, and in some cases, crumbly or even cracked

AROMA CUES

Semi-hard cheeses range in aromas. They might smell sweet and butterscotchy for Goudas and Swiss-style cheeses, or they might be barnyardy and gamy like some Pecorinos, or they might be earthy, musty, and yet nutty like most farm-house and many cave-aged cheeses are.

- Butterscotch
- Buttery
- Baked potato-like(!)
- Caramel
- Earthy
- Fruity
- Floral
- Gamy
- Mushroomy
- Musty
- Toasted nuts
- Pungent

FLAVOR CUES

- Acidic
- Barnyardy
- Beefy
- Butterscotchy
- Brown butter
- Caramel
- Earthy
- Fruity (apples, apricots, cherries, pears and other fruits)
- Gamy
- Garlicky
- Goaty
- Grassy
- Hay
- Herbaceous
- Meaty
- Musty
- Nutty (hazelnuts, almonds, or walnuts)
- Oily (primarily applicable to sheep's milk cheeses)
- Rich
- Rustic
- Sharp
- Sheepy
- Spicy
- Sweet butter

MOUTHFEEL

This style of cheese really provides something to sink your teeth into. It starts off firm with a lot of body or density, but almost immediately the cheese will soften and maybe even become creamy. That soft, creamy texture will usually linger in your mouth for a long time. Some words you might apply to the way a semi-hard cheese feels in your mouth include dense, smooth, toothsome, or waxy.

Semi-hard cheeses are almost always quite complex. This leads to long-lasting flavors and sensations after you've swallowed the cheese and a lingering memory of the cheese.

A FEW NOTEWORTHY SEMI-HARD CHEESES

ENGLAND

Lincolnshire Poacher

If you are a cheddar lover, then you might think cheddar cannot be improved upon. Then again, you might change your mind after one bite of Lincolnshire Poacher. This English cheese, which is made similarly to cheddar, is relatively new, having been developed about fifteen years ago by a dairy farmer named Simon Jones. His recipe, developed in conjunction with a Welsh cheesemaker, proved immediately popular. In fact, demand was so great that Jones's brother Tim joined him to run the marketing side of the operation. The cheese shares much of the processing method with cheddar, but its flavors are more mellow and sweet than cheddar, and its texture is creamier. Lincolnshire Poacher is at its best on a cheese board surrounded by a few walnuts and some dried apple slices or perhaps a plum jam.

FRANCE

Comté Marcel Petite

Comté is on the precipice of a revival. Although it never went away, the 80-pound wheels of cheese made in the Jura Mountains in eastern France have gotten new life in large part because of discoveries about how to age them.

Founder Marcel Petite owned an army fort, which he converted into a cheese-aging facility in the 1960s. That facility now houses about 60,000 wheels (that's 4,800,000 pounds!) of Comté, which his *affineur* brings to maturity. The wheels we get in the United States are handpicked by cheese expert Daphne Zepos, whose well-honed palate ensures nutty and buttery cheeses for us.

Comté is a well-known melting cheese, and for the most part, that was always its best use. But while the Comté Petite is no less than sublime when it is melted (see page 150 for a recipe using Comté), it is a magnificent stand-alone cheese too. The tiny crystals in the more mature cheeses (aged twelve to fourteen months), are better than candy. But it's the almost beefy and pistachio-nut-like flavors in this cheese that are totally compelling.

ITALY

Bitto

One taste of Bitto, and you will never forget it. Made in the province of Lombardy in northern Italy, Bitto is a raw cow's milk cheese made in the mountains each summer and aged in the valleys below. It is a DOP cheese, meaning that it must be made to certain government-mandated specifications to be called Bitto. One of those specifications is that it can be made with up to 10 percent goat's milk. The flavors of Bitto, whose name comes from a nearby river, inspire visions of the pasture the cows have grazed on and the cream their milk has produced. Although the cheese is aged for at least six months and up to ten years(!), my favorite age for Bitto is two years. By then it has gotten quite firm, but it hasn't lost hints of its earlier days when the cheese is ever-so-slightly tangy and a little like unsalted butter. As it ages, though, it develops unmistakable nutty notes and hints of caramel. Although fairly rare in the United States, it is a delicious cheese and certainly available to any retailer that asks.

SPAIN

Garrotxa

Aged goat's milk cheeses are few, but those that do exist are usually special because it takes a certain dedication to make them. Part of the reason for this is that fresh goat cheese is sold so readily, that dedicating the milk to an aged cheese requires patience and money. Fortunately a few cheesemakers throughout Catalonia in northeast Spain are doing just that. They have created this 2-pound pasteurized gem of a wheel that has a fairly hard, grayish rind and a paste that is a bit flaky but also firm. This unusual combination of textures makes Garrotxa a great cooking cheese (see page 154 for a recipe), but also a satisfying addition to a cheese board. The cheese has the signature goat's milk tanginess, but it also has complexity from its floral and almost tarragon-like flavors. If you ask for it, just say *gah-ROTCH-ah*.

UNITED STATES

California
Bellwether Farms: San Andreas

California's most famous earthquake fault provided the inspiration for this cheese's name, and it turns out to be apt. One taste of it, and some might say it rocks their world. This sheep's milk cheese was California's first and was developed by cheesemaker Liam Callahan, whose mother Cindy Callahan purchased the farm and sheep in the 1990s. The cheese is modeled after another Bellwether cheese called Carmody, which is made with cow's milk. The raw sheep's milk cheese is uncooked and unpressed, and is aged about three months to become semi-hard. One of the most surprising (and delicious) features of San Andreas is its pronounced tanginess. Usually sheep's milk cheeses aren't quite as tangy. In this cheese, the signature buttery and earthy sheep's milk characteristics swoop in to balance the lemony sensation, much like a well-balanced wine. The texture starts off firm but immediately becomes creamy in the mouth. Liam and Cindy have worked extremely hard to make all their cheeses standouts, and this is no exception.

Vermont

Thistle Hill Farm: Tarentaise

Another American treasure is this organic Jersey milk cheese made in North Pomfret, Vermont. John and Janine Putnam began making cheese around 2000 with the goal of making a French alpine cheese similar to the well-known Beaufort. They named their cheese after a valley in the Savoie region where the Tarine cows roam and where Beaufort is produced. In addition to its 14-carat-gold color, (owing to the Jersey milk as well as the rubbing process the cheese undergoes during aging) the cheese is unusual because it is made in a copper cheese vat. Few cheeses are made that way in the United States but the Putnams got special permission to do so. They now make their award-winning raw milk cheese (it consistently wins first place in its category at the annual American Cheese Society competition) in that vat and drain it in special molds from France. The cheese looks rich, and it tastes it too. When it reaches about six or seven months, it develops butterscotch flavors, but its grassy and nutty flavors are never far away.

 If you can't find

Comté, use **Gruyère**

Cantal, use **Montgomery, Fiscalini**, or **Cabot cheddar**, or use **Mimolette**

Fontina, use **Fontal, St. Nectaire, Pecorino Fresco (sheep's milk)**, or **Chimay**

Mimolette, use **aged Gouda** or **aged cheddar**

Storing Semi-Hard Cheeses

Semi-hard cheeses are easy to store. As with other firm cheeses, you want to strike a balance between retaining moisture and allowing the cheese to breathe. I have found the easiest way to do this is to wrap the cheese first in parchment paper or waxed paper. Then wrap it tightly with plastic wrap, and place the cheese in the drawer of the refrigerator. This method of wrapping accomplishes two things: it ensures that your cheese does not dry out, and it prevents the plastic wrap from touching the surface of your cheese. Plastic is a problem because it imparts unwanted, petroleum-like flavors to the cheese. The reason the stores wrap their cheeses in plastic is because you, as the consumer, need to be able to see the cheeses. The likelihood of your buying a cheese you cannot see is much smaller even though some cheeses do indeed come that way. Also, the plastic will preserve the semi-hard and hard cheeses longer because it will not let out the moisture. But when you get a cheese home, be sure to take it out of the plastic wrap it came in and wrap it as described above.

 Semi-Hard Cheese and Wine Pairing ☆☆☆☆☆

Semi-hard cheeses are unquestionably your best bet for wine compatibility. Because these cheeses are so well balanced, they pair with the widest variety of wines, whether white or red. Semi-hard cheeses will very often pair nicely with an otherwise tough-to-match Chardonnay as well as with an equally hard-to-match Cabernet Sauvignon.

While you can have fun pairing cheese with wine, there are some cheesemakers that have done it for you in the form of wine-soaked cheeses. A few of those you are likely to find include:

- Ubriaco (Italy)
- Murcia al Vino (Spain; also sometimes called "Drunken Goat")
- Purple Moon (Fiscalini Cheese Company/ California)

Bellwether Farms San Andreas

TAKE-HOME TEST: GETTING TO KNOW SEMI-HARD CHEESES

Because there are so many semi-hard cheeses, this assignment could be endless. So I would like you to concentrate on a cheese that tends to be America's favorite and maybe yours too: cheddar. Cheddars vary so much, and the only way to really tell how they differ is by tasting them side by side. Although this assignment calls for specialty cheddars, you can do the exercise even if you can't get all the cheeses. Just try to get the best quality cheddars or cheddar-like cheeses you can find (see substitution suggestions below).

THE ASSIGNMENT

Buy

- 2 to 4 ounces vacuum-packed sharp cheddar (no rind), at room temperature

- 2 to 4 ounces Fiscalini Bandage-Wrapped, Cabot Clothbound, Westcombe, or Keen's cheddar (or use Cheshire, Wensleydale, Gloucester, or Leicester), at room temperature

- 2 to 4 ounces Montgomery cheddar, (or use Cheshire, Wensleydale, Gloucester, or Leicester), at room temperature

- 2 to 4 ounces Parmigiano-Reggiano (yes, this is part of the cheddar assignment), at room temperature

- 1 bunch grapes

Lay out the cheeses so that they can be easily identified.

1) Start by smelling and then taking a taste of the vacuum-packed cheddar. Notice its aroma is very mild, almost nonexistent. The flavors are more assertive than the aromas. Mostly they are sharp or possibly even a little bitter at the end. Take a grape or two to cleanse your palate before moving on.

2) Next move on to the Fiscalini cheddar (or similar cheese). Break off a piece and make sure to take in its earthy aromas. Take a taste. Depending on the age and the producer of the cheese, you should detect a few little crystals in the texture as well as earthy and nutty flavors. Take a grape and then go back to the first cheese. They both say cheddar, but do the cheeses taste similar?

3) The next cheese, the Montgomery cheddar, is considered by many to be the finest of all English cheddars and possibly of all the cheddars in the world. See for yourself. It has damp and musty aromas but also a hint of sweetness too. Take a bite. Although it is much more similar to the second cheese, it still has its own unique characteristics. It is a little buttery, somewhat tangy, but mostly it's very earthy. Take another grape and move on.

4) I put the Parmigiano-Reggiano in this exercise because, texturally, it is not terribly different from the Montgomery. But by tasting a completely different cheese, it helps bring the main cheese, into better focus. So take a taste of the Parmigiano-Reggiano. It is both salty and sweet (see chapter 7 on hard cheeses for more on the characteristics of Parmigiano-Reggiano and other hard cheeses) and, as you can see, quite different from the cheddar. At the same time, the slightly granular texture of both cheeses and their inherent earthiness makes them seem more similar. Still, side by side, the Parmigiano-Reggiano has a sharper aroma and a sweeter flavor than the cheddar, which has long-lasting flavors that tend more toward the savory, earthy, and grassy end of the flavor spectrum. Grab another grape.

5) Finally, taste the first cheddar one last time. Following the Parmigiano-Reggiano, the cheese labeled "sharp" suddenly doesn't seem so sharp at all. If anything, it is relatively mild.

THE LESSON

A cheese may say cheddar, but that could mean many things on the flavor spectrum. It could be sharp and even bitter, earthy and grassy, fruity and floral. By tasting these cheddars side by side, I hope you were able to get in closer touch with the characteristics you prefer in cheddar cheese as well as a couple of specific highly regarded cheddars. In turn, this should give you greater confidence in your cheddar choice next time you go to buy it.

TRIO OF SHEEP'S MILK CHEESE SANDWICHES

I'm a big fan of sheep's milk cheese, but because there isn't a lot of it made in the United States, many people here are not familiar with it. So I decided that creating an hors d'oeuvre that called for different sheep's milk cheeses might help reveal their magical qualities. Most of the cheeses and other ingredients are available at well-stocked grocery stores. If you can't find all of the cheeses, the recipe is just fine when made with the same cheese for all three sandwiches.

Each sandwich recipe serves 4 as a meal or 6 to 8 as an hors d'oeuvre.

MANCHEGO, QUINCE PASTE, AND SERRANO HAM ON OLIVE BREAD

Manchego and quince paste, called *membrillo*, is a classic Spanish combination. The heartiness of the cheese matches perfectly with the quince. Although quince paste is now widely available, usually displayed near the cheese case, if you cannot find it, you can substitute apple butter. Although the texture is entirely different (*membrillo* is firm and gel-like), the tart-sweet flavors of the butter also pair nicely with the cheese and other ingredients on this sandwich.

8 sandwich-size slices olive bread

4 ounces quince paste (also called *membrillo*), cut into 8 slices (use 4 tablespoons quince jam or apple butter)

4 ounces Manchego cheese, cut into 12 slices

2 ounces Serrano ham, sliced paper-thin (or use prosciutto),

Spread 4 slices of bread with the quince paste. Top with cheese, ham, and remaining slices of bread. Cut into quarters for an hors d'oeuvre or into halves for sandwiches.

OSSAU-IRATY, PIQUILLO PEPPERS, AND AIOLI ON ITALIAN BREAD

This sandwich calls for Italian bread, which means a thick and hearty bread. You may use any bread you like, just be sure it has some weight to it to stand up to the richness of the sandwich ingredients.

1 large clove garlic

¼ teaspoon kosher salt

½ cup mayonnaise

8 sandwich-size slices Italian bread

4 ounces Ossau-Iraty cheese, cut into 12 slices (or use Manchego, Idiazabal for a smoky flavor, or, for a cow's milk cheese, use Gruyère)

8 piquillo peppers, drained (or use roasted red peppers)

Place the garlic and salt in a food processor and process until almost pastelike. Add the mayonnaise and pulse just until mixed. Set aside.

Spread the bread slices with the aioli. On 4 slices place the cheese and peppers. Top with remaining slices, aioli side down. Cut into quarters for an hors d'oeuvre or into halves for sandwiches.

VERMONT SHEPHERD AND MAPLE SYRUP ON WALNUT BREAD

Vermont Shepherd is one of the original aged farmhouse sheep's milk cheeses made in this country. It is delicious but made only during the summer when the sheep are grazing. If you can't find it, other sheep's milk cheeses, such as Ossau-Iraty or Pecorino Toscana work just fine.

8 sandwich-size slices walnut bread

¼ cup best-quality maple syrup, preferably from Vermont

4 ounces Vermont Shepherd cheese cut into 12 slices, (or use Ossau-Iraty, P'tit Basque, or Manchego)

Spread the bread slices with the syrup. Place the cheese on 4 slices and top with remaining bread, syrup side down. Cut into quarters for an hors d'oeuvre or into halves for sandwiches.

COMTÉ PISTACHIO SOUFFLÉ

When I first tried a piece of 14-month old Comté, I knew then that I had never tasted a French mountain cheese like this before, or at least not one like it. All I could say was "wow" when I ate and ate and ate it. One night, I took out a few pistachio nuts to eat along with the cheese because the buttery, rich quality of the cheese reminded me specifically of pistachios. The cheese and nuts harmonized so beautifully that I thought I had happened upon a song. That memorable combination gave rise to this soufflé recipe, which features both ingredients.

- 4 tablespoons (½ stick) unsalted butter
- ¾ cup unsalted pistachio nuts, lightly toasted
- 2¼ cups milk
- 3 tablespoons flour
- ¾ teaspoon kosher salt
- Freshly ground pepper

- 4 egg yolks, at room temperature and lightly beaten
- 8 ounces Comté cheese, coarsely grated (or use Gruyère, Emmentaler, Ossau-Iraty, or Manchego)
- 6 egg whites, at room temperature
- Pinch cream of tartar

Preheat the oven to 375°F.

Butter a 2½-quart (10-cup) soufflé dish or casserole or ten 8-ounce ramekins with 1 tablespoon butter. Finely chop ¼ cup of the nuts and coat the dish(es) with the nuts. Set aside.

In a small saucepan simmer the milk and remaining pistachios over medium-low heat, until hot but not boiling. Turn off the heat and let sit for 15 minutes. Transfer to a blender and mix until the nuts are finely ground.

In a medium-size saucepan, melt the remaining 3 tablespoons butter over medium-low heat. Whisk in the flour, stirring constantly so it doesn't burn. Slowly add the pistachio milk, whisking constantly until the mixture thickens, about 5 minutes. Add the salt, and pepper to taste. Cook over very low

heat for 10 minutes, stirring occasionally. Remove from heat. Cool slightly. Stir in the egg yolks and cheese. Cover with plastic wrap and set aside.

In a medium-size bowl, beat the egg whites and cream of tartar together until thick, soft peaks form. Fold one-quarter of the egg whites into the yolk-milk mixture. Gently fold in the remaining egg whites just until the whites are coated with yolk mixture and are about the size of large grapes.

Pour into prepared dish and bake on the middle rack of the oven for 35 to 40 minutes, or until the soufflé has risen 2 to 3 inches above the sides of the dish and the top of the soufflé is a deep brown color. Serve immediately.

Serves 8

SEUPA VAPELLENENTSE
(ITALIAN MOUNTAIN SOUP)

Fontina Val d'Aosta is a cheese made in the mountains of northern Italy, an area that gets very cold in the winter. Hearty food is a must for the cheesemakers and others who live there, and the regional recipes often feature local cheeses. While admittedly not the prettiest-looking soup you will ever make, this sort of soup-stew is reminiscent of Tuscan bread soup in that the bread is layered with greens and, in this case, cheese, and the amount of broth called for is just enough to moisten and make the bread steamy. The result is hearty and flavorful, the perfect anti-dote to a cold winter and a hankering for melted cheese.

---

1 teaspoon salt

12 ounces green cabbage, cored and cut into ½-inch strips, longest strips cut in half crosswise

2 ounces pancetta, finely chopped

1 tablespoon plus 2 teaspoons unsalted butter

Freshly ground pepper

6 slices stale 7-grain or whole wheat bread, ¼-inch-thick

4 ounces Fontina d'Aosta cheese, coarsely grated (or use Gruyère)

2 cups low-sodium beef broth

1 cup low-sodium chicken broth

Preheat the oven to 325°F.

In a 4-quart ovenproof pot, boil 2 quarts of water with 1 teaspoon salt. Add the cabbage and blanch for 2 minutes. Drain immediately. Wipe the pot dry.

Combine the pancetta, cabbage, and 1 teaspoon of the butter in the pot and cook over medium-high heat, stirring occasionally, until the pancetta is cooked through and some of the edges of the cabbage just begin to brown, about 10 minutes. Give a few twists of black pepper and stir to mix. Transfer the cabbage mixture to a plate. Set the pot aside.

To assemble: Place two slices of bread on the bottom of the pot. Put one-third of the cabbage mixture on the bread (it will not cover it). Sprinkle with one-third of the cheese. Repeat with remaining bread, cabbage, and cheese. You will end up with three layers. Pour both broths around the sides of the pot and over the top. They will not cover the mixture.

Dot the remaining butter on the top slices of bread. Cover and bake for 1 hour. Let cool about 10 minutes and serve.

Serves 6 to 8

MOM'S SAUSAGE-STUFFED TOMATOES WITH PROVOLONE

My mother is a great cook and this recipe is a real winner. With juicy tomatoes, savory sausage, and two types of Provolone, this is a dish that tastes as good as it looks.

8   firm ripe tomatoes (about 6 ounces each)

1   cup low-sodium chicken broth

¾   cup water

1   cup uncooked orzo

2   tablespoons olive oil

½   large onion, finely chopped

4   cloves garlic, finely chopped

½   pound sweet Italian sausage, crumbled

1   tablespoon finely chopped fresh oregano

4   ounces regular (not sharp) provolone cheese, coarsely grated

½   cup pine nuts, lightly toasted

1   teaspoon kosher salt

Freshly ground pepper

½   cup finely grated aged provolone, (or use Parmigiano-Reggiano, Asiago)

¼   cup chopped fresh Italian parsley

Preheat the oven to 350°F.

Cut ¼ inch off the tops of the tomatoes. Gently scoop out the pulp, leaving a ¼-inch-thick wall. Be careful not to break the walls or bottom skin. Let drain upside down on a paper towel.

Bring the chicken broth and water to a boil in a medium-size saucepan. Add the orzo slowly, and return to a boil. Reduce heat to simmer and let cook 12 to15 minutes, stirring occasionally, until the pasta has absorbed the liquid, is firm, and is not sticking together.

In a large sauté pan, warm the oil over medium heat. Add the onion and cook slowly until soft but not browned, about 8 minutes. Add the garlic and cook about 2 minutes until soft, not browned. Add to the orzo.

Put the sausage in the skillet and sauté over medium heat, stirring constantly and breaking up large pieces until lightly browned. If it seems fatty, drain on paper towels. Let cool slightly. In a medium bowl, combine the sausage and orzo mixture with the oregano, regular Provolone and pine nuts. Stir just until combined. Add salt and pepper to taste.

To assemble: Lightly salt the inside of the tomatoes. Spoon about ⅓ cup of the orzo into each tomato, pressing firmly to fill as much as possible. Place in a casserole dish or pie plate just large enough to hold tomatoes in one layer. Top with the aged Provolone.

Bake for 15 to 20 minutes, or until the tomatoes feel slightly soft to the touch but still holdi their shape and the cheese is melted. Sprinkle with parsley.

Serves 8

Fettuccine with Spring Peas and Garrotxa

You may be perplexed when you see the word "Garrotxa." Although popular among cheese aficionados, this Catalonian cheese is only now becoming more widely available. It is not the least bit goaty but it does have the signature tanginess, which is why I chose it. The lemon juice and the tang from the crème fraîche play beautifully with the sweetness of the peas and the sweet/tart flavors in the cheese. This is a very light and refreshing pasta that celebrates spring along with one of the best cheeses in the world.

---

1 tablespoon plus ½ teaspoon kosher salt

½ cup whole or 2% milk (do not use nonfat)

2 tablespoons butter

½ teaspoon sugar

1 cup shelled fresh peas (about 1 pound in the pod), or use frozen spring peas

8 large leaves red leaf lettuce, cut in half lengthwise, then finely sliced (make sure the lettuce is dry before using)

2 tablespoons fresh lemon juice

½ pound fettuccine

6 ounces crème fraîche

2 ounces Garrotxa cheese , finely grated, (or use goat gouda, Manchego, or aged Mahón)

1 tablespoon julienned lemon zest (a channel zester is the perfect tool for this)

2 ounces Garrotxa cheese, thinly shaved (a vegetable peeler works well)

Freshly ground pepper

Fill a 4-quart saucepan about halfway with water and add 1 tablespoon of the salt. Bring to a simmer.

In a large sauté pan, heat the milk and 1 tablespoon butter over medium heat until the butter melts. Add the sugar, ½ teaspoon salt, and peas. Turn heat to very low, cover and simmer for 10 minutes. Stir in the lettuce and lemon juice. The mixture will curdle a little; it will come together at the end. Cover and cook 5 minutes more. Keep warm.

Meanwhile, make the pasta. Bring the water to the boil, add the pasta, and cook according to the package directions, about 10 minutes, or until the pasta is tender but still offers slight resistance in the bite.

To assemble: Add the pasta, crème fraîche, grated cheese and remaining 1 tablespoon butter to the pea mixture and stir over high heat until the pasta is well coated and the mixture is piping hot. Transfer to a platter or individual plates. Sprinkle with lemon zest and top with the cheese shavings. Add pepper and serve right away.

Serves 4

TURKEY AND EMMENTALER BURGERS

I was inspired to create this recipe for turkey burgers by my friend Mark Petersen, who manages to coax out more moisture from the notoriously lean meat than should be possible. He says the key is to use the dark meat of the turkey and an egg. His solution also makes for a bit of a messy preparation because the meat and egg are sticky. The results however, particularly when crowned with the flavorful cheese, make the effort entirely worthwhile.

4 English muffins

2 teaspoons unsalted butter, at room temperature

1⅓ pounds ground turkey (use dark or thigh meat if possible)

1 egg, lightly beaten

2 tablespoons Dijon mustard

6 green onions, finely chopped

1 teaspoon kosher salt

¾ teaspoon freshly ground pepper

8 ounces Emmentaler cheese, cut into 8 slices (or use Comté, Gruyère, or Swiss, coarsely grated)

2 beefsteak tomatoes, cut into ¼-inch slices

Preheat the broiler, placing the rack 6 inches below the heating element, or set an outdoor grill to medium.

Butter the English muffins and broil or grill until the butter has melted and the muffins are toasted. Set aside.

In a medium bowl, combine the turkey, egg, mustard, onions, salt, and pepper and mix lightly. Form the mixture into 4 patties about ¾ inch thick (they will be a little sticky. To help form the patties, handle as little as possible and wet your hands in between forming each patty).

To broil: Lightly oil a broiler pan. Put the burgers on the pan and broil for 3 to 4 minutes, or until the burgers are light brown and feel firm but still slightly springy to the touch. Turn, place

2 slices of cheese (or one-quarter of the grated cheese) on each burger, and cook 3 to 4 minutes more, or until the burgers feel firm but still give just a little when pressed (for medium). Cook about 2 minutes longer for well-done.

To grill: Place the burgers on the grill, cover, and cook 3 to 4 minutes, or until the undersides are brown but not dark. Turn burgers, place 2 slices of cheese (or one-quarter of the grated cheese) on each burger, cover, and cook 2 to 3 more minutes, or until the burgers feel firm but still give slightly when pressed for medium rare. Cook about 2 minutes longer for medium or well-done.

Serve with sliced tomatoes and extra Dijon on the side.

Serves 4

MIMOLETTE AND APPLE-CRANBERRY GALETTE

Cheddar and apple may be a classic combination, but that does not mean that cheddar is the only cheese that pairs successfully with apples. Mimolette, which looks nearly identical to a cantaloupe before it is cut, is a French cheese based on a Gouda recipe. Its deep orange color is reminiscent of what many Americans think of as cheddar, which explains why Mimolette is often characterized that way. The cheese has become popular and is fairly easy to find in stores with good cheese selections. Otherwise, use an aged Gouda or cheddar.

For the dough

2 cups flour

2 tablespoons sugar

¼ teaspoon salt

8 tablespoons (1 stick) unsalted butter, very cold, cut into ½-inch cubes

3 ounces Mimolette cheese, coarsely grated (or use aged Gouda or cheddar)

1 egg, separated

¼ cup ice water

For the filling

⅓ cup dried cranberries

½ cup apple brandy, such as Calvados (or use hot water)

¼ cup plus 1 tablespoon sugar

2 tablespoons fresh lemon juice

½ teaspoon cinnamon

1½ pounds tart-sweet apples such as Jonathan, Braeburn, or Gala, peeled, cored, and cut into very thin slices, about ⅛-inch

1 tablespoon water

2 tablespoons decorating sugar, also called sanding sugar (or use regular sugar)

¼ cup heavy cream

To make the dough: Combine the flour, sugar, and salt in the bowl of a food processor and pulse the mixture 3 times. Add the butter and cheese using on/off turns just until the mixture looks clumpy and the butter is the size of large peas.

Lightly beat the egg yolk and 2 tablespoons of the ice water together. Add the mixture to the dough and pulse 5 times. Add remaining ice water and pulse just until the mixture holds together. Test this by taking a small lump and rolling it between your thumb and fingers. It should form a small ball. If it falls apart easily, add more water 1 teaspoon at a time.

Turn the dough out onto a large piece of plastic wrap and flatten into a disk. (Handle the dough as little as possible. You don't want your warm hands to soften the butter.) Wrap the plastic around the disk and refrigerate for at least 1 hour and up to 2 days. Let soften at room temperature for about 10 minutes before proceeding.

Preheat the oven to 350°F.

continued

To make the filling: Place the cranberries in a small heat-proof bowl. Pour the apple brandy over them and let sit for about 15 minutes. Drain the liquid and set aside the cranberries.

In a large bowl, toss together the sugar, lemon juice, and cinnamon. Add the apples and cranberries; mix well. Let stand 15 minutes. Stir well before proceeding.

To assemble: In a small bowl, mix together the egg white and water. Set aside.

Cut out a piece of parchment paper about 16 inches long, and place it on your work surface. Lightly flour the parchment and roll out the dough to a 15-inch round. Transfer the dough and parchment to a baking pan or sheet. Don't worry if the dough is a little larger than your pan because you will be folding in the sides of the dough to make a 13-inch round.

Arrange the apple slices and cranberries on the dough leaving a 2-inch border. Gently fold the 2-inch border of the galette toward the center to encase part of the filling, crimping the edges a little as you go. (Repair any gaps or cracks so that the galette won't leak while baking.) You should end up with a "window" of filling about 9 inches in diameter, with the crust overlapping the edges of the filling.

Pour 2 tablespoons of the accumulated apple juices over the apples. Brush the folded-over edges with the egg white mixture. Sprinkle the crust with the sanding sugar.

Bake until the border is golden and the apples are tender, 35 to 40 minutes. Let cool for about 20 minutes.

Just before serving, whip the cream with the remaining 1 tablespoon sugar. Serve the galette warm or at room temperature.

Serves 8

CHEDDAR, SHALLOT, AND
BLACK PEPPER SCONES

If you like black pepper, you'll love these scones. Although the amount of pepper may not seem like much, a little goes a long way. Because of the spiciness and the abundant shallots, you want to choose a full-flavored cheddar that will stand up to the other ingredients. Cabot Vintage Choice cheddar is a great choice because it is assertive but not bitter. If you can't find it, choose another Cabot cheddar or any cheddar, preferably one labeled "aged." Sharp cheddar is okay too.

1 tablespoon olive oil	8 tablespoons (1 stick) unsalted butter, cut into small pieces
3 large shallots, thinly sliced	6 ounces Cabot Vintage Choice cheese, coarsely grated (or use Westcombe, Montgomery, Grafton Classic Reserve, or Fiscalini cheddar; or use your favorite aged cheddar)
3 cups unbleached flour	
2 tablespoons baking powder	
½ teaspoon baking soda	
1 tablespoon sugar	
2 teaspoons coarsely ground black pepper	1¼ cups plain yogurt, preferably whole milk or lowfat (do not use nonfat)
1 teaspoon salt	

Preheat the oven to 425°F. Butter a large baking sheet or line with a silicone mat such as Silpat.

In a medium-size sauté pan, warm the oil over medium heat. Add the shallots and cook until limp but not brown, 5 to 7 minutes. Add a little salt to taste. Set aside to cool.

In a large bowl, whisk together the flour, baking powder, baking soda, sugar, pepper, and salt. Work in the butter using your fingers or a pastry blender. Mix in about 1¼ cups of the cheese and half the shallots. Add the yogurt and stir just until combined.

Transfer the mixture to a floured sur-face and, using floured hands, knead just until the dough comes together. Pat the dough into a rough circle until it's about ½ inch thick. Cut the dough into triangles with each side measuring approximately 3 inches. Top the dough with remaining cheese then the remaining shallots.

Place on the baking sheet 2 inches apart. Bake for 12 to 15 minutes, or until the scones are a light golden color. Let cool for at least 10 to 15 minutes before serving. Store in an airtight container for up to 2 days at room temperature, or freeze for up to 2 months.

Makes about 12 scones

Clockwise from top: Pecorino
Pepato, Vella Dry Jack,
Parmigiano-Reggiano

CHAPTER 7

HARD

CHEESES

Use Hard Cheeses for

- Cheese courses
- Entertaining
- Pasta
- Salads
- Casseroles
- Vegetables

What Are They?

Argentina
Argentine Reggianito

France
Mimolette (extra-aged)

Greece
Kefalograviera (sheep's milk)

Holland
Beemster Classic Extra-Aged
Beemster XO
Old Amsterdam
Parrano
Prima Donna (See also semi-hard cheeses)
Saenkanter

Italy
Bra Tenero (See also semi-hard cheeses)
Fiore Sardo
Montasio (See also semi-soft and semi-hard cheeses)
Monte Veronese (See also semi-soft cheeses)
Parmigiano-Reggiano
Pecorino Romano (See also semi-hard cheeses)
Pecorino Sardo (See also semi-hard cheeses)
Piave Vecchio
Provolone Piccante or Sharp (See also semi-hard cheeses)

Mexico
Cotija (See also fresh cheeses)

OFF THE BEATEN PATH

Greece
Kefalotyri

Myzithra (See also fresh cheeses)

Italy
Castelmagno
Crotonese

Spain
Aged Mahón (See also semi-soft and semi-hard cheeses)

Switzerland
Sbrinz

United States
Parmesan
Pecorino
Provolone (See also semi-hard cheeses)
Romano

California
Achadinha: Capricious (goat's milk)
Three Sisters Farmstead Cheese Company: Serena
Vella Cheese Company: Dry Monterey Jack, Special Select Dry Jack, Monterey Jack

Georgia
Sweet Grass Dairy: Myrtlewood

New York
Sprout Creek Farm: Toussaint, Barat

Vermont
Blythedale Farm: Cookeville Grana

Wisconsin
Bel Gioioso: American Grana, Parmesan, and Romano
Sartori Foods: SarVecchio Parmesan

You know it's a hard cheese when . . .

- The cut surface appears to be like rough granite rather than smooth
- Its rind is hard as a rock (or close to it)
- It ranges in color from straw to yellow to bright gold
- It has visible crystals that look like tiny white splotches
- It appears as if no knife in the world would cut it
- It is described as *grana*, *stagionato*, *vecchio*, *stravecchio*, and sometimes *piccante*

The Explanation

As the description implies, hard cheese is just that—hard. This is your cue that popping a large chunk in your mouth may not be the first thing to do with it, although you certainly won't break any teeth trying. In fact, many hard cheeses are fantastic stand-alone cheeses, but we'll get to that later. What is certain about hard cheese is that a little goes a long way because of its flavor intensity and oftentimes its saltiness. This is why these cheeses most often are found grated over pasta and risotto, shaved on top of salads, or the nutty and crunchy crust on a cheesy casserole. It is also why they are commonly referred to as *grana* cheeses. This translates to grain or grainy, and refers to the texture of the cheese. This textural feature explains why these cheeses lend themselves to grating.

 A Word about Parmesan

The cheese Parmigiano-Reggiano is the undisputed king of grating cheeses. The word "Parmesan" is used either to describe the family of cheeses similar to Parmigiano-Reggiano or by makers of other Italian-style grating cheeses. They are not legally allowed to use that name because the cheese is not made in the region of Italy from which the heralded cheese comes nor is it made to the strict standards specified for that cheese. Quite honestly, most cheeses that go by the name Parmesan are usually inferior to the Italian original. That does not mean they do not merit attention. But you usually cannot expect the same flavor profile or depth of flavor from them.

Hard cheeses get that way from the moment the milk arrives in the cheese room. In many cases, some of the milk that is used to make hard cheeses such as Parmigiano-Reggiano, is skimmed of its cream. This makes for a slightly lower fat cheese, and it sets the cheese up for long-term aging. Also contributing to the hard texture of the cheese is the fact that the curds are heated at high temperatures, which serves to extract moisture (whey). This helps with aging because the drier and smaller the curds, the drier the final cheese. Many hard cheeses are brined for long periods of time, perhaps weeks. While this is the means of salting the cheeses, it also serves to toughen the exterior and make it able to withstand long periods in the aging room without cracking.

The most famous of all hard cheeses is Parmigiano-Reggiano, which is a cheese that cannot be sold for at least twelve months after it is made, although it is usually aged longer, even as long as three years. Over that period, this so-called king of cheeses is magically transformed into compact layers of curds that are perfumed with pineapple, exploding with pungent aromas, and rife with crunchy crystals, each of which acts as an enticement toward the next nibble.

You will not find as many choices of hard cheeses as you do with other styles, due to the fact they have to be aged longer. That means these cheeses require time and storage — two luxuries most cheesemakers don't have. Besides, inventory on the shelf is inventory not paid for. Still, there are plenty of hard cheeses to choose from.

 ### What Are Those Crystals Anyway?

A by-product of cheese aging is the breakdown of protein. You have probably experienced this phenomenon but not known what it was. For you, it was when you bit into a cheese and discovered the delightful little crystals that seemed like sugar. To me, these are the ultimate payoff in a *grana*-style cheese. In almost all hard cheeses, the crystals are the result of the proteins breaking down, a process called proteolysis. The particular amino acid that breaks free is called tyrosine, but to anyone who enjoys those crystals, it's called a bite of heaven.

You might also find crystals in cheddar cheese, but these are entirely different. The crystals found in cheddar are generally not the result of proteolysis (which explains why they are not tyrosine) and are instead probably the effects of certain starter cultures. Called calcium-lactate crystals, these tiny white crystals tend to colonize the surface of the cheese and, to the untrained eye, may look as if the cheese is developing some type of white mold. While this is not the case, many cheesemakers, particularly the large manufacturers, have traditionally tried to avoid this. However, because people usually like these crystals, many cheesemakers are no longer discouraging their development.

Pick a Pecorino

In well-stocked cheese shops, you might find a variety of pecorinos for sale. While most Italian pecorinos come from Sardinia (called Pecorino Sardo), you will also see Pecorino Romano (which can be made in Sardinia as well) or Pecorino Toscano, among others. Unless you try these cheeses side by side, it is hard to remember the differences. For now, here are the dominant flavor characteristics some of the best known pecorinos.

Fiore Sardo—This is the queen of Sardinian pecorinos and translates to "flower of Sardinia." The unpasteurized cheese is fairly gamy and salty, is lightly smoked, and among the most heralded of all Sardinian sheep's milk cheeses.

Pecorino Romano—Think salt, and you'll remember this style of pecorino. It might also be a little sharp or spicy too. It is best used as a grating cheese rather than a table cheese.

Pecorino Toscano or **Pecorino di Pienza** Pienza is a town within Tuscany, and some of the most famous pecorinos hail from there. The Tuscan pecorinos range in flavor from mild, sweet, floral and/or nutty to sheepy or gamy to extremely so.

Hard cheeses are made from all three milks. The best known hard sheep's milk cheese comes from Italy and is known generically as pecorino. The word *pecora* means sheep in Italian. Usually the hard pecorinos are followed by the word *stagionato*, which refers to the fact they have been aged. Although most pecorinos are not aged for very long, they do not take long to become hard cheeses because they are usually made in fairly small wheels, about 6 to 8 pounds on average. Again, though, their hard texture has to do with the fairly aggressive cheesemaking methods as well. Some pecorinos are aged for a year or two, but these tend to be the exception.

The main flavor components of hard cheeses, and the reasons we find them so enticing, is that they are both salty and sweet. How can this be? Again, the process of protein breakdown as well as fat breakdown, called lipolysis, releases compounds that result in certain flavors and aromas including fruity ones. The salt is prevalent not just because these cheeses are well salted to prepare them for their long stint on the aging shelf, but also because cheese aging is a process of moisture loss. As the moisture (whey) evaporates from the cheese, the protein and fat and other solids become more concentrated. This includes salt and consequently saltiness as well as increased graininess.

Certain hard cheeses tend to be sweeter than others. The most recognized among these are Goudas, which develop dessertlike flavors, including caramel, butterscotch, and coffee. True Parmigiano-Reggiano has a signature pineapple aroma, while some pecorinos have a slightly floral scent although not flavor.

There is one other somewhat elusive characteristic common in hard cheeses. It is called "umami" and is described as the "fifth taste" along with sweet, sour, bitter, and salty. Discovered by Japanese researchers in the early part of the 20th century, it is considered the savory taste that is not detected by the other four tastes. Sometimes it is described as the "delicious" factor. Its relevance to hard cheeses is that they are considered to be high in umami mostly because of the concentration of proteins. For those of us who enjoy these cheeses, this is inherently one of the reasons. We respond favorably to this taste.

In our culture, hard cheese is used mostly in cooking. But it should not be discounted as table cheese or cheese to serve either before or after dinner. It is elegant and bursting with flavor. As a result, a little nibble here and there goes a long way. In cooking, hard cheese won't become stretchy when heated. Instead, if you grate a hard cheese on top of a casserole, the cheese will become toasty and nutty. It will also lend a huge explosion of flavor and a crunchy texture.

ALL HARD CHEESES ARE MEANT FOR GRATING OVER SALADS, PASTA, AND RISOTTO—NOT JUST THE BEST-KNOWN GRATING CHEESES LIKE PARMIGIANO-REGGIANO AND PECORINO. FOR A CHANGE OF PACE, THINK ABOUT USING AN AGED GOAT CHEESE OR MONTEREY DRY JACK THE NEXT TIME YOU'RE LOOKING TO SPRINKLE CHEESE OVER YOUR SPAGHETTI.

The Bottom Line

Hard cheeses become that way because they have lost much of their moisture. They are at once salty and sweet, and the characteristic that distinguishes these cheeses from all the rest is their grainy texture. This is why these cheeses are most often used for grating over pasta, salads, casseroles and other finished dishes.

WHAT TO LOOK FOR WHEN BUYING HARD CHEESES

Look for cheeses whose surfaces, particularly the edges, are not dried out or discolored. You may wonder, what's the difference between a dried out cheese and one that's simply hard? A dried out one will be discolored and look opaque around the edges, almost like hard wax. Most hard cheeses will be devoid of mold, although many will have visible white crystals on the cut surfaces. Those are a by-product of aging and in fact desirable.

VISUAL CUES

- The cut surface might look a bit like a sheer granite cliff — notched in places, smooth in others
- It has a grainy looking surface
- The paste is either ivory (sheep's or goat's milk), yellow or golden

- There may be a few cracks in the paste, but it should not look completely dried out
- The description of the cheese says either *grana, vecchio, staggionato,* aged, extra-aged, *piccante,* or *stravecchio*

TEXTURAL CUES

- The rind will be pretty rocklike
- The paste will offer firm resistance if you press it

- Visible crystals here and there on the cut surface
- A few cracks or fissures in the cut surface

AROMA CUES

The aroma of hard cheeses is positively intoxicating because of the surprising sweetness.

- Butterscotch
- Caramel
- Coffee
- Floral

- Gamy (some)
- Musty
- Pineapple
- Pungent

A FEW NOTEWORTHY HARD CHEESES

HOLLAND

Saenkanter

If your idea of unadulterated pleasure is biting into a cheese and being greeted by lots of crunchy crystals, then Saenkanter is for you. The burnt orange colored cheese is usually characterized as a Gouda even though it is technically made differently, although it is almost always displayed with its Dutch cheese brethren in cheese shops. Gouda or not, this long-aged cheese (aged about three years), embodies flavors like butterscotch, coffee, and nuts. Because of these distinct dessertlike flavors, the crunchy crystals challenge you to remind yourself that those crystals are not sugar and are instead tiny proteins that form as a result of long-term aging. This feature tends to catapult Saenkanter to the top of many people's favorite cheese list, and for good reason. Although somewhat tough to find, it is a cheese you should ask for next time you visit your local store, cheese shop, or online cheese source.

ITALY

Piave Vecchio

As you hopefully know by now, the word *vecchio* translates to "aged" in the cheese vocabulary. Piave is usually sold at one of two stages of aging, *mezzano* —medium—and *vecchio*. (Occasionally you might find a young Piave labeled as fresco). The medium and aged Piave are each delicious, although the *vecchio* is particularly complex and compelling. The pasteurized part-skim milk cheese, made in the Veneto region of Northern Italy, sports the characteristic caramel-like sweetness and pronounced nuttiness of many hard cheeses, including Parmigiano-Reggiano. Unlike Parmigiano-Reggiano, though, it is mellower, not quite as pungent. Piave Vecchio is also not as granular, although it still lends itself to grating. Because Piave is less assertive than some other hard cheeses, you can enjoy it as is, or on a cheese board drizzled with olive oil and herbs. It also makes a great picnic companion.

UNITED STATES

New York

Sprout Creek Farm: Barat

Sprout Creek Farm is a terrific example of an operation not only paying special attention to the land but also to educating people about it. Although cheese is part of the operation, the 200-acre working farm also hosts numerous educational and spiritual events for the public. The cheeses made there, each the result of the combined milk from four different breeds of cows, reflect the farmers' acute attentiveness to the land by way of their grassy, haylike, and earthy flavors. Although each of their three cheeses is different, the petite Barat really shows off these characteristics and then some. It is nutty and even a little musty, and because of that, lends itself equally to grating or eating out of hand with some sweet fruit to contrast its intensity.

 **If you can't find**

Parmigiano-Reggiano, use **Grana Padano, SarVecchio Parmesan**, or **Parrano**

Piave Vecchio, use **aged Asiago, Montasio, Piave Mezzano, Manchego (sheep's milk)**

Old Amsterdam, use **Van Kaas, Rembrandt, Beemster**, or **Parrano**

STORING HARD CHEESES

Because hard cheese has already lost a great deal of moisture, your task is to try to maintain whatever moisture is left. To do this, wrap the cheese in waxed paper followed by a layer of plastic wrap. To ensure that the cheese does not dry out too quickly, put it in an airtight container with a slightly damp paper towel. Refrigerate it in the drawer of your refrigerator and change the wrapping and paper towel every few days. Scrape off any mold that may have developed.

 **Hard Cheese and Wine Pairing** ☆☆☆

In general, hard cheeses work well with wine, but because of their sweetness, you have to be careful not to pair them with a big tannic wine. They will exaggerate those tannins and strip the fruit from the wine. In fact, the tendency of a lot of people is to pair a big red wine with hard cheese. While that can work with certain pecorinos because of their dominant gamy characteristics, I tend to prefer hard cheese with a light white wine, or a light sparkling wine, whether dry or sweet. Even in Parma, the heart of Parmigiano-Reggiano country, the locals tend to pour a white wine or a very light local red wine.

For sparklers, you might consider Fran-ciocorta, a sparkling wine from northern Italy. Even better is a light sparkling red wine from the Asti region of Italy called Bracchetto d'Acqui. Also from the same area is the white wine with slight effervescence called Moscato d'Asti, which goes well with hard cheese.

If you are enjoying a pecorino, then the Sardinian white wine Vermentino or the white wine from Campania called Fiano di Avellino are nice. Otherwise, a medium-bodied southern Italian red wine such as Montapulciano d'Abruzzo from Abruzzo is a good choice.

For a completely different experience, amontillado or oloroso sherries are nice with many hard cheeses because of the nutty character in the wine as well as the cheese.

TAKE-HOME TEST
GETTING TO KNOW HARD CHEESES

In order to understand the distinct flavors in hard cheeses, it is helpful to taste them with foods that have similar flavor components, particularly fruit and nuts.

THE ASSIGNMENT

Buy

- 2 to 4 ounces Parmigiano-Reggiano cheese (do not substitute), in one piece
- 2 to 4 ounces pecorino, preferably Fiore Sardo or other Sardinian pecorino
- 2 to 4 ounces Old Amsterdam or other aged Gouda cheese
- 2 to 4 rounds of dried pineapple
- 1 Golden Delicious apple
- 4 light caramels

Put the cheeses on a plate with markers next to them to identify them if necessary.

1) First, break off a piece of the Parmigiano-Reggiano with your hands. Smell the cut piece. Initially it might have a somewhat pungent aroma. But it will soon be followed by a subtle pineapple aroma. Taste the pineapple followed by a piece of cheese. Naturally the pineapple is sweeter but you should be able to see the surprising similarities.

2) Move on to the pecorino. This will not have the pineapple-like characteristics that the Parmigiano-Reggiano had. Instead, it will smell much more earthy and possibly a little gamy. It will also be a bit nutty and fruity. Cut a piece of the apple and smell it. Smell the pecorino again. Identical? Absolutely not. Similar? Quite possibly. Now taste the cheese followed by the apple. Not only do they taste good together, the apple really brings out the floral and fruity elements of the cheese.

3) Finally, do the same exercise with the Gouda and caramel. Smell both of them first. Then take a bite of the cheese followed by a caramel. The caramel will naturally be sweeter but you can see how the two very disparate foods have an affinity.

THE LESSON

Although we tend to think of hard cheese as being salty, it has a surprising and alluring amount of sweetness. Other sweet foods will really enhance those qualities in the cheese, which is helpful to know when you are in the mood to have a "sweet" cheese.

ASPARAGUS SOUP WITH DRY JACK AND CRISPY PROSCIUTTO

When springtime comes and the first spears of asparagus stand at attention on the tables of farmers' markets and produce aisles, it's time to bring out the stockpot and make a batch of simple asparagus soup. All it takes is about 30 minutes to get the essence of asparagus into a bowl. Topped with Dry Jack (Monterey Jack cheese that has been aged for a year or more) and crispy shards of prosciutto, asparagus has never gotten such regal treatment and soup never tasted so good.

2 ounces prosciutto, sliced paper-thin

2 tablespoons olive oil

2 medium onions (about 1¼ pounds total), coarsely chopped

4 cups low-sodium chicken stock

2 pounds regular (not pencil) asparagus, bottoms snapped off, cut into 2-inch pieces

1 teaspoon kosher salt (or more to taste)

6 ounces Dry Jack Reserve cheese, preferably from Vella Cheese Company coarsely grated (or use Parmigiano-Reggiano, an American Parmesan such as SarVecchio, or any hard cheese you prefer),

½ teaspoon freshly ground pepper

Preheat the oven to 400°F.

Place the prosciutto on a baking sheet. Bake for 15 minutes, or until it is crisp and very light brown around the edges. Remove from the oven and let cool completely. The prosciutto will continue to crisp as it cools.

In a large sauté pan, warm the oil over medium heat. Add the onion and cook until it is soft but not brown, about 10 minutes. Add the stock and asparagus. Turn heat to simmer, cover, and let cook until the asparagus is quite soft and tender, about 10 minutes. Puree

the soup in batches in a blender (or use an immersion blender). Put the soup back into the pan, and salt to taste, and keep it warm.

To serve, heat the soup to hot but not steaming. (This concentrates the flavors of the soup and cheese better.) Ladle the soup into individual bowls. Sprinkle the cheese on top, keeping it concentrated in the middle of the bowl. It will melt immediately. Crumble the prosciutto and sprinkle over the cheese. Give a twist of black pepper and serve right away.

Serves 8

ACORN SQUASH WITH SARVECCHIO AND SWISS CHARD

SarVecchio Parmesan is a Wisconsin cheese aged at least 18 months, that, to me, is one of the best hard cheeses made in the United States. It has complexity and a firm yet granular texture that is reminiscent of some of the best hard cheeses made in the world. In this dish, the cheese's assertive flavors and toasty texture create the perfect contrast with the sweet flesh of the squash. If you cannot find SarVecchio, use any full-flavored hard cheese such as Parmigiano-Reggiano, Grana Padano, or pecorino.

2 large acorn squash (about 3 pounds)	wise into 1-inch–wide strips (or use green Swiss chard)
2 tablespoons olive oil	½ teaspoon salt
2 large leeks (about 1 pound), sliced lengthwise into ¼-inch slices, then cut crosswise into 1-inch pieces	8 ounces SarVecchio Parmesan, finely grated (or use aged Asiago or pecorino)
1 pound ruby Swiss chard, washed, coarse stems removed, cut cross-	½ teaspoon crushed red pepper flakes

Preheat the oven to 375°F.

Cut the squash in half crosswise. Scoop out strings and seeds and discard. Line a baking sheet with foil and grease it with a little vegetable oil. Place the squash cut side down on the baking sheet and cook until the pulp is soft but the outside of the squash is still firm, about 35 to 40 minutes. Let sit until cool enough to handle. Place a fine-mesh strainer over a bowl. Using a spoon, scoop the pulp into the strainer, leaving a ¼-inch-thick wall. Let squash drain while you prepare the rest of the dish.

Place an oven rack about 6 inches below the heating element and preheat the broiler.

In a large sauté pan, warm the oil over medium-high heat. Add the leeks and cook until limp but not brown, about 5 minutes. Add the chard, cover, and cook, stirring occasionally, for about 3 minutes, or until it is cooked through and is no longer coarse. Add the squash pulp and salt and mix well. Add 2 cups of the cheese and the red pepper flakes. Mix well. Taste and add more salt if necessary. (Since hard cheeses are often quite salty, don't overdo the salt.)

Stuff the squash shells with the mixture. Top with the remaining cheese. Broil until the cheese has browned, about 2 minutes. Let cool for about 15 minutes, and then serve.

Serves 4

EGGPLANT, FAVA, AND PECORINO SALAD

Although there are several elements in this salad, it comes together quickly and easily. All you have to do is cook the eggplant for a few minutes and blanch the beans. All the elements can be prepared in advance, assembled on individual plates, and served whenever you're ready. The only last-minute steps are to toss the greens with the dressing and top with the cheese. Although this dish is much prettier as a composed salad, feel free to mix all the ingredients except the cheese together to make a tossed salad. Before serving, top with the cheese.

This recipe calls for Pecorino Romano, which adds a piquant note to the otherwise rich and creamy ingredients. If you prefer a less salty sheep's milk cheese, then choose a Sardinian or Tuscan pecorino, or head to Spain and use Manchego or Zamorano.

---

8 ounces Asian or Italian eggplant, cut diagonally into ¼-inch slices

¼ cup plus 2 teaspoons olive oil

1½ teaspoons salt

Freshly ground pepper

2 Roma tomatoes, cut in half lengthwise

1 cup shelled fava beans (about 1¼ pounds in the pod. If you cannot find fava beans, use frozen baby lima beans)

2 cups arugula

1 tablespoon plus 1 teaspoon white wine vinegar

2 ounces aged Pecorino Romano cheese, shaved (or use aged Asiago, Dry Jack, or Parmigiano-Reggiano)

2 tablespoons pine nuts, lightly toasted

Preheat the broiler, placing the rack 6 inches below the heating element.

In a medium bowl, mix together the eggplant, 2 tablespoons of the olive oil, ½ teaspoon of the salt, and pepper to taste. Brush the tomatoes with a little olive oil and sprinkle with salt.

Set a cooling rack on a baking sheet and coat the rack with cooking spray or oil (alternatively, use a lightly oiled broiler pan). Put the eggplant slices and tomatoes on the rack and broil for 2 to 3 minutes or until the eggplant starts to turn almost black in just a few places (you do not want to burn them, but giving them a crisp exterior makes for a great textural sensation with the creamy center. The tomatoes will have a few black spots as well.) Turn the eggplant and broil about 2 more minutes, or until the eggplant slices are dark on the outside and the tomatoes have softened. Set aside and let cool.

If using fresh beans, remove them from their pods by snapping off the top and using your thumb to slit open the pod. For fresh or frozen beans, put them in a medium pot of boiling, salted water, and cook for 2 minutes. Drain. For fresh beans, let sit until cool enough to handle. To remove the beans from their outer skin, grasp the little tongue end of the bean with your thumb and forefinger, and with your other thumb and forefinger, tear a little slit at the top of the bean. Simply pinch the tongue end together, and the bean will slip out. Repeat with remaining fava beans and place in a small bowl. Drizzle with 2 teaspoons oil and sprinkle with salt, to taste. Mix gently and set aside.

In a large bowl, toss the arugula with the remaining 2 tablespoons olive oil, the vinegar, the remaining 1 teaspoon salt, and pepper to taste.

To assemble: Distribute the eggplant slices on one-third of each of 4 salad plates. Put a pile of arugula, next to the eggplant, put the beans, and finally place 1 tomato half on the plate. Distribute the cheese shavings over the entire salad and sprinkle with the pine nuts. Give a twist of black pepper and serve.

Serves 4

SPICED GAME HENS WITH AGED GOUDA AND COUSCOUS

At first glance, this recipe may not look cheesy, and in fact, it does not taste overwhelmingly cheesy either. But the Gouda in the stuffing adds a savory and slightly piquant flavor that really brings out the sweetness of the dried apricots and the spiciness of the rub. For best results, be sure to use a full-flavored cheese.

For the rub

1 teaspoon cinnamon

1 teaspoon ground coriander

1 teaspoon ground cumin

1 teaspoon Hungarian sweet paprika

½ teaspoon cayenne

2 teaspoons kosher salt

For the stuffing

1 teaspoon olive oil

½ large onion, cut into ¼-inch dice

½ cup chicken broth (or use water)

¼ teaspoon salt

⅓ cup couscous

¼ cup coarsely chopped dried apricots

2 tablespoons raw pistachios, coarsely chopped

¼ teaspoon cinnamon

⅛ teaspoon ground cumin

3 ounces aged Gouda cheese such as Saenkanter, Old Amsterdam, Winchester aged Gouda, Van Kaas, or Vincent, coarsely grated

4 game hens

Preheat the oven to 400°F.

To make the rub: In a small bowl, stir together all the rub ingredients. Set aside.

To make the stuffing: Put the oil in a medium-size saucepan and warm over medium-high heat. Add the onions and cook until limp but not brown, about 5 minutes. Add the chicken broth and salt and bring to a boil. Add the couscous and cover. Turn off the heat and let stand about 5 minutes. Add the apricots, pistachios, cinnamon, and cumin. Stir once or twice. Add the cheese and mix until well incorporated.

Let cool completely. (You can make the stuffing up to one day ahead. Cover and refrigerate.)

To prepare the game hens: Rub all sides of the game hens with the rub, getting it into all the hidden areas beneath the wings and under the legs. Put about ¼ cup stuffing in the cavity of each hen. (You may have some extra. Put it in a casserole, add a little chicken stock, cover and bake for about 15 minutes alongside the game hens.)

Put the hens breast side up in a baking pan and roast for 50 to 55 minutes or until the skin is golden and the juice runs yellow when you prick the thigh with a fork. Let rest for 10 to 15 minutes before serving. Strain any pan juices and drizzle around the birds before serving.

Serves 4

BRUSSELS SPROUTS SALAD WITH AGED ASIAGO AND PANCETTA

This recipe is a cross between a side and a salad. It is saladlike because of the vinegary dressing, yet it is served warm. However you characterize it, this dish is not short on richness or flavor, guaranteed by hearty cheese shavings on top.

1½ teaspoons kosher salt

1 pound Brussels sprouts, stems trimmed, sprouts quartered lengthwise (if some outer leaves fall off, use them)

2 ounces pancetta, coarsely chopped

½ medium red onion, cut into ¼-inch slices

1 tablespoon red wine vinegar

1 tablespoon plus 1 teaspoon extra-virgin olive oil

½ teaspoon kosher salt

Freshly ground pepper

4 hard-boiled eggs sieved or grated with a Microplane or the small holes of a box grater

2-ounce piece of aged Asiago cheese (or use Parmesan, Piave, or Manchego)

Bring 1 quart of water and 1 teaspoon of the salt to a boil in a 2-quart pot. Add the Brussels sprouts and cook for 3 minutes, or until bright green and tender but still firm to the bite. You want them slightly undercooked as they continue to cook as they cool. Drain immediately.

Put the pancetta in a large sauté pan, and cook over medium-high heat until crisp and brown around the edges, about 7 minutes. Using a slotted spoon, transfer to a paper towel-lined plate. Remove 2 teaspoons of the fat from the pan and reserve for the dressing. If you don't have that much just remove as much as you can, but leave 2 teaspoons of fat in the pan to cook the onions.

Using the same pan, turn the heat to medium and add the onions. Cook, stirring occasionally, until soft and slightly caramelized, about 8 minutes. Add the Brussels sprouts to the pan just to warm through.

In a small bowl, whisk together the vinegar, the rendered fat, olive oil, ½ teaspoon salt, and pepper to taste.

In a large bowl, toss the Brussels sprouts–onion mixture, pancetta, and half of the egg with the dressing. Let sit for about 15 minutes to allow the flavors to meld. Transfer to individual plates. Sprinkle with remaining egg. Using a vegetable peeler, shave slices of cheese over each salad. Top with a few twists of black pepper and serve.

Serves 4

ZUCCHINI, TOMATO, AND GRANA PADANO GRATIN

The red and green colors of this dish are as bright as a spring day in Provence, which is the place that lends its name to the herb blend used to season this gratin. It is easy to make, and can be assembled up to 6 hours in advance, covered, and kept at room temperature. However, do not add the cheese and bread crumbs until you're ready to bake the dish. This casserole is equally good warm or at room temperature, making it a perfect do-ahead dish.

- ½ cup fresh bread crumbs
- 1 tablespoon plus 2 teaspoons olive oil
- 1 large red onion cut into ¼-inch slices
- 2 shallots, cut into ¼-inch slices
- 1 clove garlic, minced
- ¾ teaspoon kosher or coarse sea salt
- ½ teaspoon freshly ground pepper
- 2 medium zucchini, cut on the bias into ½-inch disks
- 5 ripe medium tomatoes (about 1½ pounds), cut crosswise into ½ inch slices
- 2 teaspoons herbes de Provence, crumbled
- 3 ounces Grana Padano cheese, finely grated (or use American Parmesan, Parmigiano-Reggiano, or an aged crottin)

Preheat the oven to 425°F.

Have ready a 1-quart rectangular or oval gratin dish or shallow casserole (an 11-inch glass pie plate will also work).

In a small baking pan, mix the bread crumbs with 2 teaspoons of the olive oil. Bake for 5 to 7 minutes, or until bread crumbs are toasted. Set aside.

Heat 1 tablespoon of the olive oil in a large sauté pan over a medium heat. Add the onion and shallots and sauté for 10 minutes, stirring occasionally. Add garlic and cook until soft but not brown, about 2 minutes. Add ¼ teaspoon salt and ⅛ teaspoon pepper. Spoon the onion mixture into the bottom of the gratin dish.

Assemble the gratin by alternating slices of zucchini and tomato over the onions at a 45° angle to one end of the dish. Do this by starting with one slice of zucchini, laying it at an angle against the end of the dish and leaning a slice of tomato against the zucchini. Continue overlapping in this fashion. Sprinkle with the herbes de Provence and remaining ½ teaspoon salt and ⅜ teaspoon pepper. Cover with foil and bake for 30 minutes. Remove foil, sprinkle with the cheese, then the bread crumbs over the gratin, and bake an additional 15 minutes, or until zucchini feels soft but firm when pierced with a fork and cheese is golden brown.

Place on a cooling rack and let sit for 5 to 10 minutes. Cut and serve.

Serves 4 to 6

Clockwise from left: Rogue River
Blue, Stilton, Montbriac

CHAPTER 8

BLUE

CHEESES

Use Blue Cheeses for

- Casseroles
- Cheese courses
- Entertaining
- Fondue
- Grilled cheese sandwiches
- Polenta
- Pasta
- Risotto
- Vegetables

What Are They?

Australia
Roaring Forties Blue

Denmark
Blue Castello
Saga

England
Huntsman (See also semi-hard cheeses)
Shropshire Blue
Stilton

France
Bleu d'Auvergne
Fourme d'Ambert
Montbriac
Roquefort (sheep's milk)
St. Agur

Germany
Cambozola (See also soft-ripened cheeses)

Ireland
Cashel Blue
Crozier Blue

Italy
Gorgonzola Dolce
Gorgonzola Dolcelatte
Gorgonzola Piccante

New Zealand
White Stone Cheese Company: Windsor Blue, Moeraki Bay Blue

Spain
Cabrales (cow, goat, and sheep's milk)

Monte Enebro (goat's milk; see also soft-ripened cheeses)
Peñazul
Picon (cow, goat, and sheep's milk)
Valdeon (cow, goat, and sheep's milk)

United States

California
Point Reyes Farmstead Cheese Company: Original Blue

Iowa
Golden Ridge Cheese Cooperative: Schwarz und Weis, Harmony Blue
Maytag Blue

Massachusetts
Great Hill Dairy: Great Hill Blue
Westfield Farms: Classic Blue Log (goat's milk), Hubbardston Blue (See also soft-ripened cheeses)

Minnesota
Faribault Dairy Company: Amablu, St. Pete's Select

New York
Old Chatham Sheepherding Company: Ewe's Blue

Oregon
Rogue River Creamery: Crater Lake Blue, Oregonzola, Rogue River Blue, Echo Mountain (cow and goat's milk)

Vermont
Jasper Hill Farm: Bayley Hazen Blue

Wisconsin
Bel Gioioso Cheese: Gorgonzola
Roth Käse: Buttermilk Blue
Sartori Foods: Glacier Point Gorgonzola

England
Beenleigh Blue
Harbourne Blue (goat's milk)

France
Bleu de Gex

Italy
Blu del Moncenisio

United States

California
Marin French Cheese Company: Le Petit Bleu
(*See also* soft-ripened cheeses)

Massachusetts
Berkshire Blue

Minnesota
Shepherd's Way Farm: Big Woods Blue
(sheep's milk)

New York
Lively Run Goat Dairy: Cayuga Blue (goat's
milk)

Texas
Mozzarella Company: Deep Ellum Blue

Vermont
Green Mountain Blue Cheese: Boucher Blue,
Gore-Dawn-Zola

Washington
Estrella Creamery: Wynoochee River Blue

Wisconsin
Carr Valley Cheese Company: Virginia Pine
Native Blue, Virgin Pine Native Sheep Blue
Hook's Blue Cheese

 You know it's a blue cheese cheese when . . .

- It has blue, green, dark blue, gray lines and/or veins interspersed throughout the paste
- The blue veining is the dominant characteristic of the paste
- The amount of veining, blue "dots," or lines is fairly consistent even if the cheese doesn't have a lot of veining

THE EXPLANATION

The blue cheese family is a big one. That's the reason that most stores, whether dedicated cheese shops or supermarkets, sell a wide variety of blue cheeses. American cheesemakers are making all kinds of styles, and every cheesemaking country has its own traditional blue cheeses. Blue cheeses are made with all three types of milk, with goat's milk blue cheese being the least common. But despite the variation within this family, blue cheeses are quite possibly the easiest to understand because they all share the characteristic blue mold flavors even though the mold strains may differ.

The mold strain that is used most often is *Penicillium roqueforti*, which was originally derived from moldy bread. To make blue cheese, cheesemakers add strains of this mold along with starter cultures to the milk and proceed with cheesemaking according to their particular recipe. Blue cheese parts ways from all the other cheeses a few days or sometimes weeks after the cheese has been made. At that point, the cheesemaker will usually pierce the cheese (also called needling) for the purpose of introducing air into the interior. The air interacts with the *Penicillium roqueforti* to create the signature blue veins. The more the air can circulate within the paste, the more veining will occur. Some cheeses are not pierced and develop blue mold naturally because of ambient mold spores in the aging facility or because there are enough air spaces within the cheese that, together with the mold that has been added to the milk, create the veins naturally.

The way the curds are managed also facilitates air (and therefore mold) movement. If the curds are pressed only lightly or not at all, then that leaves more space for the air to circulate between curds. Likewise, if the curds are larger, they will not be as compact as small, drier curds. Either way, the blue mold has more opportunity to do its dance within the cheese.

Most blue cheeses are made with the mold *Penicillium roqueforti*, but there is another blue mold called *Penicillium glaucom* that is used primarily in Gorgon-

 ### What to Do with Wet Cheese

Often you will see foil-wrapped blue cheeses that seem to be downright wet. This is particularly true of authentic Roquefort. The moisture is the whey continuing to drain. While it is not exactly a flaw in the cheesemaking and more likely is the consequence of sending the delicate, high-moisture cheese in a ship across the Atlantic, it is at the least inconvenient not to mention a soggy mess. To remedy this, set the cheese on a paper towel–lined plate or container to absorb some of the moisture and put the cheese in the refrigerator. After it has sat there for an hour or two, remove the paper and wrap the cheese as instructed in the section on storing blue cheeses.

zola cheese (although it is also found in or on cheeses that may be exposed to a natural source of the mold in the aging room or cave). In Gorgonzola, this mold usually produces veins that tend toward greenish rather than blue hues and in fact are called *erborinato*, which is Lombardian dialect for "parsley" (Lombardy is the official home of Gorgonzola).

If there is any single characteristic common to almost all blue cheeses it is that they are salty. After that, they are most easily understood when they are divided by texture. Generally, they are soft-ripened (creamy), creamy-crumbly, or firm.

Creamy Style

The creamiest blue cheeses include Cambozola, Saga Blue, and Blue Castello, all of which have the bloomy rind found on soft-ripened cheeses. In this way, they can be thought of as two styles of cheese in one. Like other soft-ripened cheeses, the blue versions are very creamy and their blue mold flavors are quite mild. Also in this category is the popular Montbriac, which has a grayish rind because it is covered with ash, but like other soft-ripened cheeses, become creamier as it ages.

Creamy-Crumbly Style

Other creamy-leaning blue cheeses, the ones I call creamy-crumbly, include the famous Roquefort as well as Gorgonzola Dolce, Gorgonzola Dolcelatte, Point Reyes Blue Cheese, Maytag Blue, Bleu d'Auvergne, Roaring Forties Blue, and St. Agur, among others. You can identify these because they usually have a thin rind or no rind and they look moist. Tasting them you will notice that they encompass the widest range of flavors including tangy, sweet, sometimes pungent, and noticeably salty.

Firm Style

These cheeses range in flavor from smoky to earthy to beefy and, except for Gorgonzola Piccante, tend to be mellower in flavor. Examples of firm blue cheeses are Fourme d'Ambert, Shropshire, and Stilton.

The easiest way to identify which cheese is which at the store is to know that the creamy-crumbly cheeses are usually packaged in foil, while the natural rind cheeses like Stilton are wrapped in plastic or displayed as whole wheels. Also, the crumbly style has a visible tan/light brown (inedible) rind. The soft-ripened, creamy blue cheeses are usually displayed with blue cheeses rather than the soft-ripened cheese.

One important point about blue cheese: A higher amount of veining does not necessarily equate to strong flavors. Some cheeses such as Original Blue from Point Reyes have relatively little veining and yet are quite tangy and unmistakably blue cheeses, while others have quite a bit of veining, but taste rather sweet. St. Agur is an example of this type of blue cheese.

The Bottom Line

The diversity of blue cheeses makes this style a fun challenge for anyone who likes them, but possibly frustrating for those who are shy about blue cheese. Bear in mind though, that like other styles, the flavors in blue cheese are most easily discerned by looking at their texture. Creamy equates to mild, creamy-crumbly translates to tangy and piquant, and firm means earthy, meaty, and nutty.

Most blue cheeses are not as strong as you might expect. But if you're a reluctant blue cheese eater, use the cheeses you *do* like outside the blue cheese family as your guide. That is, if you like soft-ripened cheeses, then look for soft-ripened blues, which are generally mild. If you like firmer, earthier cheeses, choose Stilton or other similar cheeses. If you're not a big blue cheese fan, then stay away from the Roquefort-like cheeses, which are usually the most pungent.

WHAT TO LOOK FOR WHEN BUYING BLUE CHEESES

Choosing blue cheeses might be confusing, since their predominant feature is mold, which can be intimidating. After all, we instinctively stay away from moldy food. Still, once you learn a few tricks, you can figure out what to buy pretty easily. One thing to remember about the firmer style of blue cheese is that it is inherently crumbly, so don't be put off by a less-than-neat slice of the cheese.

VISUAL CUES

Soft-ripened	Creamy-crumbly	Firm
• White, velvety, and vibrant rind—not rust or gray colored (except for ash-covered styles) • Supple, not saggy, paste • Little veining	• Creamy-looking, not dry • White or tan paste • Should not be wet • No yellowish or extensive pink tones in the paste • No white mold growth on the paste • Blue, dark blue, bluish-gray, or greenish-gray veining	• Extensive veining • Crumbly-looking (think dry cookie dough) • Little to no cracking of the rind • Tan, dark tan, or golden paste (or orange) • Dark green, dark blue, or dark gray veining

TEXTURAL CUES

Soft-ripened	Creamy-crumbly	Firm
• Rind should be smooth, not saggy, yet a little soft to the touch • Paste should feel fairly soft to the touch • Firm when young, softer when it ages	• Paste should be firm but not hard in cheeses that don't have any visible moisture • Cheeses with visible moisture should have a soft but not squishy paste • Will have lots of tiny "divots," which should be uniform throughout	• Paste will have a somewhat craggy smooth-looking surface and will break or crumble when cut • Firm to touch but not rock hard

AROMA CUES

Because blue cheeses tend to have assertive aromas, it is good to know how the different categories of blue cheese should *not* smell as well as how they should.

Soft-ripened	Creamy-crumbly	Firm
• Should *not* smell ammoniated	• Should *not* smell ammoniated or particularly strong	• Should *not* smell excessively strong or gamy

Blue cheeses *should* smell:

• Baconlike • Beefy • Buttermilk-like • Crème fraîche-like	• Fresh milk-like • Grassy • Herbaceous • Pungent	• Smoky • Sweet • Toasted nuts

FLAVOR CUES

Blue cheeses are far more than musty, salty cheeses. They encompass a wide range of flavors, which is why is it worthwhile tasting a variety of blue cheeses instead of just sticking to your favorite. A new favorite could be just around the bend.

• Bacon	• Grainy	• Peppery
• Brown butter	• Grassy	• Pungent
• Buttermilk	• Hay	• Salty
• Butterscotch	• Herbaceous	• Smoky
• Buttery	• Lactic/milky	• Spicy
• Caramel	• Minty	• Sweet
• Earthy	• Musty	• Tangy
• Floral	• Nutty	• Yeasty

MOUTHFEEL

Because the styles of blue cheese vary, so does the mouthfeel of each one. For the soft-ripened or ash-covered style, the predominant texture is creamy or maybe even silken. For the creamy-crumbly style, the cheese will look a little crumbly, but it will almost melt in your mouth and become cream. The harder style might have a few crystals in it and it might be a bit gritty. Overall it will be similar to the mouthfeel of a semi-hard cheese.

FINISH

The exciting thing about a well-made blue cheese, regardless of style, is that it will create many different flavors and sensations and almost always a long finish. It can be earthy, floral, pungent, and sweet at the same time.

The textural differences serve to present variations on the blue cheese theme. A soft-ripened blue cheese will usually be mild, yet the creaminess creates a lasting impression and also mitigates the pungency. A creamy-crumbly blue cheese encompasses a big range of blue cheese flavors, but most often leave either a tangy or pungent impression and finish. The firm style will be nutty, a little sweet, and possibly smoky.

A Few Noteworthy Blue Cheeses

IRELAND

Cashel Blue

This Irish cheese, originated and still made near Cashel in County Tipperary, is Ireland's first farm-produced blue cheese. Made on only one farm by Jane and Louis Grubb, the pasteurized cow's milk cheese straddles the line between crumbly and creamy. It is crumbly at about six weeks, but as it ages to about six months it tips the scales on the creamy side. Its flavors are buttery, creamy, tangy, and surprisingly sweet. The unpressed cheese is made in cylindrical wheels weighing between three and four pounds and has a natural rind. Cashel Blue has become more readily available in stores with well-stocked cheese counters as has the Grubbs' newest venture, Crozier Blue. Similar to Cashel Blue, this lovely cheese is made with sheep's milk from their nephew's farm.

NEW ZEALAND

Whitestone Cheese Company: Windsor Blue

This double- (almost triple) crème blue cheese cannot keep the "blue" ribbons away. In 2006, it won the Cuisine Champions Award, which meant it was judged the best New Zealand cheese among a field of 500 cheeses. Made by the Whitestone Cheese Company in Oamaru on the South Island of New Zealand, Windsor Blue is all about cream, butter, and sweetness. The cheese is made with Whitestone's homegrown culture that is added to the pasteurized milk. It is hand-salted and then aged for about two months.

The accolades for the Whitestone cheeses couldn't be bestowed upon nicer people. Owner Bob Barry, who started the company in 1987, is one of the most hospitable people I have ever met, having opened his door—and cheeses—to my mother and me when we visited one summer. His combination of business acumen, exacting standards, and a good palate has put Whitestone Cheese Company on the international map, not just New Zealand's.

Although the company makes many delicious cheeses, including their original cheese called Farmhouse (a delicious bloomy-rind cheese), Windsor Blue is Whitestone's flagship cheese and the one most readily available in the United States.

Oregon

Rogue Creamery: Echo Mountain

Echo Mountain is a seasonal cheese made by southern Oregon's heralded cheese company, Rogue Creamery. Although the creamery also makes cheddar cheese, their claim to fame is blue cheese. Echo Mountain, named for a now defunct dairy in the area, is one of their newest cheeses and is comprised of 20 percent organic goat's milk and 80 percent organic cow's milk, an unusual combination in the American blue cheese world. As you might expect from a blue cheese made with goat's milk, even a relatively small amount as this one is, this cheese is tangy, earthy, and grassy. The cow's milk lends the richness and buttery and nutty notes to the cheese. Overall the cheese is floral, nutty, and a little peppery. Despite the fact Echo Mountain is available only seasonally, it is worth waiting for in the same way that Rogue Creamery's flagship cheese, Rogue River Blue, is. That cheese, wrapped in grape leaves that have been macerated in pear eau de vie, is aged for nine months. Because of its popularity, stores run out of it fairly quickly. Be on the lookout for Echo Mountain when it hits the stores in January each year (it is made only in the summer months when the goat's milk is available and released a few months later), and Rogue River Blue beginning in August or September each year, and you might be lucky enough to score a piece.

 If you can't find

Roquefort, use **St. Agur** or **Gorgonzola Dolce**

Montbriac, use **Cambozola** or **Camembert**

Stilton, use **Fourme d'Ambert, Shropshire, Huntsman**, or **Gorgonzola Piccante**

Maytag Blue, use **Point Reyes Blue, Buttermilk Blue**, or **Crater Lake Blue**

STORING BLUE CHEESES

Although many blue cheeses come wrapped in foil, this is probably not the best way for you to store them at home. Foil tends to maintain any wetness that may already be in the cheese. Instead, store blue cheeses the way you would the other styles of cheese.

Put creamy, creamy-crumbly, or medium-firm blue cheeses unwrapped in an airtight plastic container with a few holes poked in it and store in the refrigerator drawer. Wrap firm blue cheeses, such as Stilton or Bayley Hazen Blue, in waxed paper surrounded with plastic wrap and store in the refrigerator drawer. Alternatively, you can put this type of cheese in a resealable plastic bag because that type of bag breathes. However, I would encourage you to wrap the cheese in waxed paper first so that it doesn't pick up any plastic odors or flavors.

 Blue Cheese and Wine Pairing ☆☆☆

Blue cheeses of all types lend themselves to a variety of wines. One classic pairing is Stilton with port. This is a fine pairing because the strength of the cheese can hold its own against the sweetness and high alcohol content of the wine. Port is also a good companion for other types of blue cheese providing your cheese and wine have the same degree of saltiness or tanginess and sweetness respectively. So if the cheese is only mildly salty or tangy, then choose a port style that is only moderately sweet. Otherwise, the wine will overtake the cheese. If port isn't your thing, then almost any dessert wine, including a cream sherry, works nicely with most blue cheeses.

The other end of the spectrum from sweet wines is, of course, dry ones, in particular, sparkling wines. The acidity and bubbles serve to lift the richness and saltiness of a blue cheese right off your tongue to create a perfect creamy yet bubbly texture in your mouth. The resulting flavors—kind of yeasty and toasty—are unbeatable.

Many dry white wines work with blue cheeses too. In particular, a fruity Chenin Blanc is nice and because of their relative fruitiness, some California Sauvignon Blancs make good matches with blue cheese, particularly the medium-firm ones.

I do not recommend red wines. The creaminess in most blue cheese, along with the pungent aromas, flavors, and salt tend to make red wine taste excessively bitter. Even high-alcohol reds, which have a perceived sweetness, end up tasting this way.

TAKE-HOME TEST
GETTING TO KNOW BLUE CHEESES

It's hard to imagine that blue cheeses could have so many different flavors, but when you try them side by side with foods that have those actual flavors, you begin to see the similarities.

THE ASSIGNMENT

Buy

- 2 to 4 ounces Point Reyes Blue cheese (or use Maytag Blue or Buttermilk Blue)
- 2 to 4 ounces Montbriac or Cambozola cheese
- 2 to 4 ounces Stilton cheese, preferably Colston Bassett
- 1 lemon, cut in wedges
- 2 ounces crème fraîche
- 2 slices bacon, cooked until crisp

Lay the cheeses out on a plate in the order listed. Mark them or make sure you have a good memory so that you know which is which. Put the remaining ingredients on a separate plate.

1) Start with the tangy blue, Point Reyes Blue. Take a taste. Notice how tangy it is? I call this "blue cheese dressing on a fork" because it has the richness and tanginess of blue cheese dressing. Take a taste of lemon. Needless to say, that is sourer than the cheese, but it isn't as different as you might expect.

2) Move on to the Montbriac. Take a taste of the cheese without the rind. Notice that it is mild, but you still detect the blue cheese flavors. Take a taste of the crème fraîche. It is richer and obviously does not have any blue mold flavors or aromas, but the richness of the crème fraîche and cheese should match quite closely.

3) The next matchup is the Stilton and the bacon. First taste the Stilton. It has a wide variety of flavors, including brown butter, nuts, and yes, bacon. Once you try the bacon you might think that it is much more bacon-y than the cheese, and you would be right. But the cheese still has similar smoky notes, which is important to note.

THE LESSON

This assignment is intended to make two main points. First, you should have noticed that blue cheeses vary tremendously in both flavor and texture. Second, by tasting blue cheeses next to foods with similar flavors, it is easier to develop a visceral memory of the flavor distinctions between some of the styles.

À Côté's Mountain Gorgonzola, Pear, and Walnut Pizzettas

Sometimes the smaller neighborhood restaurants are the ones that make the biggest splash. At À Côté in Oakland, California, one of the reasons is chef Matt Colgan's flatbread. While the crust in this recipe is not exactly cracker-thin like Matt's restaurant creations, he kindly shared this rendition, which is equally good. The sweetness of the crust shows off his magical use of ingredients by combining salty, creamy blue cheese with juicy pears and crunchy walnuts. This is unquestionably a pizzetta (little pizza) that will instantly rise to the top of your favorites list. Note that the dough for this recipe must rest for 4 hours or overnight. Alternatively, buy pre-made, refrigerated pizza dough.

Two 8-ounce balls of pizza dough (see page 198; or use high-quality refrigerated or frozen pizza dough)

2 ripe pears (Comice and French butter pears work well) cut into ¼-inch slices

3 ounces Gorgonzola Piccante cheese (or use any firm blue cheese that crumbles such as Fourme d'Ambert)

½ cup walnuts, coarsely chopped

1 tablespoon plus 1 teaspoon finely chopped fresh thyme

Kosher salt

Freshly ground pepper

2 tablespoons olive oil

1 tablespoon plus 1 teaspoon finely chopped fresh chives

Preheat the oven to 500°F. Put a pizza stone in the oven if you have one.

Roll each ball of dough into an 8-inch round. Lay them on a baking sheet or a floured baking peel. Distribute the pear slices evenly on each round. Sprinkle the cheese over the pears. Follow with the walnuts, thyme, and salt and pepper to taste (the cheese is salty, so be conservative with the salt). Brush the edges of the crust with olive oil.

If using a pizza stone and baking peel: Put the pizzettas on the peel and slide them onto the pizza stone. Cook for 8 minutes or until the dough is golden and the cheese begins to look creamy.

If you are not using a stone and peel, put the pizzettas on a baking sheet but cook them about 2 to 3 minutes longer.

Remove from the oven and garnish with the chives. Serve right away.

Serves 6 as an appetizer

À CÔTÉ'S PIZZA DOUGH

This is a fantastic, all-around pizza dough, but bear in mind that it takes about five hours prep time, so plan ahead—it is best to make the dough the day before. That way all you have to do is roll it out when you're ready. This recipe makes enough dough for four pizzettas, even though the preceding recipe makes two, using two balls of dough. Save the remaining dough for another time or double the topping ingredients to make four pizzettas. See note below about freezing the dough.

---

1   packet (.25-ounce) dry
    active yeast
1   tablespoon sugar
1¼ cups whole milk

3   to 3½ cups bread flour
1   tablespoon salt
2   tablespoons olive oil

Oil a large bowl, preferably ceramic, and set aside.

Fit a stand mixer with a dough hook. Place the yeast and sugar in the mixing bowl. Heat the milk just until it begins to feel warm (it should feel like warm bath water). Add the milk to the yeast mixture, stir, and let proof until very foamy, about 10 minutes.

Add 3 cups flour, salt, and oil, and mix until the dough forms a very loose ball around the hook, about 5 minutes. The dough should be soft but not too sticky. If necessary, add more flour until the dough is a little tighter, keeping in mind that you want to do this slowly so that the dough does not get tough. It should form around the hook loosely with about ¾ of the dough wrapped around the hook and the rest on the bottom of the bowl.

Knead the dough in the mixer for 5 minutes. Transfer to the prepared bowl. Turn the dough to coat with oil and cover with plastic wrap or a thin towel. Let rise for 1 hour.

Meanwhile, prepare a sheet pan with parchment paper sprinkled liberally with flour. Punch the dough down and divide it into four 8-ounce balls. Place the balls of dough on the baking sheet, wrap in plastic wrap, and let proof in the refrigerator for at least 4 hours or overnight.

Makes dough for 4 pizzettas

Note: If you don't plan to use all the dough at once, you can freeze the balls of dough after you shape them. Defrost overnight in the refrigerator to thaw and rise.

WALNUT-AVOCADO SALAD
WITH FOURME D'AMBERT

Years ago, I was dining at the hugely popular Aspen, Colorado, restaurant called The Wild Fig. Their signature salad at the time featured figs, walnuts, green beans, and cumin dressing. While no longer on the menu, that salad has remained at the top of my favorites list ever since. This recipe is my adaptation of that dish. I did not include figs in mine, but I did add blue cheese, which I found a surprising fit with the cumin in the dressing. Not only does this salad have wonderful flavors, it is also quite lovely looking because of the different shades and shapes of green that come from the avocado, beans, and lettuce. The ivory-colored cheese pops like a flash of light, not to mention a burst of flavor.

1 teaspoon kosher or coarse sea salt

½ pound haricot verts (or use regular green beans), ends trimmed

For the dressing

1 small shallot, finely diced

¼ cup white wine vinegar

2 tablespoons balsamic vinegar

¾ teaspoon ground cumin

¾ teaspoon Kosher or coarse sea salt

½ teaspoon freshly ground pepper

½ cup olive oil

2 heads butter lettuce, torn into bite-size pieces

½ cup coarsely chopped walnuts, toasted

1 medium avocado, cut into ¼-inch dice

1 large navel orange (about ½ pound), peeled, sectioned and each section cut in half

3 ounces Fourme d'Ambert cheese, coarsely crumbled (or use Maytag Blue, Stilton, or Gorgonzola piccante)

Bring 1 quart of water and the salt to a boil in a medium-size saucepan. Add the green beans and cook for 4 minutes, or just until they are cooked but still have some crunch left in them. Drain immediately and set aside to cool. (Can be prepared 1 hour ahead and kept at room temperature or up to 8 hours refrigerated in a dry towel).

To make the dressing: Combine the shallot, vinegars, cumin, salt, and pepper and mix well. Let sit for 5 minutes.

Slowly add the oil and whisk vigorously until well incorporated. (Can be made 1 day ahead and refrigerated.)

To assemble the salad: Toss the lettuce, beans, walnuts, and orange slices with the dressing. Add the avocado and mix gently. Distribute onto salad plates and top each salad with the cheese. Give each salad a twist of black pepper on top of the cheese and serve.

Serves 6

CRISPY CHICKEN WITH CRATER LAKE BLUE CHEESE AND SPINACH

Crater Lake Blue Cheese is made by Rogue Creamery in Central Point, Oregon, a creamery that has been around since the 1930s. The creamery got new life in the 1990s when partners Cary Bryant and David Gremmels bought it from the venerable cheesemaker, Ig Vella, who remains a contributing partner. Rogue Creamery blue cheeses are unquestionably among this nation's best, and the Crater Lake Blue, robust yet perfectly balanced, is a great cooking or stand-alone cheese. Paired with chicken and spinach as it is in this dish, the cheese struts its stuff beautifully while not overpowering any of the other elements.

Panko, or Japanese bread crumbs, can be found in Asian markets and in most supermarkets. I like them because they're especially crunchy. If you cannot find them, substitute coarse, toasted bread crumbs.

¾ cup apple juice (or use water)

½ cup currants

¼ cup olive oil

1 large clove garlic, sliced paper thin crosswise

1 pound spinach, washed, and patted dry (let a little water cling to the leaves)

2¾ teaspoons kosher or coarse sea salt

¼ teaspoon crushed red pepper flakes

1 cup Japanese panko (or use corn flake crumbs)

¼ cup finely grated American Parmesan, Asiago, or Dry Jack cheese

1 teaspoon freshly ground pepper

2 eggs, beaten

4 boneless, skinless chicken breast halves (about 2 pounds) pounded slightly to a ½-inch thickness

2 tablespoons unsalted butter

6 ounces Crater Lake Blue cheese, crumbled and divided (or use Original Blue or other tangy and creamy blue cheese)

Preheat the oven to 400°F.

In a small saucepan, heat the apple juice until almost boiling. Place the currants in a small heat-proof bowl. Pour the apple juice over them. Let sit for 20 minutes, then drain. Set aside.

In a large sauté pan, heat 2 tablespoons of the oil over medium heat.

Add the garlic and cook for 1 minute, stirring constantly. Add the spinach and cover. Cook for 3 minutes, or just until the leaves begin to turn a vibrant shade of green but are not quite cooked through. Uncover and turn off heat. (The spinach will continue to cook after the heat has been turned off.) Add ¾ teaspoon of the salt, red pepper flakes, and half of the currants. Toss gently (tongs work well), and set aside.

To prepare the chicken: Mix together the panko, Parmesan cheese, remaining 2 teaspoons of the salt, and ½ teaspoon pepper. Transfer the mixture to a flat plate. Put the beaten eggs in a shallow bowl. Have a large plate ready. Dip the chicken breasts into the eggs and then coat with the bread crumb mixture. Put them on the plate.

Line a large baking sheet with paper towels.

In a large sauté pan, heat the oil and butter together over medium-high heat, until the butter begins to bubble. Sauté the chicken breasts for 5 minutes on one side, or until the undersides are crispy and brown. Turn and cook 4 to 5 minutes more, or until the other side is also crispy and brown and the chicken is cooked through. Transfer to the paper towel-lined baking sheet to drain. Remove the paper towels and discard.

Sprinkle two-thirds of the blue cheese on top of the chicken. Bake for 5 minutes, or until the cheese has melted.

Warm the spinach on medium-high heat for 2 minutes. Distribute the spinach among 4 dinner plates. Sprinkle with remaining blue cheese. Place the chicken on top of the spinach, sprinkle with remaining currants, and serve right away.

Serves 4

PEPPERCORN-CRUSTED RIB-EYE STEAKS WITH BLUE CHEESE-CHIVE BUTTER

The combination of blue cheese and a good steak results in classic comfort food. In this case, the addition of peppercorns takes the idea behind another classic steak dish, steak au poivre, and combines it with the creamy but pungent blue cheese butter that soothes the spiciness. The addition of chives makes it seem like all-in-one steak house fare. All you need is the baked potato.

4 tablespoons (½ stick) unsalted butter, at room temperature	¼ cup black peppercorns
2 ounces creamy-style blue cheese, such as Gorgonzola, Amablu, Ewe's Blue, or Roquefort, at room temperature	4 boneless rib-eye steaks, 10 to 12 ounces each, at room temperature
2 tablespoons finely chopped chives	Salt

Using an electric mixer or wooden spoon, mix together the butter, cheese, and chives. Place the mixture on a large piece of plastic wrap about 14 inches long. Bring the long sides of the plastic wrap together and fold inward toward the butter mixture. Gently roll the butter mixture into a log about 6 inches long and 1½ inches in diameter. Twist the sides tightly against the ends of the log and refrigerate until firm, at least 1 hour or overnight.

Put the peppercorns in a large resealable plastic bag. Place the bag on a large cutting board (to preserve your countertop). Using the bottom of a heavy-bottomed skillet or a meat mallet, pound the bag to coarsely crack the peppercorns. (Alternatively, you can crack the pepper with two or three pulses in a spice grinder or mini-prep food processor. Just be sure not to grind the pepper too fine.) Pour the cracked pepper onto a large plate.

Gently press both sides of each steak into the peppercorns. Generously salt the steaks and set aside while you prepare the pans. (You can prepare the steaks to this point up to 6 hours ahead. Cover and refrigerate. Bring to room temperature before proceeding.)

Remove the butter log from refrigerator and cut into ¼-inch slices. Set aside.

Heat two large cast-iron skillets over high heat for 5 minutes. If you don't have cast-iron skillets, use two large lightly oiled sauté pans. Do not use nonstick pans. If you have just one skillet or sauté pan, cook the first 2 steaks about 2 minutes less. Keep the cooked steaks warm in a low oven while you cook the rest.

Put two steaks in each pan, being careful not to crowd them. Otherwise they will steam and prevent the crisp crust from forming. Cook for 5 to 6 minutes or until the bottom edges begin to brown. Turn and cook 4 to 5 more minutes for medium rare. Do not turn steaks again as they will lose some of their juices and become dry.

Transfer the steaks to a platter and top each one with two pats of blue cheese butter. Let sit for 5 minutes and serve.

Serves 4

Rogue Creamery Rogue River Blue rests on a piece of classic English Stilton

FRANGELICO FIGS WITH CREAMY BLUE CHEESE

Frangelico is a hazelnut liqueur that is not cloyingly sweet despite the fact it is a dessert liqueur. Its flavors marry beautifully with the salty, creamy blue cheese. The figs add a silky texture as well as their legendary natural sweetness, making this a cheese dessert that is simple but decidedly elegant. Because it takes just a few minutes to make, it will likely become one of your stand-by desserts whenever figs are in season. Note: If you cannot get fresh figs, use dried Mission or Calimyrna figs. Because they are dried they will take a few minutes longer to cook, but their sweetness will come through.

1　cup Frangelico or other hazelnut liqueur

8　fresh figs, preferably Mission or Brown Turkey, stems removed, cut in half lengthwise

8　ounces Montbriac cheese, at room temperature, cut into 8 equal pieces (or use Cambozola, Le Petit Bleu, Saga Blue, or Brie)

¾　cup hazelnuts, toasted and coarsely chopped

In a saucepan just large enough to hold the figs in one layer, bring the Frangelico to a boil, then turn the heat to medium-low. Add the figs, cut side down, and cook for 5 minutes, or until they begin to feel soft but not squishy. Drain the figs, reserving the liquid, and place 2 figs on each of 4 individual plates cut side up. Top the figs with the cheese right away. (This ensures that the cheese will begin to melt.)

Meanwhile, put the liquid back into the pan over a high heat. Reduce the liqueur until it is a syrupy consistency, 1 to 2 minutes. Watch carefully to make sure it doesn't burn. Sprinkle the hazelnuts on top of the figs and drizzle the syrup over them. Serve right away.

Serves 4

Clockwise from top: Durrus, Livarot,
Cowgirl Creamery Red Hawk

CHAPTER 9

WASHED-RIND

CHEESES

USE WASHED-RIND CHEESES FOR

- Entertaining
- Gratins
- Casseroles
- Eggs
- Fondue
- Grilled cheese sandwiches
- Polenta
- Pasta
- Risotto
- Vegetables

WHAT ARE THEY?

Belgium
Chimay

Canada
Oka
Sir Laurier d'Arthabaska

Denmark
Esrom

France
Abondance (*See also* semi-hard cheeses)
Affedelice
Beaufort (*See also* semi-hard cheeses)
Bethmale (goat's milk cheese)
Chaumes
Epoisses
L'Edel de Cleron (*See also* soft-ripened cheeses)
Livarot
Mariolles
Morbier
Munster
Pont l'Evêque
Port-Salut (*See also* semi-soft cheeses)
Raclette
Reblochon
Tête de Moine
Tomme du Berger
Vacherin Mont d'Or

Germany
Butterkäse
Limburger
Schlosskäse
Tilsiter

Ireland
Gubbeen

Italy
Bierkäse
Brescianella
Brescianella Stagionato
Taleggio

Spain
Urgelia

Switzerland
Appenzeller (*See also* semi-hard cheeses)
Raclette
Tilsiter
Vacherin Fribourgeois (*See also* semi-hard cheeses)

United States
Wisconsin
Brick (*See also* semi-soft cheeses)
Butterkäse (*See also* semi-soft cheeses)
Limburger

OFF THE BEATEN PATH

England
Stinking Bishop

France
Chaubier (cow and goat's milk)
L'Ami du Chambertin
Langres
Soumatrain

Italy

Robiola di Valsassina

United States

California

Cowgirl Creamery: Red Hawk

Marin French Cheese Company: Schloss, Schlosskranz-Herz

Colorado

Haystack Mountain Goat Dairy: Red Cloud, Snowdrop (goat's milk)

MouCo Cheese Company: Colorouge

Connecticut

Cato Corner Farm: Hooligan

Indiana

Capriole Goat Cheese: Mont St. Francis (goat's milk)

Michigan

Leelanau Cheese Company: Raclette (*See also* semi-hard cheeses)

North Carolina

Goat Lady Dairy: Gray's Chapel, Providence (goat's milk)

Texas

Mozzarella Company: Blanca Bianca

Vermont

Dancing Cow Farm: Bourrée, Sarabande

Green Mountain Blue Cheese: Brother Laurent

Jasper Hill Farms: Winnimere

Twig Farm: Twig Wheel (goat and cow's milk)

Virginia

Meadow Creek Dairy: Grayson

 You know it's a washed-rind cheese when . . .

- It has an orange, pinkish, reddish, or orangish-brown rind

- It is semi-soft, creamy, and often spoonable

- It smells like dirty gym socks, the barnyard, or worse (and that's a *good* thing)

- It is generally in small wheels or squares

- It is in the refrigerated section of the cheese store rather than on the countertop

- It feels tacky or sticky when you touch the surface

- It is saltier than most other cheeses

OR

- It is a large wheel (9 to 10 pounds or more)

- It has a brownish rind tinged with pink or orange

- It is semi-hard

The Explanation

Technically there are two subcategories of washed-rind cheeses, but one comprises the bulk of cheeses in the category and is the one most cheesemongers refer to when they say "washed-rind." These are the creamy, small-format (about 4 ounces to 3 pounds) cheeses that sport orange, pinkish, reddish, or orangish-tan rinds (or some variation). The other subcategory of washed-rind cheeses is quite different from the former in that it is comprised of large (9- to-10 pound), aged cheeses. These include France's Beaufort, Abondance, raclette, Comté, Swiss Gruyère, America's Pleasant Ridge Reserve and Tarentaise among others. These cheeses are usually rubbed and/or washed with a saltwater-bacteria solution during the aging process, which encourages the growth of certain bacteria and the characteristic "multi-hued" rind, but because they are aged several months and their texture is semi-hard, they are rarely referred to as washed-rind cheeses. Therefore, for the purposes of this chapter, I will be mostly referring to the creamy style of washed-rind cheeses, not the semi-hard ones.

 What's in a Name?

In this country, we have a much-loved cheese called Muenster. It is modeled after a cheese that was created during medieval times by the monasteries in the Alsace region of France and in Germany. In fact, the word Muenster comes from the Latin word, *monasterium*.

However, the Muenster produced in this country and whose name stems from the German spelling (Alsatian Munster is spelled without an "e" after the "u"), is completely different than the European versions. Here, the cheese is typically made in a loaf shape and is rather bland in flavor and aroma. Also, instead of being produced like an authentic washed-rind cheese, it is made to look like one by being brushed with paprika or with a harmless orange dye. Its chief attribute is that it is a great melting cheese.

In Europe, the wheel-shaped munster cheese is very strong–stinky in fact–but it is one of the best tasting washed-rind cheeses produced. While it has an unmistakable gym socks smell, the creamy texture and meaty flavors are far more seductive than the aroma is dissuasive.

Regardless of the type of Muenster/Munster you prefer, just remember that while they may share the name, that's where the similarity begins and ends. If you buy the Alsatian version assuming it is similar to the American one, you'll be in for the type of surprise you probably will *not* appreciate.

To create a soft, creamy-style washed-rind cheese, it is necessary to keep the curds larger than for aged or harder-style cheeses. The larger curd size retains the moisture, which helps create the creaminess. Washed-rind cheeses are drained of their whey only through gravity, not with the use of presses as some semi-soft and most semi-hard cheeses are. This aids in the retention of moisture and, in some cases, creates a texture with a smattering of small eyes.

The biggest distinction between washed-rind cheese and all other cheese is that, as the name implies, it is literally washed during the ripening process. The washing is done with a saltwater solution, but cheesemakers and *affineurs* (cheese agers) often strive for certain flavors and textures that come from a particular wash solution with which they will finish the cheese. For example, in the case of Epoisses, a brandy called marc de Bourgogne made from the "leftovers"(skins and seeds) from white wine making is rubbed on the cheese shortly before sending the cheese to market. The resulting cheese does not taste like wine, but the brandy creates certain beneficial bacterial processes that positively affect the flavor and texture of this heralded cheese.

The washing solution itself, however, is not in and of itself the reason that certain flavors and aromas and colors are conferred to washed-rind cheeses. The "mystery ingredient" in washed-rind cheeses is bacteria known as *Brevibacteria linens* or *B. linens*, as they're usually called. Sometimes the bacteria are in the air, but usually they are introduced into the brine solution and/or the aging room so as to maintain controlled *B. linens* activity, at least at first. These *B. linens* act as protectors of the cheese by preventing bad molds from infiltrating the cheese while allowing the good molds and bacteria to ripen the cheese. Equally important, the *B. linens* create the distinctive color on the surface of washed-rind cheeses. And yes, they also create the strong aromas that almost always accompany this style.

Whether made from cow, sheep, or goat's milk, a washed-rind cheese will always share the characteristic tan, orange- or pink-colored rind, creamy texture, small eyes in the paste (except for the ones with soupy textures like Epoisses), and fairly pungent aroma. Another common characteristic among washed-rind cheeses is saltiness. While not all are terrifically salty, the salt is unquestionably a hallmark of this style of cheese because of the brine. On average, washed-rind cheeses are aged anywhere from about three weeks to two months, during which time they develop a range of flavors including nutty, beefy, and mushroomy, among others.

Perhaps the best-known washed-rind cheeses are Taleggio, Epoisses, Munster, and Red Hawk from Cowgirl Creamery in California. There are many others, and because of their growing popularity in this country, new ones are being introduced every day.

Smear-Ripened: The Story of Brick Cheese

An American original, brick cheese is an example of what is known as a smear-ripened cheese, which is a relative of washed-rind cheese. Invented in the 1800s by a Swiss teen named Joe Jossi who ran his family's Limburger factory, brick was created as a milder alternative to the pungent Limburger that he and his family also produced. In fact, when brick was first created, it was referred to as the "married man's Limburger" because of its relative mildness. (Limburger is still made at the same factory, known as Chalet Cheese Co-Op in Monroe, Wisconsin, and is the only producer of Limburger in the country. Although invented in Limburg, Belgium, Limburger is produced primarily in Germany today.)

Brick starts out like many other washed-rind cheeses in that it is dipped in a brine and *B. linens* solution. But that is where the similarity begins and ends. The cheese curds are put in brick-shaped molds and pressed with bricks to extract the whey. Not only is this method unique, it is also unusual in the family of washed-rind cheeses because most are not pressed. Once brick goes into the aging room, it is constantly rubbed with a smelly solution of whey and brine. The longer it is aged, the stinkier it becomes. Young brick, however, is extremely mild and because of that, makes a great cooking or sandwich cheese. The more aged version is a terrific addition to a cheese board.

Traditional brick cheese is still made exclusively in Wisconsin. Among the producers are Widmer Cheese Cellars and the previously mentioned Chalet Cheese Cooperative. Joe Widmer is a third-generation cheesemaker whose Swiss grandfather started making brick around the turn of the 20th century in Theresa, Wisconsin. Joe has continued the tradition by adhering to the original methods of making brick cheese and doing so almost entirely by hand.

Ask most Wisconsinites and they will tell you that aged brick cheese (read: strong) is best served with pumpernickel bread, mustard and raw(!) onions. Alongside you will usually find a pale ale or dark beer or sometimes apple cider. Limburger is served the same way.

The Bottom Line

The large curd size, the relatively short aging period, and the constant washing of the rind adds up to creamy, aromatic cheeses in the main category of washed-rind cheeses. The subcategory within the washed-rind cheese family is those cheeses whose paste is firmer, like a semi-hard cheese, but whose aromas and pinkish or orange-tan rinds indicate they have gone through a washed-rind process. (Note: You may also see washed-rind cheeses referred to as mold-ripened, surface-ripened [not to be confused with the style], or smear-ripened cheeses.)

What to Look for When Buying Washed-Rind Cheeses

The spectrum of washed-rind cheeses practically looks like a box of Crayola crayons, or at least those on the warm-color side.

Visual Cues

- Pale pink, darker pink, tan, light orange, or bright orange
- Might have stripes or striations and natural white mold interspersed with tan or light orange colors as in Livarot, Pont-l'Evêque, Reblochon, and Brescianella
- Possible specks of mold, but rind should be mostly mold-free

- Cut surfaces should be free of visible white mold
- Rind should be fairly smooth with few to no cracks or dry areas
- May be saggy, but that is because of the semi-soft texture
- Square or small (4- to 8-ounce) wheel

Textural Cues

The creamiest styles of washed-rind cheeses are usually packaged in wooden boxes because they are so delicate. As a result, you can't touch them and have to rely on how they look and smell to determine if you want them.

- Creamy, often oozy, bursting at the seams
- Should give readily when gently pressed in the middle
- Might be saggy, but paste should still be smooth-looking, not dried out
- Surface is tacky or sticky

- Surface might look a little like sandpaper—slightly gritty and tan-colored with hints of orange or pink peeking through (think Taleggio)
- Paste will be creamy and will usually have tiny eyes

Aroma Cues

The cheese may smell very strong, perhaps even offensive (think old gym socks), but it should not smell of ammonia.

- Barnyardy
- Beefy
- Mushroomy

- Toasted nuts
- Truffly

Washed-rind cheeses will usually taste milder than they smell. If you avoid the rind these cheeses will taste milder.

• Barnyardy	• Gym socks(!)	• Tart
• Beefy	• Milky	• Truffles
• Buttery	• Mushroomy	• Yeasty
• Earthy	• Nutty	
• Gamy	• Salty	

MOUTHFEEL

The creamy style naturally has a creamy mouthfeel. These cheeses linger on your tongue and the roof of your mouth. They're not sticky, just mouth-filling.

FINISH

The best of the washed-rind cheeses have a long and languorous finish. These cheeses may start out mild and get increasingly more pronounced, or they may start out fairly strong and remain that way. Either way, they are likely to leave a lasting memory, both in terms of flavor and in your experience of tasting these never-boring cheeses.

A FEW NOTEWORTHY WASHED-RIND CHEESES

BELGIUM

Chimay Grand Cru

A cheese developed by Trappist monks in the Chimay area of Belgium, this mild yet delicious cheese is washed with either the beer of the region, Chimay (developed by the same order of monks), or a simple saltwater solution. The former is called Chimay Trappiste with Beer. The cheese is creamy, has obvious but not too much salt, and a fantastic crunchy exterior owing to the aging process. Although technically a washed-rind cheese, Chimay is milder than most other washed-rind cheeses and is an all-around pleasing, easy-to-eat cheese.

FRANCE

Vacherin Mont d'Or
It is lucky that this cheese comes along in winter because it can light up a holiday table all on its own. No other food needed. The spruce bark-wrapped oozing gem is made in the area known as Franche-Comté not far from the Swiss border. In fact, the term Vacherin Mont d'Or has been a source of confusion since the name was used to identify the same cheese made by the Swiss. As a result, the French cheese also goes by the name Vacherin du Haut-Doubs. The cheese is traditionally made with raw milk, and surely isn't a day over two months when it is sold. Because of the bark that encircles it, the cheese tastes a bit smoky, and the paste is like nut-studded vanilla ice cream. It isn't sweet, but it has that milky, creamy quality. Because it is a washed-rind cheese, Vacherin Mont d'Or can also have a faintly gamy aroma, although the cheese itself is usually tame.

IRELAND

Gubbeen
Located in County Cork in west Ireland, Gubbeen—the name of the farm and of the cheese that is made there—is the Gaelic word for "small mouthful." This refers to the bay on which the farm is situated. Owners Tom and Giana Ferguson make the cheese with milk from their own herd of cows, which is made up of different breeds. The pasteurized milk cheese is made from the morning milk, and once the cheese goes into the aging room, it is washed daily with a brine solution until it is sent to market. The result is a golden-colored semi-soft cheese with absolutely lovely milky and somewhat musty flavors. There are several other washed-rind cheeses made in Ireland (Ardrahan and Durrus are two others), and they are all excellent.

ITALY

Brescianella Stagionata
There are two primary square-shaped washed-rind Lombardian (northern Italy) cheeses—Taleggio and the smaller Brascianella. There are others, but they are more rare. Although Brascianella isn't as widely distributed as its Lombardian cousin, it is available in many cheese shops and Italian delicatessens. As you know, the word *stagionata* means aged, and when the word follows Brascianella, it tells you you're in for a great cheese. Like many other washed-rind cheeses, Brascianella Stagionata has a pinkish-orange rind and fairly strong aroma. It parts

ways with other washed-rind cheeses, though, when you taste it. For one, it is a little mellower. In fact, whenever I present this cheese in seminars, it is invariably one of the favorites even among those who are usually thumbs-down on washed-rind cheeses. Its creamy texture, which is inherent to the *stagionata* version, and yeasty and beefy flavors are instantly appealing.

SPAIN

Urgelia

I don't know which is more seductive about Urgelia—the crunchy rind or the silky texture of the paste. Or maybe it is the combination of the two. All I know is that this slightly salty, relatively mild washed-rind cheese is easy to fall in love with. Thank goodness its commercial name is easy to pronounce (er-HAIL-ya) because this cheese's full name, L'Alt Urgell y la Cerdanya, which refers to its provenance in the Pyrenees in the northwest part of Catalonia, is a mouthful. Urgelia is pasteurized, pressed, and brined before being aged for at least six weeks. During the aging period, the cheese is exposed to the special bacteria known as *Brevabacteria linens*, which confer flavor and the signature orange color to the rind. Urgelia is almost impossible to eat in small quantities and is equally at home on a cheese board and in the kitchen. It is an excellent cooking cheese because of its beautiful melting properties and assertive yet balanced flavor.

UNITED STATES

Michigan

Leelanau Cheese Company: Raclette

When they were making raclette in the Swiss Alps, Anne and John Hoyt may not have been planning to do so in the United States, but today their raclette is making the American cheese landscape infinitely richer. The Hoyts are the owners/cheesemakers of the Leelanau Cheese Company at Black Star Farms on Michigan's northern lower peninsula. They make just one cheese. A blue ribbon winner at the American Cheese Society annual competition in 2006, the Hoyts' is unequivocally the best raclette in this country and quite possibly anywhere. They make the pasteurized milk cheese throughout the year from the milk from just one farm. The labor-intensive cheese is made in nine-pound wheels and is aged from four to nine months. The longer-aged version tastes like nuts drizzled with browned butter and the young milder version is a perfect melting cheese, just the way raclette is intended to be eaten.

The word raclette comes from the French verb "*racler*," which means "to scrape" and refers to both the cheese and the dish with the same name. For that dish, half-wheels of raclette are held close to a fire or other heat source to melt the surface. The runny cheese is then quickly scraped onto a plate for eating with the typical accompaniments of cornichons, potatoes, and other vegetables. No matter how you slice it, the Leelanau Cheese Company's raclette is a cheese worth eating at any stage of ripeness.

Dancing Cow Farmstead Cheese: Sarabande

When Matt Jennings, co-owner of the excellent cheese shop called Farmstead in Providence, Rhode Island, asked if he could send me a new cheese that he was certain would knock my socks off, naturally I said yes. It is rare when I am introduced to a cheese that makes me lose my breath, but the cheese Matt sent me, Sarabande, is one such cheese. Made with the milk from grazing cows on Dancing Cow Farm in Bridport, Vermont, this unpasteurized milk cheese is remarkable for its flavor, texture, and the innovation it represents.

Owners Karen and Steve Getz are relatively new to dairying and even newer to cheesemaking, having sold their first cheese in 2006, but their love of good food and responsible land management clearly informs their cheese.

Sarabande, named after a Baroque-period Spanish dance (appropriately enough, all the names of the Dancing Cow cheeses have a dance theme), is unusual in a number of ways. For one, the pyramid-shaped molds in which the cheese is shaped are usually reserved for goat's milk cheeses, not cow's milk. Also unusual is that a cheese like this is typically made with pasteurized milk in the United States because it is challenging to age such a small, delicate cheese for the sixty- day time period legally required for raw milk cheeses. But the Getzes, along with their business partner, Jeanne Finnerty, with whom Karen shares cheesemaking duties, have somehow figured out how to do it. The result is a cheese with a slightly tacky yet crunchy, burnt-orange colored rind and a creamy golden-colored paste that tastes of grass, nuts, and caramel. The aroma is nutty, toasty, and a bit beefy. As I told Matt and Karen after tasting the cheese, it is the "velvet glove" of cheese — voluptuous and powerful. And delicious.

Meadow Creek Dairy: Grayson

To make a superior washed-rind cheese takes perseverance and unyielding dedication. Grayson is the result of both those qualities. Cheesemaker Helen Feete and her husband Rick, of Meadow Creek Dairy in Galax, Virginia, worked for years to get Grayson just right. Consider it done. The raw Jersey milk cheese looks like Taleggio but has its own unique sweet, nutty, beefy, and brown butter flavors. The texture is semi-soft, a bit springy rather than completely oozy, and is excellent on its own, perhaps with a few toasted walnuts, or as the star ingredient of a gourmet fondue. Because the Feetes are steadfast custodians of the land, they practice rotational grazing with their Jerseys. This means the cows graze on pasture until they are moved (rotated) to another part of the farm to allow the grass they have just grazed to grow back. The land, the cows, and those of us who eat the cheese made from their milk are the beneficiaries.

 If you can't find

Epoisses, use **Affidelice, l'Ami du Chambertin**, or **Rocchetta**

Gubbeen, use **Reblochon, St. Nectaire**, or **Oka**

Grayson, use **Taleggio, Pont l'Evêque, Munster**, or **Teleme**

Reblochon, use **Taleggio, Red Hawk**, or **Camembert**

Winnimere, use **Vacherin Mont d'Or, l'Edel de Cleron**, or **Epoisses**

Grayson

STORING WASHED-RIND CHEESES

The longer you keep a washed-rind cheese, the more pungent it will become. But don't be too quick to throw it away. Instead, cut away the rind, let the cheese sit out for a half hour or so, and try it again. It will still be fairly strong, but some of the flavors and aromas you may have found too pungent will have dissipated.

To store the creamy style of washed-rind cheese, put the unwrapped cheese in a plastic container, poke a few holes in it, and snap the lid on. If you don't have a plastic container, then wrap the cheese in waxed paper followed by plastic wrap. You want to be sure that the cheese can breathe a little because it will deteriorate very quickly otherwise. Store in the drawer of the refrigerator.

 Washed-Rind Cheese and Wine Pairing ☆☆☆

Because washed-rind cheeses are often salty and pungent, their wine partners are a little harder to find. Still, there are some very good pairings if you think beyond some of the wines you are most familiar with. For white wines you might consider an Austrian Grüner Veltliner, French Aligoté, or a Spanish Verdejo. If you cannot get these, then think floral yet dry—a German Riesling or an Oregon or Alsatian Pinot Gris. The stronger the cheese, the more floral you want your wine. That's why in Alsace, where Munster comes from, the typical wine pairing is either the local Pinot Gris, Gewürztraminer, or Riesling.

A word about Chardonnay and washed-rind cheeses: In general, the richness of Chardonnays makes them fine matches for washed-rind cheeses, particularly those from France. However, you are best off staying away from oaky Chardonnay. Instead, French Chablis, Macon, or St. Veran make nice choices as do lightly oaked California Chardonnays such as Saintsbury and J. Lohr.

If you're looking for a red wine to pair, then you will have to take into account just how pungent your cheese is. If the cheese is on the strong side, stick with white wine. A red with lots of oak and tannins, such as Cabernet Sauvignon or Syrah, will taste just like oak and tannins and nothing more with a washed-rind cheese. A somewhat lighter yet fruity red wine, such as a California Pinot Noir or an Italian Lagrein (a grape from northeast Italy getting increasing recognition) are often good matches for washed-rind cheeses.

Finally, don't overlook sweet wines. Choose from the region where your cheese is made. If you've selected a Spanish cheese, then consider a sweeter-style sherry such as an amontillado or oloroso. In Italy, Moscato d'Asti is a terrific choice because of its slight effervescence and sweetness, while several of the French washed-rind cheeses will work with Alsatian Rieslings and Gewürztraminers, many of which have residual sugar, or sweetness.

TAKE-HOME TEST: GETTING TO KNOW WASHED-RIND CHEESES

Sometimes a way to remember the flavor characteristics of an unfamiliar food is to compare it with similar food that you *do* know. Washed-rind cheeses particularly lend themselves to this exercise because there are two common descriptions for most washed-rind cheeses: roasted nutlike and beefy.

For this assignment, I'm just going to concentrate on the nutty component. I decided that you could get a better handle on the flavor characteristics of a few washed-rind cheeses by doing side-by-side comparisons with certain nuts. While you may not remember which cheese tastes most like, say, walnuts when you're done with this, you will remember that this family of cheeses will more than likely have a roasted nut flavor of some type. I think you will also see that many of these cheeses do not taste nearly as strong as they smell. Many of the creamy styles of washed-rind cheeses are salty, though.

I have selected a few creamy washed-rind cheeses and a couple of semi-hard washed-rind cheeses too. Although they are very different in texture, you will see that they all share that roasted nut characteristic. I think it's very important to pay attention to texture, not just flavor. Not only is texture a huge component in your overall impression and enjoyment of cheese, it also helps you remember your cheeses. Think about it. Washed-rind cheeses are semi-soft or creamy, some of them have a little crunch in the rind, and some are a little sticky. Those are all textural descriptions and yet they are integral to knowing what a washed-rind cheese is all about.

THE ASSIGNMENT

Buy

2 to 4 ounces Fontina d'Aosta cheese (or use the highest quality raclette, preferably French; do not subsitute another type of Fontina for this as the substitutes do not have the same flavor attributes. If you can't find one of these two cheeses, then skip this part of the exercise. Your grade will not be lowered).

- 2 to 4 ounces Comtè cheese (or use Gruyère)
- 2 to 4 ounces Taleggio cheese
- Half or whole wheel of Epoisses cheese (you'll have some left over, or use Affidelice, l'Ami du Chambertin, ripe Red Hawk, or Soumatrain)
- 2 tablespoons hazelnuts, lightly toasted
- 2 tablespoons pistachio nuts, lightly toasted
- 2 tablespoons walnuts, lightly toasted
- 2 tablespoons almonds (with skins), lightly toasted

1) Start with the Fontina d'Aosta. Take a taste of the cheese without the rind. Now taste just half a hazelnut. (Hazelnuts are full-flavored nuts, so for the purposes of this exercise it's best to go easy.) Now go back to the cheese. Notice any flavor similarities between the cheese and the nut? Fontina d'Aosta has dominant hazelnut characteristics, which is why the cheese and the nut taste similar. Texturally, of course, they are almost opposite, as is the case with all cheese and nut comparisons. In some ways, though, it is that contrast that helps get you in closer touch with the texture of the cheese—the crunchiness of the nut accentuates the creaminess or firmness of the cheese, depending which style of washed-rind cheese you're tasting.

Now try a taste of the cheese with the rind. Although I wouldn't necessarily recommend eating the rind of Fontina d'Aosta because it makes the cheese taste bitter, it is educational because you will see how much stronger the cheese tastes with the rind. A bite of hazelnut mitigates its strength a little, although for some people, that stronger flavor is a favorable attribute. Let's move on.

2) Take a taste of Comté without the rind. Now eat a pistachio. Once again, notice the similarity in flavor (and contrasting texture) between the cheese and nut. Whereas hazelnuts have a stronger, almost butterscotch-like flavor, pistachios are much more buttery. The combination of the buttery and of course nutty quality brings out those two dominant characteristics of the Comté.

3) Now do a matchup with Taleggio and the walnuts. Taste the Taleggio without the rind. Pay attention to the flavors that continue after you have swallowed the cheese. Although texturally you will notice a creamy sensation in your mouth, the lingering flavors you may taste will be a little like walnut bread —somewhat earthy with a slightly sour note. Now taste a walnut. The walnut will probably be more full-flavored than the Taleggio, but the similarity in flavor characteristics is unmistakable. Now try the cheese *with* the rind. You will notice a significant textural contrast between the two. The rind might have a crunchy quality, and compared with the paste, could taste slightly bitter though not overpoweringly so. Try another walnut. Notice how together with the rind, the cheese and walnuts harmonize with one another?

4) Finally, pair the Epoisses and the almonds. To start, dig past the rind into the creamy center of the cheese. Take a small spoonful, avoiding the rind. Now try the nut. You may find that the nut is a bit overpowering for the creamy center, although it does mitigate some of the saltiness of the cheese. Now try the cheese with the rind followed by another almond. Just as with the rind of Taleggio together with walnuts, Epoisses meets the almond head-on. What's more, it demonstrates just how almondy Epoisses really is.

You can try this exercise again, only this time switch the cheese and nut combinations. You will find that the hazelnuts certainly taste good with Epoisses, but they also overwhelm it. Likewise, Epoisses tastes good with walnuts, but the creaminess of the cheese accentuates the bitterness in the skin of the walnuts. Does this mean you should only pair certain nuts with certain washed-rind cheeses? Definitely not. It just means that some pairings are more successful than others.

THE LESSON

Washed-rind cheeses, whether creamy or semi-hard, share nuttiness in common. In addition, their rinds mirror the bitterness found in the skins of nuts, which makes nuts all the better as a match because the bitter elements shared by the cheese and the nuts go a long way toward neutralizing one another.

I hope that a by-product of this assignment was that you experienced the phenomenon of washed-rind cheeses smelling stronger than they taste. Among this group of cheeses, you probably found that Epoisses was the strongest smelling and tasting. If that is not to your liking, then perhaps something like the delectable winter cheese Vacherin Mont d'Or will appeal to you more. Or, if that is still too strong, then go for a surface-ripened cheese like Rocchetta or La Tur. You'll love the mildness of these cheeses as well as their Epoisses-like silken texture.

Epoisses

PAIN D'ÉPICES AND EPOISSES

When my dear friend and fellow cookbook author Cheryl Jamison tasted this bread, she declared it the best-ever accompaniment for the regal Epoisses. Coming from someone who has spent a lot of time in Burgundy — the place where both Epoisses and *pain d'épices* originate — I thought that was quite an endorsement. Note: This bread is good the first day but is even better after a day or two when the flavors have had a chance to develop. For best storage, wrap in foil and then in plastic.

1 cup milk	¼ teaspoon salt
¾ cup packed brown sugar	1¼ teaspoons ground cinnamon
1 cup honey	¾ teaspoon anise seed
2 cups all-purpose flour	½ teaspoon ground ginger
1¼ cups whole wheat flour	¼ teaspoon nutmeg
2 teaspoons baking powder	2 large eggs, lightly beaten
½ teaspoon baking soda	1 wheel (about 9 ounces) Epoisses cheese, at room temperature

Preheat the oven to 400°F. Butter and lightly flour a 9 x 5 x 3-inch loaf pan.

In a medium-size saucepan, combine the milk, sugar, and honey, and bring to a boil. Immediately reduce heat to a simmer. Cook, stirring occasionally, until the sugar has melted and the mixture comes together, about 10 minutes. It will be a little clumpy. Let cool to lukewarm.

In a large mixing bowl, whisk together the flours, baking powder, baking soda, salt, and all of the spices. Make a well in the center. Pour a little of the milk and sugar mixture into the well, and using a wooden spoon, stir to incorporate the dry ingredients. Continue until the wet and dry ingredients are combined. Add the eggs and stir just until they are mixed in. The batter will be fairly thick. Pour the batter into the prepared pan.

Bake for 15 minutes, then reduce the oven temperature to 325°F. Continue baking until a toothpick inserted in the center of the bread comes out almost clean with just a few crumbs clinging, about 40 more minutes. (It's better to slightly undercook this bread as it keeps it from becoming overly dry.) Let cool for 30 minutes then turn the bread out onto a rack to continue cooling completely.

To serve, cut the bread into ½-inch slices. Or, you can toast it for a crisp texture. Serve with a whole wheel of Epoisses and a spoon.

Makes 1 loaf

POLENTA WITH ITALIAN CHEESE, POACHED EGGS, AND PROSCIUTTO

Every cuisine has its comfort foods, and a bowl of steaming polenta has got to be high on the comfort scale in Italian cuisine. Mixed with an aromatic creamy cheese like northern Italy's Brescianella and topped with a soft egg, the polenta becomes the foundation for a gourmet brunch dish or a unique and wonderful dinner. This is pure, unadulterated comfort food in any language.

2 cups low-sodium chicken stock

2 cups water

1 teaspoon salt

1 cup polenta

4 ounces Brescianella cheese, rind removed, coarsely chopped (or use Taleggio, Reblochon, or other washed-rind cheese; or use mozzarella)

1¼ teaspoons finely chopped fresh rosemary (or use ½ teaspoon dried and crumbled)

4 eggs

4 paper-thin slices (about 2 ounces) of prosciutto

Freshly ground pepper

Have 4 shallow serving bowls ready.

To make the polenta: In a saucepan, combine the chicken stock, water, and salt, and bring to a boil. Add the polenta in a steady stream, stir once or twice, cover, and turn heat to simmer. Let cook until all the liquid has been absorbed by the polenta, about 10 minutes. Add the cheese and rosemary and stir just until the cheese has mostly melted. Keep covered over very low heat.

Meanwhile, poach the eggs. Place a small container, such as a metal measuring cup next to the stove. In a 2-quart saucepan, bring about 1 quart water to a boil. Break each egg into the measuring cup and gently pour the egg into the water. Repeat with remaining eggs. Cook for 4 to 6 minutes, depending how you like your egg yolks. For a runny yolk, cook just 4 minutes. For a hard-cooked egg, cook about 6 minutes.

Working quickly, ladle the polenta into the bottom of each bowl. Using a slotted spoon, scoop up an egg and place it in the middle of the polenta. Drape a piece of prosciutto on the side of the egg, sprinkle with black pepper, and serve right away.

Serves 4

CHIMAY BREAD

Chimay is the name of both a cheese and an ale made in Belgium. Like many cheeses and beers, they have roots in the monastery, in this case, the Chimay monastery. When you see Chimay cheese, it might be labeled Grand Cru, Bière (or beer), or Grand Classic. My favorite is the Grand Cru because of its assertive yet sweet flavors, qualities that lend themselves particularly well to this easy-to-make bread. The use of the Red Chimay Ale is a natural in this classic beer bread recipe, but do be sure to use that or another fruity ale rather than the Chimay Blue or Chimay Triple, which can make the bread taste bitter.

---

3 cups self-rising flour

2 tablespoons sugar

5 ounces Grand Cru Chimay cheese, rind removed, coarsely grated (or use Chimay Grand

Classic, St. Nectaire, Oka, or cheddar)

12 ounces beer, preferably Red Chimay Ale (or use any fruity ale)

Preheat the oven to 350°F. Oil a 9 x 5-inch loaf pan. Set aside.

In a large bowl, mix together the flour and sugar. Add 4 ounces of the cheese (about 1¼ cups) and mix to coat. Add the beer and stir just until the dough comes together. Transfer the dough to the loaf pan, smooth it out and sprinkle with the remaining cheese.

Bake for 50 to 60 minutes, or until a toothpick or skewer inserted in the bread comes out clean. Let cool for at least 45 minutes. Slice and serve.

Makes 1 loaf

TALEGGIO AND MUSHROOM RISOTTO

Taleggio is the classic washed-rind cheese originally from the Lombardy region of Italy. Unlike some washed-rind cheeses, Taleggio is assertive but not overwhelmingly strong. It is square-shaped and starts off very mild, becoming stronger as it ages. The raw milk version of the cheese is much more flavorful, and I highly recommend that you seek it out. Whether raw or pasteurized, the earthy, nutty, and creamy qualities of the cheese matched by similar qualities in the mushrooms create a deliciously creamy and nutty risotto.

continued

1 ounce dried porcini mushrooms

1½ cups very hot water

½ pound brown or white mushrooms, stems trimmed, cut into ½-inch pieces

1 tablespoon olive oil

2 tablespoons finely chopped fresh thyme (or use 2 teaspoons dried)

About 8 cups low-sodium chicken stock

1 medium yellow onion, coarsely chopped

2 cups Arborio or Carnaroli rice

Salt

Freshly ground pepper

½ pound Taleggio cheese, rind removed, coarsely cut into small chunks (this is easiest when the cheese is cold); or use Brescianella or Reblochon

3 tablespoons unsalted butter

2 ounces Parmigiano-Reggiano, Grana Padano, or other hard cheese, finely grated

In a heat-proof bowl, soak the porcini in the water for 20 minutes, or until softened. Remove the mushrooms and squeeze the liquid back into the bowl. Rinse the mushrooms to remove grit. Strain the liquid through a coffee filter or paper towel-lined strainer into a large saucepan. Add the chicken broth and bring to a boil. Reduce the heat to medium-low and maintain a slow simmer.

In a large (4-quart) saucepan, warm the oil over medium-high heat. Add the onions and cook, stirring occasionally, until they are translucent, about 5 minutes. Do not let them brown. Add the porcini and fresh mushrooms and cook until the fresh mushrooms are soft and most of their liquid has cooked away, about 7 minutes. Add the rice and stir constantly until it begins to look slightly opaque around the edges, about 5 minutes.

Using a ladle or glass measuring cup, add about 1 cup of the hot stock mixture to the rice and stir vigorously. Once the rice has absorbed the liquid, add another cupful. Stir vigorously after each addition of stock. Continue adding stock just until the rice grains are opaque and firm but tender to the bite, 15 to 20 minutes. It may not take all of the stock or it could take more—it depends on the rice. If you need more liquid, add near-boiling water.

After the last ladleful of stock has been added, add a generous amount of salt and pepper. Mix well. Add the Taleggio, butter, and thyme and stir just until the cheese and butter have melted. Add half the grated cheese and stir to mix.

Divide the risotto among individual bowls or plates, sprinkle with the remaining grated cheese, and give a few twists of black pepper. Serve immediately.

Serves 6

GRAYSON AND ROASTED GARLIC PIZZA

The name of this pizza refers to a magnificent cheese made in Grayson County, Virginia, by Meadow Creek Dairy (see page 217 for more about Meadow Creek Dairy). Because the cheese can be a bit hard to come by, feel free to use one of the substitutes listed below. You will be rewarded by the combination of the sweet shallots and garlic and the full-flavored cheese. Don't be alarmed if the amount of cheese looks skimpy when you assemble the pizza. Once you cook it, you will have no problem tasting the cheese or enjoying its silky texture.

1 recipe pizzetta dough (see page 198), or use 12 to 14 ounces purchased pizza dough

1 whole bulb garlic

3 tablespoons olive oil

¾ pound shallots, peeled and cut into ¼-inch thick slices

¼ teaspoon kosher salt plus more to taste

Freshly ground pepper

8 ounces washed-rind cheese such as Grayson, Taleggio, Pont l'Evêque or St. Nectaire, cut into approximately ¼-inch thick slices (easiest to cut when cold); or use Gruyère

Prepare the pizzetta dough as directed in the recipe. Combine 3 of the dough balls into 1 large ball (save the remaining dough for another use).

Preheat the oven to 500°F. Put a pizza stone in the oven if you have one.

Cut off the top ¼ inch of the garlic bulb to expose the cloves. Rub with ½ teaspoon of olive oil. Wrap the garlic in foil and roast for 45 minutes. Let cool to room temperature.

In a large sauté pan, warm 2 tablespoons of the oil over low heat. Add the shallots and cook, stirring occasionally, for about 45 minutes. They should turn a golden color but should not brown. Be patient! If they stick, add a little bit of water. Add ¼ teaspoon salt and pepper. Mix well, and set aside.

On a lightly floured work surface,

roll out the pizza dough to a 14-inch round. Brush the dough with remaining olive oil. Squeeze the garlic out of its paper skin and spread on the dough to within 1 inch of the edges. (Use all the garlic, about 1 tablespoon.) Top with the shallots, followed by the cheese.

If using a pizza stone and baking peel, put the pizza on the peel and slide it onto the stone. Cook for 8 minutes or until dough is golden and cheese is melted and bubbly. Sprinkle with a little extra salt (unless cheese is salty already) and a twist or two of pepper.

If you are not using a stone and peel, place the pizza on a baking sheet or pizza pan and cook the pizza about 2 to 3 minutes longer.

Serves 6 to 8 as an appetizer; 4 as a main course

REBLOCHON AND POTATO *TARTIFLETTE*

Rumor has it that this recipe was created by the promoters of Reblochon and therefore is not deeply rooted in the culinary traditions of the Savoie where Reblochon is made. Regardless, this gratinlike dish is one you will likely make over and over because of the delectable combination of onions, bacon, and melted cheese. If you do not care for a strong cheese like Reblochon or cannot get it, then use another flavorful cheese such as Appenzeller, raclette (rind removed), or almost any washed-rind or creamy surface-ripened cheese.

4 slices thick-sliced bacon cut crosswise into ¼-inch pieces (or use ¼ pound pancetta)

1 medium onion, sliced ¼-inch thick

1 pound Yukon Gold or other waxy potatoes, peeled and sliced crosswise ¼ inch thick

Salt

Freshly ground pepper

5 ounces Reblochon cheese, cut into ¼-inch slices (or use Livarot, Munster, Appenzeller, raclette, or Gruyère). If the cheese is sticky, pinch off pieces instead of cutting slices.

½ cup cream

Preheat the oven to 375°F.

In a medium-size sauté pan, cook the bacon until brown and crisp. Drain on a paper towel–lined plate. Remove all but 1 tablespoon fat. Sauté the onions in the bacon fat until soft but not brown, about 5 minutes.

Place half the potato slices in a 9-inch pie plate or shallow oval pan. Sprinkle with a touch of salt and pepper (remember that the cheese and bacon are both salty). Sprinkle half the onions over the potato slices followed by half

the bacon, and half the cheese. Repeat with remaining potatoes, onions, bacon and cheese. Pour cream over the top and around the edges.

Cover with foil and bake for 30 minutes. Remove foil and cook for 20 minutes or until the potatoes are soft and the *tartiflette* is brown and bubbly. Let sit 15 minutes before serving. This allows the cream and potatoes to set up (otherwise, it's too runny).

Serves 8 to 10

CHAPTER 10

ENTERTAINING

WITH

CHEESE

In this country, we are slowly transitioning from using cheese solely as an ingredient to making it the focal point of a party or one of the courses on a dinner menu. Western Europeans have known for centuries what we are beginning to learn for ourselves — that cheese can and often should stand alone.

THE CHEESE COURSE

Following are a few basic questions and answers to help you understand how to use cheese in the context of entertaining.

What is a cheese course? It is a course during the meal in which cheese is the focus. It can kick off the meal as an hors d'oeuvre or appetizer, or it can follow the meal as a course between dinner and dessert, or it can be dessert itself.

Do you serve other foods with a cheese course? Accompaniments with cheese can enhance the entire experience of eating the cheese (see recipes that follow in this section). But the cheese should be the star. Good cheese accompaniments include olives, toasted nuts, dried fruit compotes, dried fruit, ripe fresh fruit, caramelized onions, and chutney.

Do you serve bread or crackers with a cheese course? Many people like to serve crackers with cheese, and while I am not opposed to that (as long as they do not have seasonings), I find that slices of plain baguette make the best host for cheese. It is neutral and does not interfere with the flavors in the cheese. Olive oil-brushed baguette slices that are toasted are also still fairly neutral but add nice flavor and texture to milder cheeses. Likewise, very thin slices of toasted walnut bread are good with creamy cheeses, strong (washed-rind) cheeses, and blue cheeses.

How many cheeses should be part of a cheese course? My belief is that less is more. One great cheese is often enough because it will command all your attention. On the other hand, sometimes it is nice to have a variety, in which case I recommend serving no more than three cheeses.

The other consideration is where the cheese course falls in the meal. If it is served before, then you can serve two or three cheeses as wheels or wedges, and people can help themselves. If you are presenting the cheese following a meal, particularly a big meal, then a small portion of just one great cheese is enough, although you can certainly opt to serve small portions of two or three cheeses if you prefer.

How much cheese do I serve per person? It depends when and how you are serving your cheese course. If you are serving it before the meal, then plan on 1 to 2 ounces of each cheese per person. This may not seem like a lot, but with the accompaniments and with the food that is presumably to come, it is more than enough.

For an after-dinner cheese course, you really need only 1 to 2 ounces of cheese (*total*) for each person. This means that if you are doing the after-dinner cheese course featuring Manchego, Cantal, and Gruyère, you can plan on about ½ to ¾ ounce of each cheese per person. Because you can slice these cheeses very thin, a little does go a long way. You don't want your guests to feel as though they have eaten too much.

How do you decide which cheeses to serve? In general, I like to offer lighter cheeses before a meal and more complex, flavorful cheeses following a meal. It may seem as if the opposite should be true, but to me starting a meal with a full-flavored cheese and ending it with a mild one is the equivalent of starting with a piece of roasted prime rib and following it with a piece of steamed fish. You can select the cheeses based on milk type, style of cheese, availability, personal preference, and so on. See some suggestions on the next page.

Is one knife enough if you're serving a group of cheeses? No. You want a different knife for each cheese. Otherwise, your fresh goat cheese will end up tasting like the rest of the cheeses on the plate, particularly if you are serving a blue cheese. In fact, if you have a particularly strong or runny cheese, serve it on a separate plate.

Do you serve all the cheeses on one platter or plate them individually? This is entirely up to you. I like to plate the cheeses individually for an after-dinner cheese course because it is cumbersome to pass a big platter of cheese and attempt to cut the cheeses at the same time. Plus, it puts your wine glasses in peril. By cutting and plating the cheeses ahead of time, you are allowing them to come to room temperature and getting the work out of the way; all you have to do is serve. If you do this, be sure to cover the plates loosely with plastic wrap so the cheeses won't dry out.

What types of platters are best for serving cheese? Wooden boards are especially good for serving cheese. They are sturdy, which allows you to bear down on a cheese with a knife and not worry about the plate slipping. Ceramic, glass and marble boards and platters are okay too, but bear in mind that they might get scratched. One of the best types of cheese boards now widely available is made from bamboo. They come in all shapes and sizes, are easily cleaned, and best of all, are made with a renewable wood.

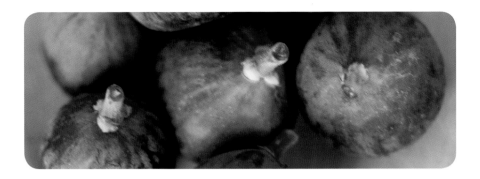

A FEW SUGGESTIONS FOR CHEESE COURSES

Before Dinner

Cheeses: Fresh goat cheese, soft-ripened cow's milk cheese such as Brie
Accompaniments: Green and black olives, dried apricots, and toasted walnuts
Bread/cracker: Olive oil crostini

Cheese: St. Marcellin
Accompaniment: Marinated mushrooms
Bread/cracker: Baguette slices

Cheeses: Cheddar (because you are serving just the one cheese, use the best cheddar you can find)
Accompaniments: Mango chutney, toasted pecans
Bread/cracker: Neutral (not seasoned) cracker

Cheeses: Soft-ripened goat cheese such as Humboldt Fog or Haystack Peak, soft-ripened or surface-ripened sheep's milk cheese such as Pérail or Queso de la Serena, and double- or triple-crème soft-ripened cow's milk cheese such as Fromager d'Affinois, St. André, or Explorateur
Accompaniments: Fresh cherries, apple slices, thin slices of prosciutto
Bread/cracker: Baguette slices
Note: This cheese course is just as appropriate—and good—following a meal

After Dinner

Cheese: Comté
Accompaniments: Toasted pistachio nuts, apple slices
Bread/cracker: None

Cheese: Epoisses
Accompaniment: Fig compote or jam
Bread/cracker: Toasted walnut bread

Cheeses: Soft and creamy blue cheese such as Montbriac or St. Agur, medium-firm blue cheese such as Maytag Blue, firm blue cheese such as Fourme d'Ambert or Stilton
Accompaniments: Dried or fresh figs, dried cherries, toasted walnuts
Bread/cracker: Toasted walnut bread or baguette slices

Cheeses: Manchego, Cantal (or cheddar), Taleggio
Accompaniments: Quince paste (called *membrillo*) or other fruit paste, fresh or dried cherry compote, lightly toasted almonds
Bread/cracker: Neutral or no cracker or bread

THE SKINNY ON KNIVES

The large array of cheese knives in all shapes and sizes can be confusing. Here's what the different knives are for.

(A) **Long knife with large holes in the blade and a forked tip:** This is called a skeleton knife and is used for soft cheeses because they cannot stick to the holey blade.

(B) **Short, stubby, quasi-triangular knife with a pointed tip:** This is a hard cheese knife used for digging out chunks of cheese rather than cutting nice, neat slices.

(C) **Medium-size (about 4 inches) knife with forked tip:** This is an all-purpose cheese knife and can be used for soft or semi-hard cheeses. The forked tip is for you to pick up the piece of cheese you have just cut and transfer it to your plate. Think of it as a built-in toothpick. Just don't eat from it.

(D) **Two-handled knife:** This type of knife is fairly new to consumers, although retailers have used it for a long time. It is quite long, usually about 12 inches from side to side, with handles on either side of the blade. This allows you to cut large pieces of semi-hard and hard cheeses because you can bear down on them with equal pressure from both sides of the blade using a see-saw motion.

(E) **Offset cheese knife:** This is best for soft cheeses, although it can be used for almost all others too, except for hard cheeses. The advantage of the offset shape is that it allows you to cut the cheese without the risk of your knuckles ending up in the cheese or getting the knife handle gooey. All that can touch the cheese is the blade.

(F) **Cheese plane:** This is a rounded-corner triangle with a thin horizontal opening on the wide base end of the knife. This opening has sharp edges and is meant for shaving semi-hard and hard cheeses.

How to Cut Cheese

Cutting cheese can be a little tough if you have a large piece or a whole wheel. That is why starting with good knives is extremely helpful. If there is any rule about cutting cheese, it is that you should not cut it in cubes. It doesn't interfere with the taste ofthe cheese, but it does hurt its image because cubes are usually the cheeses we find on deli platters and most of the time these are no more than commodity cheeses. Beyond that, the following are some general cheese-cutting guidelines.

Cylindrical cheeses: Cut in horizontal slices about 1 inch thick, then cut each slice into triangular wedges.

Round cheeses (wheels): If thick, cut in half horizontally. Proceed by cutting each half into ¼-inch-thick slices across the diameter of the cheese. Cut each slice into triangles.

Soft cheeses: These are easiest to cut when cold. Bring to room temperature before serving. If the wheels are large, such as a full-size Brie, cut the cheese in quarters. Cut crosswise across each quarter, then cut thin slices from each section.

If the cheese is a small wheel, simply cut it into equal size wedges about ½ to ¾ inch thick.

Rectangular cheeses: If the rectangle is small, cut crosswise into ¼-inch slices. If it is a large rectangle (wider than 3 inches across), cut the cheese in half lengthwise, then crosswise into ¼-inch slices.

BALSAMIC-GLAZED PINEAPPLE WITH PARMIGIANO-REGGIANO

As I have written more than once in this book, true Parmigiano-Reggiano has a distinctive pineapple aroma when you cut into it. For that reason, bringing the fruit together with the cheese seemed like a natural pairing. And because Parmigiano-Reggiano, made in the Emilia-Romagna region of Italy, is often paired with balsamic vinegar, which is produced in that area's Modena province, I decided to combine all three ingredients to create a cheese course. This recipe is the result, and it's as easy as it is delicious.

¼ cup balsamic vinegar

1 tablespoon sugar

1 fresh medium-size pineapple (about 3 pounds) or use fresh

peeled and cored pineapple found in the produce section

8 ounces Parmigiano-Reggiano cheese, cut into 8 chunks

Place an oven rack 5 to 6 inches below the heating element and preheat the broiler. Line a baking sheet with a silicone mat, such as Silpat. Alternatively, lightly butter the pan. Set aside.

In a small bowl, mix together the vinegar and sugar. Set aside.

Cut the top plus about 1 inch off the pineapple. The exposed surface should be free of any brown or tough spots. Cutting crosswise, cut eight ¼-inch-thick slices. Cut off the rind plus any prickly brown spots around the edges of each slice. Cut each slice in half and remove the core. You should end up with 16 pieces. (Save any leftover pineapple for another use.) Drain well before using.

Place the pineapple on the prepared baking sheet and brush both sides of each piece with the balsamic mixture. Broil for 3 to 4 minutes, or until the edges of the pineapple look crisp but not burned and the middle has turned golden. Turn slices and repeat. Remove pineapple from oven and transfer to a lightly greased cooling rack. Let cool completely.

To serve, put a piece of cheese on each of 8 individual serving plates along with 2 slices of pineapple. Alternatively, put the cheese and pineapple slices on a platter and pass.

Serves 8

CHEWY PAN FORTE

Pan forte is a super-sweet and nutty confection that originally comes from Italy. Although it is great on its own with a cup of tea, it is also extremely versatile when it comes to matching cheeses with it. Because of its sweetness, I tend to like either stronger-flavored or super-creamy cheeses with it. I suggest a cheese called Morbier in this recipe because it is somewhat assertive and has a soft and somewhat creamy texture. Feel free to experiment with your favorite cheeses, though.

2 tablespoons canola or other vegetable oil

1 cup flour

1 tablespoon unsweetened cocoa powder

1 teaspoon cinnamon

¼ teaspoon nutmeg, preferably fresh grated

1¼ cups almonds, toasted

1¼ cups hazelnuts, toasted

1 pound total of the following dried fruit: prunes, apricots, white figs (Calmyrna), regular and golden raisins, all but raisins cut into ½-inch pieces

2 ounces candied orange peel, cut into ¼-inch pieces (if you cannot find it, make your own or substitute 1 teaspoon orange zest)

¾ cup honey

1 cup sugar

Confectioners' sugar for dusting

8 ounces Morbier cheese, cut into 8 slices (or use any washed-rind, triple-crème cheese, or aged cheddar)

Oil the bottom and sides of a 9-inch springform pan with 1 tablespoon of the oil. Cut out a piece of parchment paper to fit the bottom of the pan and place inside the pan. Oil the parchment. Set aside.

Preheat the oven to 300°F.

In a large bowl, whisk together the flour, cocoa powder, cinnamon, and nutmeg. Mix in the nuts, fruit, and orange peel.

Combine the sugar and honey in a small saucepan over low heat. Stir until sugar dissolves. Bring mixture to a boil, then reduce the heat to low. Cook without stirring to soft-ball stage (240°F on a candy thermometer), or until the syrup looks thick like mapel syrup but not as thick as molasses (if the syrup is overcooked it becomes nearly impossible to mix with the dry ingredients).

Pour the syrup into the nut mixture and stir to coat. The mixture will be very sticky, but keep stirring until it comes together into a ball. If it doesn't, wet your hands and use them to finish bringing the mixture together. Transfer to the prepared pan and smooth the surface. Bake for about 1 hour or until firm and the surface has lost its sheen. Let cool completely or preferably overnight.

Run a damp sharp knife around the edges and remove the side of the pan. Dust with confectioners' sugar. Cut the *pan forte* into thin slices, about ½-inch thick. Serve with the cheese and additional hazelnuts, if you like.

The cake will last about 1 month wrapped in plastic and stored at room temperature.

Makes about 38 slices

Dried Fig and Cherry Compote with Red Hawk

Nothing is easier to make than a dried fruit compote. Best of all, compotes are great with cheese, particularly stronger ones. Red Hawk is an organic washed-rind cheese made by the venerable Cowgirl Creamery in California. It happens to go particularly well with this compote, but if you can't find it, use any washed-rind cheese or other full-flavored cheese such as blue cheese.

2½ cups water

1½ cups sugar

⅓ cup fresh lemon juice (juice from about 1 large lemon)

12 ounces dried Black Mission figs (2½ cups), stemmed and quartered

4½ ounces dried tart cherries (1 cup) (if you can, stay away from the presweetened style)

1 wheel (about 12 ounces) Cowgirl Creamery Red Hawk cheese, cut into 12 wedges (or use Alsatian Munster, Taleggio, or for a milder flavor, use Brie)

In a medium-size saucepan, combine all ingredients except the cheese. Bring to a simmer over medium-high heat until the sugar is dissolved. Reduce the heat to medium and simmer, stirring occasionally, until fruit is tender and juices are reduced to a medium-thick syrup, 75 to 90 minutes. You should end up with about ½ cup of liquid. The liquid will still seem soupy but it will gel as the mixture cools. Let cool to room temperature. (Maybe made up to 4 days in advance, covered and refrigerated. Bring to room temperature before serving.)

To serve, place a wedge of cheese on its side on each of 12 individual serving plates. Place a dollop of compote next to the cheese and serve. Alternatively, put the cheese on a platter and a bowl of the compote on the side and let people help themselves.

Makes 4 cups or 32 two-tablespoon servings to serve 12 or more

Note: You will have more compote than you need for one wheel of cheese. Save the compote for other uses — it will last about 2 months in the refrigerator — or if you're having a big get-together, this is the perfect accompaniment to a group of cheeses instead of just one.

APPENDIX

CHEESE LIST

Following is an alphabetical list of cheeses you're likely to find in a cheese store. The style of the cheese is in parentheses, and you can assume it's a cow's milk cheese unless otherwise specified.

Abbaye de Bellocq (semi-hard; sheep's milk)

Abondance (semi-hard, washed-rind)

Affedelice (washed-rind)

Appenzeller (semi-hard, washed-rind)

Argentine Reggianito (hard)

Asadero (semi-soft)

Asiago (semi-hard)

Asiago Fresco (semi-soft)

Banon (surface-ripened; goat's milk, sometimes mixed with cow's milk)

Beaufort (semi-hard)

Beecher's Handmade Cheese: Flagship (semi-hard)

Beemster Classic (semi-hard, hard)

Beemster Classic Extra-Aged, XO (hard)

Bel Paese (semi-soft)

Bethmale (washed-rind; goat's milk)

Bierkäse (washed-rind)

Bleu d'Auvergne (blue)

Blue Castello (blue)

Boerenkaas (semi-hard; farmhouse Gouda)

Boschetto al Tartufo Bianchetto (semi-hard; cow and sheep's milk)

Bra Tenero (semi-hard, hard)

Brebiou (surface-ripened)

Brescianella (washed-rind)

Brescianella Stagionato (washed-rind)

Brick (semi-soft, washed-rind)

Brie (soft-ripened)

Brillat-Savarin (soft-ripened)

Brin d'Amour (semi-soft, semi-hard; sheep's milk)

Brinata (soft-ripened; sheep's milk)

Bucheron (soft-ripened)

Burrata (fresh/*pasta filata*)

Butterkäse (semi-soft)

Buttermilk Blue (blue)

Cabécou (surface-ripened)

Cabrales (blue; cow, goat, and sheep's milk)

Caciocavallo (semi-hard)

Caciotta (semi-hard; sheep's milk)

Caerphilly (semi-soft)

Cambozola (soft-ripened, blue)

Camembert (soft-ripened)

Cantal (semi-hard)

Cashel (blue)

Chabichou de Poitou (surface-ripened)

Champignon (soft-ripened)

Chaource (soft-ripened)

Chaumes (washed-rind)

Cheddar (semi-hard)

Cheshire (semi-hard)

Chèvre (fresh goat cheese)

Chihuahua (semi-soft)

Chimay (washed-rind)

Classic Blue Log (soft-ripened, blue; goat's milk)

Colby (semi-soft, semi-hard)

Comté (semi-hard, washed-rind)

Cooleeny (soft-ripened)

Cotija (fresh/pressed, hard)

Cottage cheese (fresh/soft)

Cougar Gold (semi-hard)

Coulommiers (soft-ripened)

Cravanzina (surface-ripened; cow and sheep's milk)

Cream cheese (fresh/soft)

Crescenza (fresh and semi-soft)

Crottin de Chavignol (surface-ripened)

Crozier Blue (blue; sheep's milk)

Edam (semi-soft)

Emmentaler (semi-hard)

Epoisses (washed-rind)

Esrom (semi-soft, washed-rind)

Etorki (semi-soft; sheep's milk)

Explorateur (soft-ripened)

Farmer's cheese (fresh/pressed and nonmelter)

Feta (fresh/brined; sheep, goat, cow, or mixed milk)

Fiore Sardo (hard)

Fontal (semi-soft)

Fontina (semi-soft)

Fontina Val d'Aosta (semi-hard)

Fourme d'Ambert (blue)

Fromage blanc (fresh/soft)

Fromager d'Affinois Florette (soft-ripened; goat's milk)

Garrotxa (semi-hard; goat's milk)

Gjetost (fresh/whey, semi-hard)

Gloucester/ Double Gloucester (semi-hard)

Goat cheese (fresh/soft; also known as fresh chèvre or chèvre)

Goat Gouda (semi-hard)

Gorgonzola Dolce (blue)

Gorgonzola Dolcelatte (blue)

Gorgonzola Piccante (blue)

Gouda (semi-soft, semi-hard, hard)

Graviera (semi-hard; sheep's milk)

Great Hill Blue (blue)

Gruyère (semi-hard, washed-rind)

Halloumi (fresh/nonmelter; sheep, sheep and goat, and/or cow's milk)

Havarti (semi-soft)

Herbed goat cheese (fresh/soft cheese; also known as chèvre)

Humboldt Fog (soft-ripened)

Huntsman (semi-hard, blue)

Iberico (semi-soft; goat and cow's milk)

Ibores (semi-hard; goat's milk)

Idiazabal (semi-hard; sheep's milk)

Istara (semi-hard; sheep's milk)

Jarlsberg (semi-hard)

Kasseri (fresh/*pasta filata*, semi-hard; sheep and goat's milk)

Kefalograviera (hard; sheep's milk)

La Tur (surface-ripened; sheep, cow, and goat's milk)

Lagioule (semi-hard)

Lancashire (semi-hard)

Le Chevrot (surface-ripened)

L'Edel de Cleron (soft-ripened, washed-rind)

Le Gariotin (surface-ripened)

Le Lingot (surface-ripened)

Leerdamer (semi-hard)

Leyden (semi-hard)

Limburger (washed-rind)

Livarot (washed-rind)

Longhorn

Madrigal (semi-hard)

Mahón (semi-soft, semi-hard, hard)

Majorero (semi-hard; goat's milk)

Manchego (semi-hard; sheep's milk)

Manouri (fresh/whey; sheep and goat's milk)

Mariolles (washed-rind)

Mascarpone (fresh/soft)

Maytag Blue (blue)

Midnight Moon (semi-hard; goat's milk)

Mimolette (extra-aged; semi-hard hard)

Mirabo (soft-ripened)

Montasio (semi-soft, semi-hard, and hard)

Montbriac (soft-ripened, blue)

Monte Enebro (surface-ripened, blue; goat's milk)

Monte Veronese (semi-soft, semi-hard, and hard)

Monterey Jack (semi-soft, semi-hard, hard)

Morbier (washed-rind)

Mozzarella (fresh/*pasta filata*)

Mozzarella di bufala (fresh/*pasta filata*; water buffalo milk)

Muenster (semi-soft)

Munster (washed-rind)

Murcia al Vino (semi-hard; also called Drunken Goat)

Myzithra (fresh/whey, hard; sheep and goat's milk)

Neufchâtel (fresh/soft)

Nevat (soft-ripened; goat's milk)

Oaxaca (fresh/*pasta filata*)

Oka (washed-rind)

Old Amsterdam (hard)

Original Blue (blue)

Ossau-Iraty (semi-hard; sheep's milk)

Paneer (fresh/nonmelter)

Panela (fresh/nonmelter)

Parmigiano-Reggiano (hard)

Parrano (semi-hard, hard)

Pave d'Affinois (soft-ripened)

Pecorino Fresco (semi-soft)

Pecorino Romano (semi-hard, hard; sheep's milk)

Pecorino Sardo (semi-hard, hard; sheep's milk)

Pecorino Toscano (semi-soft, semi-hard)

Peñazul (blue)

Pérail (surface-ripened; sheep's milk)

Petit Agour (semi-hard; sheep's milk)

P'tit Basque (semi-hard; sheep's milk)

Piave Mezzano (semi-hard)

Piave Vecchio (hard)

Picodon (surface-ripened)

Picon (blue; cow, goat, and sheep's milk)

Pierre Robert (soft-ripened)

Pleasant Ridge Reserve (semi-hard)

Point Reyes Original Blue (blue)

Pointe de Brique (surface-ripened)

Pont-l'Evêque (washed-rind)

Port-Salut (semi-soft, washed-rind)

Pot cheese (fresh/pressed and nonmelter)

Pouligny-St.-Pierre (surface-ripened)

Prima Donna (semi-hard, hard)

Provolone (semi-hard, hard)

Provolone, *piccante* or sharp (hard)

Quark (fresh/soft cheese)

Queso blanco (semi-soft)

Queso fresco (fresh/non-melter)

Raclette (semi-hard, washed-rind)

Reblochon (washed-rind)

Red Hawk (washed-rind)

Red Leicester (semi-hard)

Rembrandt (semi-hard)

Requesón (fresh/whey)

Ricotta (fresh/whey)

Ricotta salata (fresh/whey; sheep's milk)

Roaring Forties Blue (blue)

Robiola Bosina (soft-ripened; sheep and cow's milk)

Robiola di Roccaverano (surface-ripened; goat and/or mixed milk)

Robiola Tre Latte (surface-ripened; sheep, goat, and cow's milk)

Rocamadour (surface-ripened)

Rocchetta (surface-ripened; sheep, cow, and goat's milk)

Roncal (semi-hard)

Roomkaas (semi-soft)

Roquefort (blue; sheep's milk)

Saenkanter (hard)

Saga (blue)

Sage Derby (semi-hard)

Saint Albray (soft-ripened)

Saint-Paulin (semi-soft)

San Simon (semi-hard)

São Jorge (semi-hard)

Schlosskäse (washed-rind)

Schwarz und Weis (blue)

Selles-Sur-Cher (surface-ripened)

Shropshire Blue

Sir Laurier d'Arthabaska (washed-rind)

Sonoma Jack (semi-soft and semi-hard)

Sottocenere al Tartufo (semi-hard)

St. Agur (blue)

St. André (soft-ripened)

St. Félicien (surface-ripened)

St. Jean de Brie (soft-ripened)

St. Marcellin (surface-ripened)

St. Maure (surface-ripened)

St. Nectaire (semi-soft)

St. Pete's Select (blue)

St. Simeon (soft-ripened)

Stilton (blue)

Taleggio (washed-rind)

Teleme (semi-soft)

Tetilla (semi-soft)

Tilsit, Tilsiter (semi-soft, washed-rind)

Tomme de Savoie (semi-soft)

Tomme du Berger (washed-rind)

Ubriaco (semi-hard)

Urgelia (washed-rind)

Vacherin Fribourgeois (semi-hard, washed-rind)

Vacherin Mont d'Or (washed-rind)

Valdeon (blue; cow, goat, and sheep's milk)

Valençay (surface-ripened)

Van Kaas (semi-hard)

Vella Dry Jack

Vincent (semi-hard)

Wensleydale (semi-hard)

Westcombe Red (semi-hard)

Windsor Blue (blue)

Zamorano (semi-hard, hard; sheep's milk)

CHEESE GLOSSARY

acidity: The level of acid in milk before and after starter cultures have been added. The cheesemaker must know the acidity level before proceeding to the next phase of cheesemaking.

affineur: The "cheese finisher," or person whose specialty and responsibility is bringing cheese to maturity.

aged: A cheese that is matured to develop flavor. The term can refer to a cheese that is as young as two or three weeks, but usually it refers to cheeses that are allowed to mature for at least a couple of months or as long as several years.

aging: The process of protein and fat breakdown in cheese that creates flavors and aromas as well as textural changes.

ammoniated: The condition of overripeness, most often found in soft-ripened (bloomy rind) cheeses, where the aroma and flavor are reminiscent of ammonia.

annatto: Also known as achiote, annatto is a red-colored seed that is used to create the orange hue found in some cheddars, Colby, and other cheeses.

aroma: The smells that emanate from a cheese and the usual way of describing those smells. Aromas can be mild to overpowering, although the aroma does not always translate directly to the flavor.

bacteria: The microorganisms that circulate just about everywhere, including cheese aging rooms, which contribute to the cheese's final flavor. Bacteria are also naturally occurring in cheese but most prevalent in unpasteurized milk cheeses, and foster the aging and flavor of the cheese.

bacterial cultures: Used as starters in the cheesemaking process to bring milk to the proper acid level. They also contribute to the flavors and textures found in cheese.

barnyardy: A flavor and aroma in some cheese that is reminiscent of the smells that emanate from a barn or barnyard. Usually it is

similar to a strong, musty and even sometimes dirtlike flavor or aroma, and despite that description, can be a favorable quality.

bitter: An unfavorable component in cheese that is often detected after the cheese has been swallowed. It leaves a lingering "off" taste in the mouth that is a bit like biting into citrus peel.

bloomy rind: The white, flowery, and desirable downy surface of a soft-ripened cheese such as Camembert or Brie that is the result of a bacteria known as *Penicillium candidum*.

blue cheese: A style of cheese in which the *Penicillium roqueforti* or *Penicillium glaucom* mold is added to the curds and/or is prevalent in the aging room or cave. After the cheese is made, formed, and in certain cases, cured for a short while, it is punctured or needled. This creates a passageway for air to enter the cheese and interact with the mold to create veining. The mold that is formed in those veins and throughout the cheese is blue or blue-green.

body: Refers to the texture of the cheese. The body can be firm, pliable, soft, and springy, among other things.

Brevibacteria linens: Often referred to as *B. linens*, these are the bacteria added to the saltwater solution rubbed on washed-rind cheeses during the aging process. The moisture helps the *B. linens* to grow; they protect the cheese and also lend it its characteristic strong aromas and sometimes flavor.

brine: A solution, usually salt and water, in which certain cheeses are "bathed" for a few hours to several weeks. This process is called brining and is a means of salting the cheese as well as creating a protected exterior for longer aging.

butterfat: See **milk fat**

buttery: Pertains to the creamlike, rich flavor in cheese. Triple-crème cheeses are especially buttery because of the cream that is added to the milk to make them.

casein: The protein in milk that coagulates to form curds.

chalky: Refers to the texture of a cheese, most often found in surface-ripened goat cheeses where the paste is dry, crumbly, and mouth-coating.

cheddaring: The process by which cheddar cheese is made. After draining as much whey as possible, the cheesemaker moves the cottage cheese–like curds to the sides of the vat to mat together and create long sheets of curds that are stacked on top of each other so that their weight will push more whey out. They are usually restacked several times. The curds are then milled, or cut into tiny pieces, and scooped into molds where they will be pressed further.

cheese course: Refers to a part of a meal, either the beginning or end, in which cheese is the focus. It may consist of several cheeses or just one, and it may have popular cheese accompaniments such as toasted nuts, honey, or fresh or dried fruit.

chèvre: The French word for goat, chèvre refers to a fresh cheese made with pasteurized goat's milk, so the word chèvre is used interchangeably with the phrase goat cheese.

citrusy: A flavor characteristic that is similar to the tart, sometimes sour, and sometimes herbal qualities found in citrus fruits. It might be specific, such as orangelike or lemony. Often pertains to high-acid cheeses such as young goat cheese.

cloth-wrapped or bandaged: A cheese, usually cheddar, that is wrapped in cheesecloth and then aged.

coagulation: The point in cheesemaking when the casein, or milk protein, has clumped together to form curds.

cooked curds: A process in cheesemaking where the curds are heated, sometimes to very high temperatures, to help expel the whey. Examples of cooked-curd cheeses are Emmentaler and Gruyère.

creamy: A favorable textural consistency and/or flavor of certain cheeses, it indicates a smooth and often runny consistency. It usually refers to the ripe forms of Brie, Camembert, and other soft-ripened cheeses. Can also refer to certain fresh cheeses such as some cottage cheese, mascarpone, and crème fraîche. Also used to describe a flavor denoting rich and/or milky characteristics.

crème fraîche: Refers to cultured milk or cream, or a combination of both. The result is a thick, fresh cheese similar in consistency to sour cream. The flavor is buttery and a little tangy, and is good on fruit tarts or pies instead of whipped cream. It is also a good ingredient in cooked dishes, both sweet and savory.

curds: The solid or coagulated portions of the milk. Curds are the result of the casein or milk proteins clumping together after they are exposed to starter bacteria. The starter(s) raise the acidity level of the milk, which causes the casein molecules to bond together. The curds then undergo further solidifying once rennet is introduced, and eventually the curds become cheese.

cutting the curd: Refers to the stage in cheesemaking when the curds—at that point one continuous custardlike block—are cut with specially designed metal wires, called harps, to facilitate whey expulsion. The size of the resulting curds varies depending on the direction they are cut and the type of harp.

dry matter: The portion of the cheese that is comprised of solids. Most cheeses have at least 25 percent of their weight in dry matter or solids. The non-dry matter is the liquid portion of a cheese. For example, a young Jack cheese will be comprised of about 50 percent dry matter, while the other 50 percent is moisture. Also, the portion of the cheese that is measured for total fat content.

earthy: A generally positive term to describe a flavor that has characteristics of the earth or soil, the area where the cheese is made, and/or the feed of the animal. It may also describe a slight mustiness in the cheese.

eyes: Tiny or large holes that form in cheese as a result of certain bacteria. In Swiss cheese, eyes are encouraged by the introduction of Propionic bacteria, which produce carbon dioxide, creating gas bubbles that eventually burst and leave grape-sized eyes or holes behind. Eyes may also form when curds are not pressed or pressed only lightly, which keeps the curds from knitting tightly together, thus allowing small eyes to form.

fermentation: The process by which milk becomes cheese and other milk products such as sour cream and yogurt. Technically, fermentation is the process leading to the breakdown of carbohydrates. In the case of milk, *lactococci* or *lactobacilli* bacteria are introduced to the milk, which cause the shift of lactose to lactic acid. This conversion sets up the proper acid levels and textural consistency for the milk to be made into cheese.

firm: Refers to the body of the cheese when it is strong and smooth rather than weak or soft.

floral: The fragrant quality in cheese that can pertain to both aroma and flavor. A floral flavor is a sweet though not sugary-tasting cheese, as found in a fresh sheep's milk ricotta. Also refers to a cheese that might have a floral component added to it, such as lavender.

fresh cheese: Cheeses that have not been aged or ripened. Cottage cheese, pot cheese, and mozzarella are a few examples.

fresh milk: A flavor and/or aroma characteristic that is reminiscent of the prefermented milk. A just-made mozzarella, especially one made with the milk from a water buffalo, will have this flavor.

fromage blanc: A fresh (unripened) cultured cheese that can be made from cow, goat, or sheep's milk. Its texture falls somewhere between ricotta and sour cream, and its flavor lies somewhere between those two products as well. It is tangier than ricotta but not as sour as sour cream. It can be used as a spread and is also very good for cooking since it melts nicely and adds creaminess and body. It can be used in pastas, risotto, pizzas, tarts, and vegetable dishes or in fruit and baked desserts.

fruity: A flavor and/or aroma characteristic in many cheeses that is reminiscent of fresh fruit. The flavor or aroma can be that of a specific fruit, or more general, with notes of sweetness (though not sugar). The aroma of a cheese might also have the natural sweetness that is associated with fruit.

gamy: Refers to the flavor and/or aroma in a cheese that has strong animal-like characteristics. Can be a favorable or unfavorable characteristic, depending on the individual taster and on the cheese.

Geotrichum candidum: A yeastlike mold that is often used in surface-ripened, soft-ripened, and washed-rind cheeses. It contributes flavor and acts as a protector from undesirable molds. Cheeses with *Geotrichum candidum* can often be identified by their wrinkly rind.

grassy: Refers to a flavor and sometimes aroma in a cheese that is reminiscent of grass. Usually relates to a certain acidic element, which might be perceived as sour by some. Fresh goat cheeses often have a grassy element, which is usually considered favorable. The term can also pertain to the flavors and/or aromas that are the result of the grasses eaten by the animals.

gummy: Of or pertaining to a gumlike or chewy quality in the texture of the cheese often due to excessive moisture or condensation. It is an unfavorable characteristic.

hard cheese: A style of cheese that has been aged for a long period, and/or salted, and/or pressed, causing it to lose its moisture and become hard. Grating cheeses are hard cheeses.

heat-treated milk: The quick heating of milk at a lower temperature. Falling somewhere between raw milk and pasteurization, heat-treated milk is heated at 130°F for two to sixteen seconds. The goal is to kill off any potentially unhealthful organisms that might exist in raw milk, yet retain certain flavor and other characteristics that exist in the milk.

herbaceous: Refers to the flavor and/or the aroma of a cheese, denoting an herbal quality. This can be the result of herbs added to the cheese, or herbs used in the curing process, but usually it is the result of the way the cheese is made, the area in which it is made, and the type of feed or grasses eaten by the animals whose milk was used for the cheese.

holes: Used interchangeably with the term eyes, holes are the distinguishing characteristic of Swiss or Emmentaler cheese. They are the result of carbon dioxide bubbles that form in the body of the cheese in response to specific bacteria that are deliberately introduced into the cheese. Other cheeses, such as Havarti, have much smaller holes or eyes.

homogenization: A process that breaks down and incorporates the fat globules in milk. This prevents the cream from separating and rising to the top. It also helps in cheesemaking because less fat is lost in the whey, which means the yield will be higher. Some cheesemakers deliberately avoid homogenization because they believe the larger fat globules are beneficial to the consistency and flavor of their cheese.

hooping: The process of putting wet curds into molds or hoops. (See also molding)

hoops: Another word for the molds or containers into which fresh curds are scooped to take their shape as wheels, blocks, pyramids, etc.

lactic: The strong presence of milk in flavor and/or aroma.

lactic acid: The acid that is produced by the breakdown of lactose. That breakdown results from a starter bacteria being added to the milk or natural bacteria present in the milk.

lactose: A natural sugar present in milk.

lactose intolerant: The inability of the body to break down lactose. Symptoms of lactose intolerance can include bloating, diarrhea, and nausea.

Longhorn: A style of cheddar or Colby cheese that is so named because of its cylindrical shape.

mascarpone: A naturally sweet, spreadable cream. It is made with only two ingredients: cream and citric or tartaric acid. These ingredients are combined and left to drain, allowing all the noncream components, including the sodium, to separate out. The cream that is left is buttery in both taste and texture. It is very rich and is often used as an ingredient in sweet dishes or as a topping for desserts. It melts well and can sometimes be used in place of cream cheese, though it is creamier. Its most well-known use is in the Italian dessert tiramisu.

milk fat: The amount of fat in milk expressed as a percentage of weight.

mold: Spores that are added to the milk or the curds and/or the surface of a cheese to encourage mold growth as the cheese develops. Surface molds are sometimes sprayed on the outside of the cheese as in the case of Camembert. These types of molds are edible. Mold is also the undesirable growth that forms on the outside of old and/or poorly wrapped cheese. On semi-hard and hard

cheese, the mold can usually be cut away from the cheese, and the cheese can then be consumed.

molding: The step in cheesemaking when the curds are poured or hand ladled into molds, usually plastic, that are outfitted with tiny holes to allow for drainage of the whey. Molding also contributes to the final shape of the cheese. Sometimes the molds are muslin or nylon bags that are tied in a particular shape. These bags allow for drainage and also create the final shape of the cheese. (See also hooping).

mouthfeel: Refers to the way a cheese "feels" in the mouth. It might be smooth, dense, granular, buttery, or any number of other consistencies.

mushroomy: The flavor and/or aroma in a cheese that is reminiscent of mushrooms.

musty: Often due to mold growth, a flavor or aroma can be likened to dirt. It is earthy to the point of dank, and such flavor often lingers well after the cheese has been consumed. This flavor most often comes from the rind of a cheese, which can be cut away before eating.

natural rind: A rind that develops naturally from molds and bacteria in the cheese and/or molds found in the cheese aging room. The term is most often used in the context of aged, semi-hard cheeses such as Tomme de Savoie.

nutty: A favorable flavor and aromatic characteristic found in aged cheeses, nutty refers to the toasty and sometimes woody flavors that are found in nuts. Those same flavors can be found in certain cheeses, including Manchego, Gruyère, and Parmesan.

pasta filata: Literally "stretched curd," these cheeses are hand- or machine-stretched while still warm and made into a variety of shapes. This process creates their stringlike characteristic. Examples of pasta filata cheeses are mozzarella, Oaxaca, Provolone, and string cheese.

paste: The interior of a cheese. In French, the interior is called the pâte.

pasteurization: The process by which milk is heated to kill any unwanted or unhealthful organisms. There are two acceptable forms of pasteurization: 160°F for fifteen seconds or 145°F for thirty minutes.

Penicillium candidum: A mold that is often used in certain soft-ripened cheeses to create flavor as well as the growth of the distinctive white or bloomy rind.

perfumy: The perfumelike aroma that is emitted from certain cheeses. Aged Goudas and Gruyères often have this characteristic.

piquant: A bright, tangy, and sometimes sharp flavor characteristic. It can be detected in certain young goat cheeses and also in some cheddars. It should not be confused with bitter.

pungent: A strong and possibly acrid flavor or aroma found in some cheese. Many smear-ripened cheeses—such as brick and Limburger—and some blue cheeses might be described as pungent.

quark (or **quarg**):, A nonfat or lowfat fresh cheese whose texture lies somewhere between yogurt and a creamy cottage cheese. A staple for most Germans, quark can be used in place of sour cream or yogurt in baking. It can also be used as a tart topping on toast or fresh fruit salad.

rancid: A soapy, bitter, and "off" flavor that is usually the result of poorly handled milk.

raw milk: Refers to the milk that comes directly from the animal. A raw milk cheese is one made with milk that has not been pasteurized.

rennet: An animal, vegetable, or microbial substance that contains the enzyme rennin which is crucial to the coagulation of milk. Traditionally, rennet came from the stomach lining of a calf, but it also comes from sheep and goats. Non-animal sources include the thistle, and laboratory-made microbial rennet, the genetic equivalent of animal rennet.

rennin: The enzyme that coagulates milk.

rind: The exterior layer of the cheese which forms as the result of the activity of various molds and bacteria in conjunction with the temperature-controlled air and humidity.

ripe: A cheese that is ready to be eaten. The term refers to any cheeses that are aged regardless of the length of aging time.

ripening: Used to describe the process by which a cheesemaker allows the milk to simply sit in order to allow desirable bacteria to grow. Also often used synonymously with "aging" to denote the maturing of a cheese.

rubbery: Pertains to an undesirable quality in the texture of a cheese, suggesting a certain stiffness and a lack of the textural qualities normally found in that cheese. Certain bulk-manufactured part-skim mozzarellas are inherently rubbery as are many lowfat and nonfat cheeses. This is due to the lower fat content, cheesemaking method, and the particular protein structure found in these types of cheeses.

savory: Loosely defined as the "fifth taste" after sweet, sour, bitter, and salty. Several cheeses are characterized as savory including aged cheddar and Parmesan. (See umami.)

semi-hard cheese: A style of cheese that has about 50 percent moisture or less. Examples are Emmentaler, aged Gouda, and aged cheddars.

semi-soft cheese: A style of cheese that has between 50 and 75 percent moisture. Examples are high-moisture Jack cheese, Havarti, and American Muenster.

sharp: A flavor that straddles the line between piquant and bitter. Many bulk-manufactured American cheddars are labeled "sharp," usually referring to a step in the cheesemaking process in which the enzymes are quickly heated to boost the acid level of the cheese. This translates to a sharper cheese. In specialty cheesemaking, the sharpness also comes about because of the acid content, but the full sharp flavor manifests itself slowly as a result of the aging process.

smoky: A flavor and/or aroma that is reminiscent of smoke from a wood-burning fire. More loosely, it might simply mean an earthy component in the cheese.

soft-ripened cheese: A style of cheese that ripens from the rind inward due to the mold that has been added in the cheesemaking process and/or sprayed on the surface of the cheese once it has been molded (shaped). Evidence that a soft-ripened cheese has begun its ripening or softening is that the cheese just under the rind is soft, eventually becoming runny.

spicy: A characteristic that might be piquant and/or aromatic. Blue cheese is often described as spicy because of its mold characteristics, while a cheese that has been flavored with black pepper or chile peppers is also described as spicy.

squeakers: Refers to just-made cheese curds that are packaged and sold on the same day they are made. Invented in Wisconsin, they are called squeakers because they are said to squeak when they are chewed due to their freshness. Technically, if squeakers are sold the day after they are made, they are then referred to as day-old.

starter: Refers to the bacteria that are added to milk at the beginning of the cheesemaking process to raise the lactic acid level. This creates "sour" milk, which then helps the milk to coagulate. The starter is also responsible for much of the flavor and aroma in the final cheese.

sulfurous or sulfide flavor: The flavor and/or aroma in a cheese that is reminiscent of rotten eggs. It is thought to come about when, for some reason, an enzyme found in certain bacteria breaks down two of the sulfur amino acids in cheese.

supple: A cheese whose texture is pliable, smooth, and/or satiny.

surface-ripened cheese: The broad definition is a cheese that is ripened or aged by the molds and bacteria that exist on the surface of the cheese. The second, more narrow, definition is a cheese with a wrinkled-or "brainy-" looking rind owing to the yeast known as *Geotrichum candidum*.

sweet: Can refer to the flavor or aroma of a cheese. It usually signifies a lower acid cheese and possibly one with a less pronounced sodium component.

tangy: A term often used when describing goat cheese due to its piquant flavor. It often suggests a higher-acid cheese.

truffly: A flavor and/or aroma that is earthy, almost dirtlike, but favorably so. The characteristic pertains to the prized fungus known as a truffle.

umami: A term used to describe the "fifth taste," after sweet, sour, salty, and bitter. Identified by the Japanese and now being studied in this country, umami loosely equates to the term "savory." Aged cheddar and Parmesan cheese, among others, are said to have umami.

velvety: Pertains to the texture and/or mouthfeel of a cheese. Both the rind and the paste of a ripe soft-ripened cheese might have this characteristic.

washed-rind cheese: A style of cheese in which the rinds are literally washed with a saltwater solution to which so-called *Brevibacteria linens (B. linens)* have been added. These cheeses may be finished in the aging room with liquids such as cider, beer, or wine to lend unique flavors. Most washed-rind cheeses can be distinguished by their orangeish, reddish, pinkish, or tan colored rind—colors that form because of the presence of *B. linens*.

waxy: Refers to the appearance of a cheese that is slick and smooth and has no apparent rind. It can be a negative or positive feature, depending on the cheese.

whey: The high-protein liquid portion of milk that forms after the milk protein, or casein, begins to coagulate and becomes curds.

yeasty: A flavor and/or aroma that is reminiscent of baking bread, a good Champagne, or brewed beer. A blue cheese might have a yeasty aroma, as might certain soft-ripened cheeses.

CHEESE INFORMATION RESOURCES

American Cheese Society
www.cheesesociety.org
304 West Liberty Street, Suite 201
Louisville, KY 40202
502-583-3783

**Australian Specialist Cheesemakers'
Association**
www.australiancheese.org
Phone: +61 (3) 5727-3589
Fax: +61 (3) 5727-3590

California Artisan Cheese Guild
www.cacheeseguild.org

California Milk Advisory Board
www.realcaliforniacheese.com
400 Oyster Point Boulevard
Suite 214
South San Francisco, CA 94070
650-871-6459

Cheese from Spain
www.cheesefromspain.com/CFS/Index

Great Cheeses of New England
www.newenglandcheese.com

Maine Cheese Guild
www.mainecheeseguild.org

**New York State Farmstead and Artisan
Cheese Makers Guild**
www.nyfarmcheese.org/index.asp
9626 County Highway 21
Franklin, NY 13775
607-829-8852

Oregon Cheese Guild
www.oregoncheeseguild.com
PO Box 3606
Central Point, OR 97502
866-665-1155 ext. 156

Southern Cheese Guild
www.southerncheese.com

**Specialist Cheesemakers Association (Great
Britain)**
www.specialistcheesemakers.co.uk
17 Clerkenwell Green
London EC1R 0DP
Phone: 020 7253 2114
Fax: 020 7608 1645

Vermont Cheese Council
www.vtcheese.com
116 State Street
Montpelier, VT 05620
888-523-7484

Washington State Cheesemakers Association
www.washingtoncheesemakers.org
104 Pike Street, #200
Seattle, WA 98101
206-322-1644

Wisconsin Cheese Makers Association
www.wischeesemakersassn.org
8030 Excelsior Drive, Suite 305
Madison, WI 53717-1950
Phone: 608-828-4550
Fax: 608-828-4551

Wisconsin Milk Marketing Board
www.wisdairy.com
8418 Excelsior Drive
Madison, WI 53717
608-836-8820

Wisconsin Specialty Cheese Institute
www.wisspecialcheese.org
PO Box 15
Delavan, WI 53115
866-740-2180

CHEESE BLOGS

Cheese By Hand
www.cheesebyhand.com

Cheese Diaries
www.cheesediaries.com

Cheese Mistress
www.cheesemistress.com

Cheese Underground
cheeseunderground.blogspot.com

Curdnerds
www.curdnerds.com

Murray's Cheese Shop Blog
www.bigcheesestories.blogspot.com

Pacific Northwest Cheese Project
www.pnwcheese.typepad.com

Saxelby Cheesemongers
www.saxelbycheese.blogspot.com

Small Cheese Shops

AJ's Fine Foods
Multiple locations
602-230-7015
www.ajsfinefoods.com

Cheuvront Wine & Cheese Café
1326 N. Central Avenue
Phoenix, AZ
602-307-0022

Sportsman's Fine Wines
Multiple locations
602-955-9463
www.sportsmans4wine.com

California

24th Street Cheese Company
3893 24th Street
San Francisco, CA
415-821-6658

Aniata Cheese Company
2710 Via de la Valle, B-138
Del Mar, CA
858-847-9616
www.aniata.com

Bi-Rite Market
3639 18th Street
San Francisco, CA
415-241-9760
www.biritemarket.com

Canyon Market
2815 Diamond Street
San Francisco, CA
415-586-9999

C'est Cheese
825 Santa Barbara Street
Santa Barbara, CA
805-965-0318
www.cestcheese.com

Cheese Plus
2001 Polk Street
San Francisco, CA
415-921-2001
www.cheeseplus.com

The Cheese Board Collective
1504 Shattuck Avenue
Berkeley, CA
510-549-3183
www.cheeseboardcollective.coop

The Cheese Shop
423 Center Street
Healdsburg, CA
707-433-4998
www.doraliceimports.com/cheeseshop

The Cheese Shop–Carmel
Carmel Plaza (lower level)
Ocean and Junipero
Carmel, CA
800-828-9463
www.cheeseshopcarmel.com

The Cheese Store of Beverly Hills
419 N. Beverly Drive
Beverly Hills, CA
800-547-1515
www.cheesestorebh.com

The Cheesemaker's Daughter
127 E. Napa Street
Sonoma, CA
707-996-4060
www.cheesemakersdaughter.com

The Cheesestore of Silverlake
3926-28 West Sunset Boulevard
Los Angeles, CA
323-644-7511
www.cheesestoresl.com

Cowgirl Creamery (2 California and
1 Washington, DC location)
1 Ferry Building, #17
San Francisco, CA
415-362-9354

80 Fourth Street
Point Reyes Station, CA
415-663-9335
www.cowgirlcreamery.com

Divine Food Shop
6481 Valley Circle Terrace
West Hills, CA
866-332-7666
www.divinefoodshop.com

Farmstead Cheeses and Wines
1650 Park Street
Alameda, CA
510-864-9463
www.farmsteadcheesesandwines.com

Lazy Acres Market
302 Meigs Road
Santa Barbara, CA
805-564-4410
www.lazyacres.com

The Market on El Paseo
73-375 El Paseo Drive Suite F
Palm Desert, CA
760-341-4262
www.themarketonelpaseo.com

Oakville Grocery
Multiple locations in Northern California
707-944-8802
www.oakvillegrocery.com

Oliver's Markets (2 locations)
546 E. Cotati Ave.
Cotati, CA
707-795-9501

560 Montecito Ave.
Santa Rosa, CA
707- 537-7123
www.oliversmarket.com

Pasta Shop (2 locations)
Rockridge Market Hall
5655 College Avenue
Oakland, CA

1786 4th Street
Berkeley, CA
888-952-4005
www.markethallfoods.com

Rainbow Grocery
1745 Folsom Street
San Francisco, CA
415-863-0620
www.rainbowgrocery.org

Raymond & Co. Cheesemongers
14301 Arnold Drive
Glen Ellen, CA
707-938-9911
www.raymondcheesemongers.com

Salt Creek Wine Company
30100 Town Center Drive Suite B-2
Laguna Niguel, CA
949-249-9463
www.saltcreekwine.com

Sapphire Laguna
The Old Pottery Place
1200 South Coast Highway
Laguna Beach, CA
949-715-9889
www.sapphirelaguna.com

Say Cheese
2800 Hyperion Avenue
Los Angeles, CA
323-665-0545

Say Cheese
856 Cole Street
San Francisco, CA
415-665-5020

Tutto Latte Express
1233 Vine Street
Los Angeles, CA
323-463-1879

Venissimo Cheese
754 W. Washington
San Diego, CA

619-491-0708
www.venissimo.com

Wally's
2107 Westwood Boulevard
Los Angeles, CA
310-475-0606
www.wallyswine.com

Colorado

The Cheese Co.
5575 E 3rd Avenue
Denver, CO
303-394-9911

Cheese Importers/La Fromagerie
33 South Pratt Parkway
Longmont, CO
303-772-9599
www.cheeseimporters.com

Chez Cheese Gourmet Market
1512 Larimer Street R24
Denver, CO
303-825-3122
www.chezcheesegourmet.com

Marczyk Fine Foods
770 E. 17th Avenue
Denver, CO
303-894-9499
www.marczykfinefoods.com

Specialty Foods of Aspen/The Cheese Shop
601 East Hopkins
Aspen, CO
970-544-6656

St. Kilians Cheese Shop
3211 Lowell Boulevard
Denver, CO
303-477-0374
www.stkilianscheeseshop.com

The Truffle, Inc.
2906 East 6th Avenue
Denver, CO
303-322-7363
www.denvertruffle.com

Connecticut

Brie & Bleu
84 Bank Street
New London, CT
860-437-2474
www.brieandbleu.com

Darien Cheese and Fine Foods
25-10 Old Kings Highway North
Darien, CT
203-655-4344
www.dariencheese.com

The Olive Market
19 Main Street
Redding, CT
203-544-8134

Say Cheese Too!
Simsburytown Shops
924 Hopmeadow Street
Simsbury, CT
860-658-6742
www.saycheese-lgp.com

Florida

Bodega Blue Artisan Cheese
2114 14th Avenue
Vero Beach, FL
772-569-4400
www.bodegabluecheeses.com

The Cheese Course
1679 Market Street
Weston, FL
954-384-8183

Epicure Market
1656 Alton Road
Miami Beach, FL
305-672-0385
www.epicure-market.com

The Wine Room on Park Avenue
270 Park Avenue South
Winter Park, FL
407-696-9463
www.thewineroomonline.com

District of Columbia

Cowgirl Creamery
919 F Street NW
Washington, DC
202-393-6880
www.cowgirlcreamery.com

Georgia

Alon's Bakery
1394 N. Highland Avenue
Atlanta, GA
404-872-6000
www.alons.com

Muss & Turner's
1675 Cumberland Parkway Suite 309
Smyrna, GA
770-434-1114
www.mussandturners.com

Savor
3187 Roswell Road
Atlanta, GA
404-869-0747
www.savorgourmet.com

Star Provisions
1189 Howell Mill Road
Atlanta, GA
404-365-0410
www.starprovisions.com

The Barrelman
800 Peachtree Street, Suite F
Atlanta, GA
404-228-8817
www.enorestaurant.com/barrelman.asp

Illinois

Binny's
Multiple locations
Chicago, IL
888-942-9463
www.binnys.com

Bouffe
2312 W. Leland Avenue
Chicago, IL
773-784-2314
www.bouffechicago.com

Chalet Wine & Cheese Shop
40 E Delaware Place
Chicago, IL
312-787-8555

eatZi's Market & Bakery
Century Shopping Centre
2828 N. Clark Street
Chicago, IL
773-832-9310

Fox & Obel Food Market
401 E. Illinois Street
Chicago, IL
312-410-7301
www.fox-obel.com

Marion Street Cheese Market
101 N. Marion Street
Oak Park, IL
708-848-2088
www.marionstreetcheesemarket.com

Pastoral Artisan Cheese, Bread and Wine
2945 N. Broadway
Chicago, IL
773-472-4781
www.pastoralartisan.com

Sam's Wine and Spirits (3 locations)
Marcey Street Market
Chicago, IL
800-777-9137
www.sams-wine.com

2010 Butterfield Road
Downers Grove, IL.
630-705-9463

1919 Skokie Valley Road
Highland Park , IL.
847-433-9463

The Cheese Stands Alone
4547 N. Western Avenue
Chicago, IL
773-293-3870

Indiana

The Cheese Shop
8702 Keystone Crossing
Indianapolis, IN
317-846-6885

Iowa

New Pioneer Co-op (2 locations)
22 S. Van Buren Street
Iowa City, IA
319-338-9441

1101 2nd Street
Coralville, IA
319-358-5513
www.newpi.com

The Prairie Table, Inc.
223 E. Washington Street
Iowa City, IA
319-337-3325
www.prairietablegourmet.com

Kansas

The Better Cheddar
(also in Missouri)
Prairie Village Shopping Center
#5 On the Mall (71st & Mission Road)
Prairie Village, KS
913-362-7575
www.thebettercheddar.com

Louisiana

Cork & Bottle (2 locations)
3700 Orleans Avenue
New Orleans, LA
504-281-4384

3911 Perkins Road
Baton Rouge, LA
225-344-1414
www.cbwines.com

St. James Cheese Co.
5004 Prytania Street
New Orleans, LA
504-899-4737
www.stjamescheese.com

Maine

K.Horton Specialty Foods at the Market House
28 Monument Square
Portland, ME
207-228-2056
www.khortonfoods.com

Treats
80 Main Street
Wiscasset, ME
207-882-6192
www.treatsofmaine.com

Maryland

Atwater's
529 East Belvedere Avenue
Baltimore, MD
410-323-2396
www.atwaters.biz

Tastings Gourmet Market
1410 Forest Drive
Annapolis, MD.
410-263-1324
www.tastingsgourmetmarket.com

The Wine Source
3601 Elm Avenue
Baltimore, MD
410-467-7777
www.the-wine-source.com

Massachusetts

The Concord Cheese Shop
29 Walden Street
Concord, MA
978-369-5778
www.concordcheeseshop.com

Formaggio Kitchen (2 locations)
244 Huron Avenue
Cambridge, MA
888-212-3224
www.formaggio-kitchen.com

South End Formaggio
268 Shawmut Avenue
Boston, MA
617-350-6996
www.southendformaggio.com

Joppa Fine Foods
50 Water Street - The Tannery
Newburyport, MA
978-462-4662
www.joppafinefoods.com

Rubiner's Cheesemongers & Grocers
264 Main Street
Great Barrington, MA
413-528-0488

Wasik's The Cheese Shop
61 Central Street
Wellesley, MA
781-237-0916

The Wine and Cheese Cask
407 Washington Street
Somerville, MA
617-623-8656
www.thewineandcheesecask.com

Michigan

Holiday Market
1203 S. Main Street
Royal Oak, MI
248-541-1414
www.holiday-market.com

Vince & Joe's (2 locations)
41790 Garfield
Clinton Township, MI
586-263-7870

55178 Van Dyke Avenue
Shelby Township, MI
586-786-9230
www.vinceandjoes.com

Zingerman's
422 Detroit Street
Ann Arbor, MI
734-663-3354
www.zingermans.com

Minnesota

E's Cheese
720 Main Street, Suite 102
Mendota Heights, MN
651-452-0903
www.escheese.com

France 44 Deli & Market
4351 France Avenue South
Minneapolis, MN
612-925-3252
www.france44.com

Great Ciao Inc.
1201 Dupont Avenue North
Minneapolis, MN
612-521-8725
www.greatciao.com

Kowalski's Markets
Multiple locations in Minnesota
651-698-3366
www.kowalskis.com

Lund's and Byerly's
Multiple locations in Minnesota
952-548-1400
www.lundsandbyerlys.com

Premier Cheese Market
5013 France Avenue South
Minneapolis, MN
612-436-5590
www.premiercheesemarket.com

Surdyk's
303 East Hennepin Avenue
Minneapolis, MN
612-379-3232
www.surdyks.com

Missouri

The Better Cheddar
(also in Kansas)
Country Club Plaza
604 W. 48th Street
Kansas City, MO
816-561-8204
www.thebettercheddar.com

Cosentino's Market
Multiple locations in Missouri
816-523-3700
www.cosentinos.com

Provisions Gourmet Market
11615 Olive Boulevard
St. Louis, MO
314-989-0020
www.provisionsmarket.com

The Smokehouse Market
16806 Chesterfield Airport Road
Chesterfield, MO
636-532-3314
www.smokehousemarket.com

The Wine & Cheese Place (3 locations)
St. Louis
7435 Forsyth Boulevard
Clayton
314-727-8788

Rock Hill
9755 Manchester Road
St. Louis, MO
314-962-8150

West County
14748 Clayton Road
St. Louis, MO
636-227-9001
www.wineandcheeseplace.com

The Wine Merchant Ltd. (2 locations)
20 South Hanley
Clayton, MO
314-863-6282

12669 Olive Boulevard
Creve Coeur, MO
314-469-4500
www.winemerchantltd.com

Montana

The Gourmet Cellar
212 West Park Street
Livingston, MT
406-222-5418
www.thegourmetcellar.com

Nebraska

Broadmoor Market
8722 Pacific Street
Omaha, NE
402-391-0312
www.broadmoormarket.com

Nevada

Cheese Board & Wine Seller
247 California Avenue
Reno, NV
775-332-0840

Valley Cheese and Wine
1770 West Horizon Ridge Parkway
Henderson, NV
702-341-8191
www.valleycheeseandwine.com

Angela's Pasta and Cheese Shop
815 Chestnut Street
Manchester, NH
603-625-9544
www.angelaspastaandcheese.com

C'est Cheese
122 Lafayette Road
North Hampton, NH
603-964-2272
www.c-estcheese.com

Co-op Food Stores (2 locations)
45 South Park Street
Hanover, NH
603-643-2667

Centerra Marketplace
Route 120
Lebanon, NH
603-643-4889
www.coopfoodstore.com

Chez Cheese
10 Washington Street
Tenafly, NJ
201-568-2050
www.chezcheeze.com

Echo + Whetstone
215 Rivervale Road
Rivervale, NJ
201-664-0033
www.echoandwhetstone.com

Gary's Wine & Marketplace
Multiple locations in New Jersey
888-994-2797
www.garysmarket.com

Sickles
Harrison Avenue off Rumson Road
Little Silver, NJ
732-741-9563
www.sicklesmarket.com

Summit Cheese Shop
75 Union Place
Summit, NJ
908-273-7700

Relish Cheese Market & Sandwich Shop
(2 locations)
8019 Menaul, NE
Albuquerque, NM
505-299-0001

411 Central NW
Albuquerque, NM
505-248-0002

Adams Fairacre Farms (3 locations)
1560 Ulster Avenue
Kingston
845-336-6300

1240 Route 300
Newburgh
845-569-0303

765 Dutchess Turnpike
Poughkeepsie
845-454-4330
www.adamsfarms.com

Artisanal Fromagerie & Bistro
2 Park Avenue
New York, NY
212-725-8585
www.artisanalbistro.com

Auray Cheese Shop
1935A Palmer Avenue
Larchmont, NY
914-833-2274
www.auraycheeseshop.com

Bedford Cheese Shop
229 Bedford Avenue
Brooklyn, NY
888-484-3243
www.bedfordcheeseshop.com

Bierkraft
191 Fifth Avenue
Brooklyn, NY
718-230-7600
www.bierkraft.com

Blue Apron Foods
2 locations in Brooklyn
Brooklyn, NY
718-230-3180
www.blueapronfoods.com

The Cheese Plate
Water Street Market #302
10 Main Street
New Paltz, NY
845-255-2444

Despana
408 Broome Street
New York, NY
212-219-5050
www.despananyc.com

Di Palo's
200 Grand Street
New York, NY
212-226-1033

Fairway
Multiple locations in New York
212-595-1888
www.fairwaymarket.com

Formaggio Essex Market
Essex Street Market
120 Essex Street
New York, NY
212-982-8200
www.formaggio-kitchen.com

Honest Weight Cheese Co-Op
484 Central Avenue
Albany, NY
518-482-2667
www.hwfc.com

Ideal Cheese Shop
942 1st Avenue
New York, NY
800-382-0109
www.idealcheese.com

Ithaca Bakery
400 North Meadow Street
Ithaca, NY
607-273-7110
www.ithacabakery.com

Marshall's Cheese Shop
27 Cedar Street
Dobbs Ferry, NY
914-591-1997

Murray's Cheese (2 locations)
254 Bleecker Street
New York, NY
212-243-3289
www.murrayscheese.com

Grand Central Market
43rd and Lexington Avenue
New York, NY
212-922-1540

Saxelby Cheesemongers
Essex Street Market
New York, NY
212-228-8200
www.saxelbycheese.com

Wine Sense
749 Park Avenue
Rochester, NY
585-271-0590
www.wedefinewine.com

Zabar's
2245 Broadway
New York, NY
212-787-2000
www.zabars.com

North Carolina

A Southern Season
Highway 15-501 at Estes Drive

University Mall
Chapel Hill, NC
800-253-3663
919-929-7133
www.southernseason.com

City Beverage
915 Burke Street
Winston-Salem, NC
336-722-2774
www.citybeverage.com

Erick's Cheese & Wine
4004 Highway 105
Banner Elk, NC
828-898-9424
www.erickscheeseandwine.com

Ference Cheese Inc.
174 Weaverville Highway #A
Asheville, NC
828-658-3101

Firehouse Wine and Cellar
4622 North Virginia Dare Trail
Kitty Hawk, NC
252-261-5115
www.firehousewine.com

Ohio

The Baricelli Inn
2203 Cornell Road
Cleveland, OH
216-791-6500
www.baricelli.com

The Cheese Shop at the West Side Market
West Side Market, Corner of West 25th
and Lorain
Cleveland, OH
216-771-6349
www.westsidemarket.com

Dorothy Lane Market (3 locations)
Oakwood
2710 Far Hills Avenue
Dayton, OH
937-299-3561

Springboro
740 N. Main Street
Springboro, OH
937-748-6800

Washington Hills
6177 Far Hills Avenue
Dayton, OH
800-824-1294
www.dorothylane.com

Jungle Jim's
5440 Dixie Highway
Fairfield, OH
513-674-6000
www.junglejims.com

Oklahoma

Forward Foods
123 E. Main Street
Norman, OK
405-321-1007
www.forwardfoods.com

Oregon

Artisan Cheese Trading Co.
422 S. 33rd Place
Philomath, OR
541-207-7805
www.artisancheesetrader.com

Curds & Whey
8036 SE 13th Avenue
Portland, OR
503-231-2877
www.curdsandwhey.us

Elephants Delicatessen
115 NW 22nd
Portland, OR
503-299-6304
www.elephantsdeli.com

Foster & Dobbs
2518 NE 15th Avenue
Portland, OR
503-284-1157
www.fosteranddobbs.com

Market of Choice
Multiple locations in Oregon
www.marketofchoice.com

Pastaworks
2 locations in Portland
Portland, OR
503-232-1010
www.pastaworks.com

Steve's Cheese
2321 NW Thurman Street
Portland, OR
503-222-6014

Zupan's Markets
Multiple locations in Oregon
360-737-2728
www.zupans.com

Pennsylvania

Chestnut Hill Cheese Shop
8509 Germantown Avenue
Philadelphia, PA
888-343-3327
www.chcheeseshop.com

Di Bruno Bros.
3 locations
Philadelphia, PA
215-922-2876
www.dibruno.com

Downtown Cheese
Reading Terminal Market
Philadelphia, PA
215-351-7412

Pennsylvania Macaroni Co.
2010-2012 Penn Avenue
Pittsburgh, PA
412-471-8330
www.pennmac.com

Rhode Island

Farmstead
186 Wayland Avenue
Providence, RI
401-274-7177
www.farmsteadinc.com

Milk & Honey Bazaar
3838 Main Road
Tiverton, RI
401-624-1974
www.milkandhoneybazaar.com

South Carolina

O'Hara & Flynn (2 locations)
1640 Palmetto Grande Drive
Mount Pleasant, SC
843-216-1916

160 East Bay Street
Charleston, SC
843-534-1916

Ted's Butcherblock
334 East Bay Street
Charleston, SC
843-577-0094
www.tedsbutcherblock.com

Tennessee

Corrieri's Formaggeria
1110 Catuthers Avenue
Nashville, TN
615-385-9272
www.cfcheese.com

Texas

Central Market/H-E-B
Multiple locations in Texas
512-206-1000
www.centralmarket.com or www.heb.com

eatZi's Market & Bakery
3403 Oak Lawn Avenue
Dallas, TX
214-526-1515
www.eatzis.com

Grape Vine Market
7938 Great Northern Boulevard
Austin, TX
2nd location in Round Rock
512-323-5900
www.grapevinemarket.com

Liberty Heights Fresh
1300 South at 1100 East
Salt Lake City, UT
801-583-7374
www.libertyheightsfresh.com

Tony Caputo's Market & Deli
314 West 300 South
Salt Lake City, UT
801-531-8669
www.caputosdeli.com

Brattleboro Food Co-op
2 Main Street
Brattleboro, VT
802-257-0236
www.brattleborofoodcoop.com

Cheese Outlet Fresh Market
400 Pine Street
Burlington, VT
800-447-1205
www.cheeseoutlet.com

Cheese Traders and Wine Sellers
1186 Williston Road
South Burlington, VT
802-863-0143
www.cheesetraders.com

City Markets/Onion River Co-op
82 S. Winooski Avenue
Burlington, VT
802-863-3659
www.citymarket.coop

Hunger Mountain Co-op
623 Stone Cutters Way
Montpelier, VT
802-223-8000
www.hungermountain.com

Squash Valley Produce
2597 Waterbury-Stowe Road
Waterbury, VT
802-244-1290

Arrowine
4508 Lee Highway
Arlington, VA
703-525-0990
www.arrowine.com

Cheesetique
2403 Mt. Vernon Avenue
Alexandria, VA
703-706-5300
www.cheesetique.com

Feast!
416 West Main Street
Charlottesville, Virginia

434-244-7800
www.feastvirginia.com

Say Cheese
102 Salem Avenue
Roanoke, Virginia
540-342-3937

The Cheese Shop of Virginia
410 Duke of Gloucester Street
Williamsburg, VA
757-220-0298

The Wine and Cheese Shop
1915 Pocahontas Trail Suite D-6
Williamsburg, VA
757-229-6754
www.potterywineandcheese.com

Warwick Cheese Shoppe
Hidenwood Shopping Center
Newport News, VA
757-599-3985
www.warwickcheese.com

Beecher's Handmade Cheese
1600 Pike Place
Seattle, WA
206-956-1964
www.beechershandmadecheese.com

The Cheese Cellar
100 4th Avenue North Suite 150
Seattle, WA
206-404-2743
www.thecheesecellar.com

Cheese Louise
321 Wellington
Walla Walla, WA
509 529-5005
www.tea2cheese.com

The Cheesemonger's Shop
633 Front Street
Leavenworth, WA
877-888-7389
www.cheesemongersshop.com

De Laurenti Specialty Food & Wine
1435 1st Avenue (Pike Place Market)
Seattle, WA
800-873-6685
www.delaurenti.com

Metropolitan Market
Multiple locations in Washington
206-923-0740
www.metropolitan-market.com

Salumiere Cesario
20 North Second Avenue
Walla Walla, WA
509-529-5620
www.salumierecesario.com

Saunders Cheese Market
210 S. Washington Street
Spokane, WA
509-868-6972

The Wine & Cheese Shop
Capitol Market
800 Smith Street
Charleston, WV
304-344-1905
www.capitolmarket.net/wineandcheese

Brennan's Market
Multiple locations in Wisconson
608-833-2893
www.brennansmarket.com

House of Wisconsin Cheese
107 State Street
Madison, WI
608-255-5204
www.houseofwisconsincheese.com

Larry's Market
8737 N. Deerwood Drive
Milwaukee, WI
800-236-1307
www.larrysmarket.com

Maple Leaf Cheese and Chocolate Haus
554 First Street
New Glarus, WI
608-527-2000
www.mapleleafcheeseandchocolatehaus.com

Nala's Fromagerie
2633 Development Drive Suite 30
Green Bay, WI
920-347-0334
www.nalascheese.com

NATIONAL AND REGIONAL CHAINS
WITH NOTEWORTHY CHEESE
SELECTIONS

Balducci's
Multiple locations in MD, VA, NY, CT
240-403-2440
www.balduccis.com

Bristol Farms
Multiple locations in California
310-233-4700
www.bristolfarms.com

Dean & Deluca
Locations in NY, CA, KS, NC, DC
800-221-7714
www.deananddeluca.com

The Fresh Market
Locations nationwide
866-532-5989
www.thefreshmarket.com

Wegmans Food Markets
Locations in the Northeast
800-934-6267
www.wegmans.com

Whole Foods
Nationwide
512-477-4455
www.wholefoods.com

ONLINE CHEESE SHOPPING

Artisanal Cheese
American and International cheeses
877-797-1200
www.artisanalcheese.com

Artisan Made-Northeast
Northeast cheeses
203-264-2883
www.artisanmade-ne.com

CheeseOnline.fr
French cheeses
+33 8 74 55 71 06
www.cheeseonline.fr

Fromages.com
French cheeses
www.fromages.com

igourmet.com
American and International cheeses
877-446-8763
www.igourmet.com

METRIC CONVERSION CHART

Weight Equivalents

The metric weights given in this chart are not exact equivalents, but have been rounded up or down slightly to make measuring easier.

Avoirdupois	Metric
¼ oz	7 g
½ oz	15 g
1 oz	30 g
2 oz	60 g
3 oz	90 g
4 oz	115 g
5 oz	150 g
6 oz	175 g
7 oz	200 g
8 oz (½ lb)	225 g
9 oz	250 g
10 oz	300 g
11 oz	325 g
12 oz	350 g
13 oz	375 g
14 oz	400 g
15 oz	425 g
16 oz (1 lb)	450 g
1½ lb	750 g
2 lb	900 g
2¼ lb	1 kg
3 lb	1.4 kg
4 lb	1.8 kg

Volume Equivalents

These are not exact equivalents for American cups and spoons, but have been rounded up or down slightly to make measuring easier.

American	Metric	Imperial
¼ t	1.2 ml	
½ t	2.5 ml	
1 t	5.0 ml	
½ T (1.5 t)	7.5 ml	
1 T (3 t)	15 ml	
¼ cup (4 T)	60 ml	2 fl oz
⅓ cup (5 T)	75 ml	2½ fl oz
½ cup (8 T)	125 ml	4 fl oz
⅔ cup (10 T)	150 ml	5 fl oz
¾ cup (12 T)	175 ml	6 fl oz
1 cup (16 T)	250 ml	8 fl oz
1¼ cups	300 ml	10 fl oz (½ pt)
1½ cups	350 ml	12 fl oz
2 cups (1 pint)	500 ml	16 fl oz
2½ cups	625 ml	20 fl oz (1 pint)
1 quart	1 liter	32 fl oz

Oven Temperature Equivalents

Oven Mark	F	C	Gas
Very cool	250-275	130-140	½-1
Cool	300	150	2
Warm	325	170	3
Moderate	350	180	4
Moderately hot	375	190	5
	400	200	6
Hot	425	220	7
	450	230	8
Very hot	475	250	9

RECIPE INDEX

Page numbers in **bold** denote photographs

INDEX

Page numbers in **bold** denote photographs